PRAISE FOR MAUREEN WEBB AND ILLUSIONS OF SECURITY

"George Orwell and Michel Foucault together could not have imagined the future that Maureen Webb warns is already here—a state of global surveillance that challenges all of our most deep-seated expectations of privacy. Highly readable and critically important. Read it to see who's watching you."

—DAVID COLE, author of *Enemy Aliens: Double Standards and Constitutional Freedoms in the War on Terrorism*

"Through the various 'frozen scandals' of the War on Terror—from extraordinary rendition to torture to warrant-less wiretapping and surveillance—runs a single theme: the Bush Administration's obsessive concern with 'the preemption of risk.' In *Illusions of Security*, Maureen Webb manages to construct a broader, compelling narrative out of what had seemed the isolated abuses of a single government, and to follow that grim narrative fearlessly where it leads: to a darker, less democratic and more frightening future."

—MARK DANNER, author *of Torture and Truth: America, Abu Ghraib and the War on Terror*

"Maureen Webb exposes deep and wide how the erosion and destruction of civil liberties and human rights on an international scale may well be the death knell for democracy. She issues a provocative challenge in these pages: can we rollback the emerging police state out of our constitution and imagine a world ruled by human rights, law and mutual cooperation?"

—ARNOLDO GARCIA, National Network for Immigrant and Refugee Rights

"Tracking the myriad ways in which governments—aided by advanced technology and profit-hungry corporations—are monitoring and manipulating us, she reminds us that the only predictable consequence of it all is human suffering, with little or no increase in real security."

—ROBERT JENSEN, University of Texas at Austin professor and author of *The Heart of Whiteness* and *Citizens of the Empire*

"Maureen Webb pulls all the pieces together—special rendition, no-fly lists, biometric surveillance, warrant-less wiretaps, torture—to create a harrowing picture of post 9-11 state repression. This valuable guide makes clear how dramatically civil liberties have been attacked in recent years."

—CHRISTIAN PARENTI, author of *The Freedom: Shadows and Hallucinations in Occupied Iraq*, *The Soft Cage* and *Lockdown America*

"'Your government is spying on you, and it's going to get worse until we do something about it,' is Maureen Webb's message in her brilliant, much needed new book. In measured, lucid detail, Webb presents a wide-ranging account of the emerging global network of surveillance that is infringing on the personal privacy and civil liberties of people in the United States and worldwide."

—NADINE STROSSEN, Executive Director, American Civil Liberties Union

"*Illusions of Security* is a thorough and terrifying compendium of the threats to democracy posed by the unquestioning use of technology. Maureen Webb portrays a frightening image of high-placed officials playing with their technological toys; meanwhile the real world—and its real insecurities—elude them."

—ELLEN ULLMAN, author of *The Bug: A Novel* and *Close to the Machine*

"She has riveted our attention on the scale and capacity of the global surveillance system that has been set up since the terrorist outrages of 2001. This is a compelling book and it should be compulsory reading."

—JEREMY WALDRON, Professor of Philosophy, NYU and author of *The Dignity of Legislation and Law and Disagreement*

"Observing government surveillance of individual citizens from her perch in Quebec, human rights lawyer Webb wonders how long democracy can survive when power-hungry officials are able to persecute innocent men and women as well as the occasional terrorist. Webb focuses her criticism on the governments of Canada and the United States, but persuasively documents international cooperation on illegal, or at least immoral, high-tech information gathering. Webb devotes substantial space to the National Security Agency of the U.S. and its monitoring of international telephone traffic despite apparent lawlessness and ethical violations. Webb also writes in detail about how governments, following the lead of the Bush administration, use 'terrorism' as an excuse to 'serve agendas that go far beyond security from terrorism—namely the suppression of dissent, harsh immigration and refugee policies, increased law enforcement power,' and the consolidation of political power within governments and in exerting control over national populations."

—*Booklist*

ILLUSIONS OF SECURITY

GLOBAL SURVEILLANCE AND DEMOCRACY IN THE POST-9/11 WORLD

Maureen Webb

CITY LIGHTS
San Francisco

A City Lights Books first edition.

Library of Congress Cataloging-in-Publication Data

Webb, Maureen.
Illusions of security : global surveillance and democracy in the post-9/11 world / by Maureen Webb. — 1st ed.
p. cm.
ISBN-13: 978-0-87286-476-4
ISBN-10: 0-87286-476-6
1. Civil rights—United States. 2. Electronic surveillance—United States. 3. Intelligence service—United States. 4. Terrorism—United States—Prevention. 5. September 11 Terrorist Attacks, 2001—Influence. I. Title.
JC599.U5W364 2006
323.44'820973—dc22
2006018066

Cover design by POLLEN, New York.
Book design by Gambrinus.

www.citylights.com

City Lights Books are published at the City Lights Bookstore,
261 Columbus Avenue, San Francisco, CA 94133.

For Monia's children and mine

Contents

Acknowledgments

I have so many people to thank.

This book began its life as an analysis for an international campaign—the International Campaign Against Mass Surveillance, or ICAMS—which a group of committed people from around the world conceived of in February 2004. Soon, we hope, it will become a movement.

The International Civil Liberties Monitoring Group (ICLMG) in Canada sponsored the initial meeting of ICAMS, and it, along with Statewatch in Europe, the American Civil Liberties Union and Friends Committee on National Legislation (Quakers) in the United States, and Focus on the Global South in Asia, became an ultimate sponsor of the campaign. I would like to thank these organizations and the key people in the working group that made the campaign a reality. Thanks to Roch Tassé of ICLMG for his leadership and consummate diplomacy and for his major contribution to the corporate security complex analysis. Thanks to Ben Hayes of Statewatch for sparking the idea of the campaign and for following through with such intelligent commitment on many substantive and practical matters. Thanks to Hilary Homes of Amnesty Canada for her brainstorming and campaigning expertise. Thanks to Yap Swee Seng of Suaram for his contribution of information from Asia, and to Martine Eloy of La ligue des droits et libertés for her many fine insights. And special thanks to Brian Murphy (Interpares), Karen Seabrooke (Interpares), and Jeanne Herrick-Stare (Friends Committee on National Legislation) for their wisdom and astute editorial comments on successive drafts of the original analysis.

I would like to thank Monia Mazigh and Maher Arar, two Canadian heroes, for their exemplary grace and principle. Thanks is due also to Saida Nagti, Monia's amazing, stalwart mother, who has kept the family running through all the difficult times they have been through.

Special thanks to Kerry Pither for her leadership spearheading the public campaign for justice for Maher Arar and for the invaluable chronologies she wrote and connections she made about the Arar, Almalki, and El Maati stories. In this book I have drawn heavily from these chronologies, and they will remain critical historical documents in the years to come as we retell and reflect on these important stories.

Thanks to my family for their abiding support now and in the past: my dear father, Donald Webb, who passed away in 2002; my dear mother, Constance McDonald Webb; my special grandmother, Edith Todd Webb; and my terrific brother and sister-in-law, Michael Webb and Joanne Webb.

Thank you to Robert Chernomas for his love and support.

Thanks to Marco for the year in New York, and to my cognata Adriana, for her interest. Thanks to Columbia University and especially to philosopher Jeremy Waldron, who taught me, not what, but how, to think about rights. And thanks to the Canadian Association of University Teachers and Jim Turk for their commitment to civil liberties issues.

Everlasting thanks to Anne Hardcastle and, in memory, Judith Russell and Susan Arnold, for their friendship and mentoring. And also to Bobbie Davidson, Cathy Adlington, and Liz Soper.

Thanks to friends and neighbors—Jody, Art, Marie, Stephanie, Rosemary, Diane, Romeo, Natasha, Marc, and others—who encouraged me through this project and helped with offers to entertain my children and with computers and battery packs when the power went down on the day the manuscript was due.

And thank you to my sweet, forbearing, precious children, Lucia and Michele, who now have *all* my attention. "I'm going to tell your boss not to make you work all the time," was the only chiding I received from my four-year-old during the time I spent writing.

I would like to extend a warm thank you to publicist Stacey Lewis of City Lights, for her skillful shepherding and good humor. And finally, I would like to express my immense gratitude to my editor, Greg Ruggiero, for his vision and for the immediate faith he placed in this project and its aim. It is a privilege working with him and City Lights.

PROLOGUE

Monia's Children

◎ ◎

Eternal vigilance is the price of liberty.
—Wendell Phillips, 1852

The first time I saw Monia was on a freezing Ottawa night in February 2003. I stood with my two small children—a boy in a stroller and a little girl—on one side of the Centennial Flame on Parliament Hill, and she stood with hers like a mirror image on the other side—a little boy in a stroller almost my son's age and a brave little girl about my daughter's height. It was a meager group of people on a bitter night, and by appearances all of them were from the Arab or Muslim community except me and my kids and a politician who showed up for a sound bite.

I couldn't quite explain why I had come. Dragging my kids out to political rallies just wasn't something that I usually did. Perhaps I was attuned to Monia's story because at the time I was working on border issues at my job. But more than anything else, I was there as a mother—one who had listened to another mother's story unfold on the radio over the previous five months and tried to answer my own kids' curious questions.

"But why can't they get their papa back? Who took him? Why?"

Characteristically, my children wanted to know who the bad guys were.

At first, no one knew why or even where Monia's husband had been taken. There had already been stories of Muslim Canadians having trouble at the U.S. border and of the National Security

Entry/Exit Registration System (NSEERS) program—but never a disappearance.

Monia's husband, Maher Arar, had disappeared in New York on September 26, 2002. He had been traveling back to Canada early from a family vacation in Tunisia, flying through Zürich, then JFK International Airport, en route to Montreal. He only had a few hours to wait in JFK. No one heard from him for six days.

When his family learned that the United States had detained him in the Metropolitan Detention Center in Brooklyn, New York, they got help to arrange for a lawyer and consular access. They were assured that Maher would have a hearing, and that if he were deported from the United States, it would be to Canada—his place of residence and citizenship—or to Zürich where his flight to the United States had originated. But in the very early hours of the morning on October 8, 2002, Maher Arar disappeared again. Fourteen days later he turned up in Syria, the place where he was born but had left when he was seventeen years old. There were reports that he had first been sent to Jordan.

Maher's little boy was seven months old at the time, his little girl, five years old. They were an ordinary middle-class family. Monia had completed her doctorate in financial economics in Montreal, and Maher, his master's degree in telecommunications. They were an articulate, professional couple, who, like model Canadians, spoke English and French, as well as their native Arabic, fluently. They had worked hard to start their careers while juggling family responsibilities and had been looking forward to a comfortable future up until the day Maher disappeared.

Monia, a dignified, quiet-spoken woman, was determined to find out what had happened to her husband. She had tenaciously been writing to—and meeting with—politicians, bureaucrats, and human-rights groups for months. I began to believe, as time dragged on, that Monia's children were never going to get their papa back. In radio interviews Monia explained her will to continue simply. She could not bear to let her children grow up fatherless. She never attempted to protest on the basis of her husband's innocence, which at the time people may have viewed suspiciously. Shrewdly, she stuck to the real point: *If my husband has done something wrong, let him be charged and tried in his own country, Canada*. This was her message.

The Canadian foreign affairs minister and the prime minister claimed that they knew nothing. They made high-level inquiries with the United States. The U.S. ambassador to Canada, Paul Cellucci, said that Canadian "elements" did not want Arar returned to Canada, which was why the United States had deported him to Syria.[1] In a private meeting, Secretary of State Colin Powell reportedly "slammed" Canadian Foreign Affairs Minister Bill Graham and "told him 'it was information from your people' that led to Arar's detention."[2] The *National Post*, quoting inside sources, reported that the Royal Canadian Mounted Police (RCMP) had quietly asked U.S. authorities to arrest and deport Maher Arar when he traveled through New York City.[3]

A few days later, the U.S. Embassy released a statement that "the U.S. did not consult with any Canadian law enforcement organization. . . . Mr. Arar was on U.S. soil when he was arrested and U.S. officials made that decision on their own."[4] But, quoting unnamed sources, journalist and political columnist Robert Fife reported that the American disavowal of Canadian participation had been made under pressure from the RCMP.[5]

The Syrian ambassador to Canada said it was a matter between the Canadian government and the American government.[6] Later he told journalists that Syria was waiting for instructions from the Central Intelligence Agency (CIA) in order to lay charges against Maher Arar.[7] U.S. Ambassador Cellucci told Monia Mazigh that "[t]he United States ha[d] no authority to intervene on his behalf with either the government of Canada or the government of Syria."[8]

What had happened to Maher Arar and who had power to release him remained a mystery.

Monia was only about five months into her twelve-month quest to have her husband returned when I saw her on that cold February night at the Peace Flame rally. When she had finished her speech and the media drew away, I walked over to her with my stroller and offered her a modest donation of support. My children had become so engaged with her story that I had been able to put myself in her shoes; I felt I had to help in some small way.

Earlier, I had waffled about doing it. *What if Arar was a terrorist?* Did I want to give money to a terrorist family? Would I get in trouble? Would there be security intelligence agents watching? But in the end I came back to the point that if her husband had done something wrong, he should have been charged and tried in Canada, not *disappeared*. Monia was a mother like myself. She had been taking time away from her career to care for her infant son when her husband was disappeared, and she had been thrown into a financial crisis. I knew how quickly household expenses mounted up, how demanding it was to care for two young children, how difficult it must be to look for a job in her circumstances.

She declined our gift gracefully, saying that she was optimistic she would get work in her field and that she had drawn strength from looking across at us—another mother and her children—during her speech.

I wished her luck.

◎ ◎

Like a lot of mothers, I operate on two levels. I have my worldly or professional understanding of events and issues, and I have my maternal experience. I look for insight where they intersect. On September 11, 2001, I was in New York City, to take up a fellowship at Columbia University. I had come to set up an apartment and had plans to return to Canada on Thursday, September 14, 2001, to pack up and return to New York with my husband and two children. I heard about the plane crash into 1 World Trade Center, (the North Tower of the Twin Towers) on the morning radio show and was talking to my husband on the phone about the "accident" when another plane hit, this one crashing into 2 World Trade Center, the South Tower. It was a chilling moment. "*It's terrorists,*" I said with sudden conviction. Then the third plane hit the Pentagon and the fourth crashed short of its White House destination.

I ran over to International House, the international students' residence near the Columbia campus, and saw the Twin Towers coming down in real time on the television and learned that students had been calling on their cell phones from stairwells in the towers a short time before that. I went out onto the streets with a German lawyer, and we lined up to give blood at the nearest hospital. On that day, in that moment, I was, *we all were*—as the French newspapers said—*Americans.*

That night I lay awake in bed listening to the fighter jets roar over Manhattan. All other air transport had been grounded. I was desperate to get back to my family, and was watching the chances of my flight departing as scheduled grow slimmer and slimmer.

Later that week I joined thousands of other people in Grand Central Terminal who were trying to get back home by train. I heard stories from people who had narrowly missed being in the Twin Towers on September 11 and other stories of people who had only gone there once in their life on that day. There was a fine white dust from the crushed towers swirling on the sidewalks and streets. It was like a signature of grief.

I wept every time I saw a fire truck or a fire station that year. But as the days passed and the initial shock wore off, another emotion grew up beside the grief. It took some time before I realized what it was: *anger*. It glowed like an ember when I heard Americans ask, "Why do they hate us?' or assert: "They hate our power and our way of life, they hate our freedoms."

Not for a moment would I condone or excuse the perpetrators

of the atrocity I had witnessed, but these were maddening statements to many people who were not Americans and to a good number of people who were.

As Gwynne Dyer has, I think, insightfully observed, Americans are rightfully proud that theirs was the first large society in history to create a democratic, egalitarian form of government. The foible of many of them, however, is to believe that they invented the idea or that their values are superior to other peoples.

> [I]n the wider world, the examples of the French Revolution (which raised issues of racial, class and gender equality largely ignored by the American Revolution) and of the slowly evolving British model of parliamentary democracy have been just as influential in shaping the many dozens of democratic societies that exist today. In the past twenty years, non-Western societies of many different cultural backgrounds have demonstrated both their desire for democracy and their ability to seize it from corrupt and oppressive rulers by non-violent means, as have European countries living under totalitarian regimes."[9]

These facts are largely ignored in the American debate, so that it sounds perfectly plausible to argue[10] that "other peoples have little chance of achieving democracy without the example and perhaps the direct help of the United States, which is therefore the chief moral actor in the current era of world history."[11] And it is, perhaps, easier to mislead the American people about what its government is doing in the rest of the world, since "there is a popular assumption that America only uses force for moral reasons."[12] I used the word "foible," but perhaps it is the *tragic flaw* of Americans to believe so fervently in the destiny of their country to do good in the world. It is an idea so fixed, that it infiltrates the logic of even the most sophisticated and progressive Americans.

Meanwhile, a good number of Americans remain ignorant, or willfully blind, about the effect of their foreign policy on other communities, so that, as Gwynne Dyer observes, they can honestly confuse an attack on their foreign policy as an attack on their ideals. I thought of the people from El Salvador I had served in a legal clinic in the 1980s. They were among the many who had good reason to hate the *exercise* of American power. It was not envy; it was hard experience. American power has often been used in other countries to support brutal and corrupt regimes and to block development and democratization.[13] The United States had not deserved to be attacked in 2001, but, in the view of many people around the world, it was responsible for having, over time and through the repeated policies of successive administrations, made the world a more dangerous place.

Sanctimonious, ungrateful Canadian that I was, I brought my family back to New York.

And then the anthrax attacks started. The woman who was killed by them lived in our postal district. Like a crazy person, I would open the mail as seldom as possible. I would get dressed in old clothes and take the mail out into the sun and wind of a nearby park where I read and then disposed of it in a plastic bag. I would then come back and undress in the apartment building's broom closet and dispose of my clothes in a plastic bag, wash my hands, and change into other clothes I had stashed there. How's that for hysteria? But my little boy was five months old. I had dragged him to this newly dangerous place. I thought we were going to have to give up soon and go home. My family might be as likely to be struck by lightning as by terrorist attacks, but I would be responsible if they were harmed. *I wanted the authorities to do everything in their power to catch whoever was involved and foil new plots.*

And this is where the intersection between instinct and understanding lies. What should we responsibly do to protect ourselves from acts of terrorist violence and what can we *not* afford to do?

Like many people around the world, I have been struggling with this question over the past five years. It is not an easy one to answer and I do not seek to provide pat answers or to dismiss the legitimate role instinct plays in our responses to risk. But I do aim to weigh in on the side of understanding, since I have come to believe that it is through understanding what is really *at risk*, that we best guarantee our safety and freedom.

CHAPTER ONE

Maher Arar's Story: A Cautionary Tale

◎ ◎

. . . unaccommodated man is no more but such a poor, bare, fork'd animal as thou art.
—William Shakespeare, *King Lear*, III. iv

PROJECT A-O CANADA AND MAHER'S RENDITION TO SYRIA

Maher Arar's odyssey began, unbeknownst to him, in an Ottawa restaurant.[14] On October 11, 2001, he was having lunch with the brother of Nazih Amalki, a fellow he worked with. The wife of the brother, Abdullah, had four children in Ottawa, and Maher was asking Abdullah's advice about finding a doctor for Monia, who was pregnant.[15] After lunch, they stood outside in the rain discussing where Maher could buy a printer cartridge. Then Abdullah decided to go with Maher to the Future Shop to help him pick one.[16] The RCMP had been covertly monitoring Abdullah Amalki since 1998.[17] It was on the basis of this casual meeting that Maher Arar first became a person of interest in their investigation.[18]

The Canadian intelligence community came under intense pressure after 9/11. They had failed to uncover Montreal resident Ahmed Ressam's plot to bomb Los Angeles International Airport on New Year's Eve, 1999, and there was a widespread, though mistaken, belief among Americans that some of the 9/11 attackers had entered the United States from Canada. Canada's economy depends heavily on overland trade with the United States, and the Canadian government was doing everything it could to ensure that the Americans did not close the border.

Days after 9/11, the RCMP initiated an investigation into alleged terrorist cells in Toronto and Ottawa. They were taking over files from the Canadian Security Intelligence Service (CSIS). The investigation was code-named "A-O Canada," and it was a joint operation in which local law enforcement and various government departments and agencies were involved. The Ottawa half of the project, known as "A Canada," worked in close relationship with U.S. agencies including the Federal Bureau of Investigation (FBI) and another unnamed American agency—probably the CIA.[19] An overarching mandate of the project was "prevention." As the head of A Canada, Superintendent Mike Cabana, would later testify, "In other words, we were directed to adopt a zero tolerance and—I guess the best way to term it—leave no stones unturned. We were to do everything in our power to prevent anything else from happening."[20]

Under orders, which according to Cabana came from its most senior levels,[21] the RCMP threw aside normal protocols that required signed authorizations and limits on the dissemination of information they shared with foreign agencies. Project A Canada was told to make sure all available information was shared with its U.S. partner agencies, and there were discussions about the importance of ensuring that no one withheld information, however innocuous they thought it might be.[22] The U.S. agencies attended regular meetings in Canada[23] and in April 2002 were provided with copies of the twenty-six hard drives, hundreds of compact disks, and thousands of documents that the RCMP had seized in seven raids in Ottawa and elsewhere but did not have the manpower to analyze themselves.[24] The fruits of these raids and other correspondence and reports generated by the investigation, including the

RCMP's SUPERText database, were burned on to three CD-ROMs that were given to the U.S. agencies.[25]

Cabana would also later testify that Maher Arar was *never* a target of the investigation, only a person to whom the RCMP wanted to talk, as a possible witness.[26] But the RCMP were obviously keen to impress their American counterparts. As Justice Dennis O'Connor, the judge appointed to hold a public inquiry into the affair would later reveal, the Mounties passed to U.S. officials all kinds of misleading and downright false information about Maher Arar. At various times they called him a "target," a "suspect," a "principal subject," a person with an "important connection" to Abdullah Almalki, and a person directly linked to Almalki in a diagram entitled "Bin Laden's Associates: Al Qaeda Organization in Ottawa." The RCMP asked U.S. Customs to put Maher and Monia on U.S. border lookouts, describing them, without a shred of evidence, as "Islamic extremists suspected of being linked to the al-Qaeda movement."[27] The RCMP also gave a copy of Maher Arar's apartment rental contract to U.S. agencies. The corporate real-estate company, Minto, had voluntarily given the contact to the RCMP.[28]

The RCMP were asked if they wanted to provide questions for an interrogation of Arar and they did, not in relation to Arar himself, but to the main target of their investigation, Abdullah Almalki.[29] Wantonly, the RCMP suggested that Maher had been in the Washington D.C. area on September 11, 2001, which was patently false.[30]

The FBI and CIA then asked the RCMP to provide them with information that would support criminal charges against Arar in the United States. Apparently, the RCMP Criminal Intelligence Directorate, which Project A-O Canada reported to, also thought the object of sending questions down was to build a case against Arar, but this was a mistaken assumption. A-O Canada had nothing on Arar on which it could base criminal charges, and they were only interested in him at the time as a potential witness.[31] On

October 5, 2002, the U.S. Embassy asked the RCMP if Canada would lay charges against Arar if he were returned to Canada or if it could refuse entry to him.[32] The answer was *no* on both counts.

Over the course of his detention in the United States, the RCMP seriously considered sending officers down to New York to interview Maher Arar but did not.[33] According to Mike Cabana, they had assumed he would be deported back to Canada or to Zürich but learned through Canadian consular officials that Arar himself had been told he might be deported to Syria. Maher Arar had already been flown to Jordan when they were informed on October 9, 2002, of the fact, not by their partner agencies in the United States, but by the U.S. embassy in Ottawa.[34] In any event, when Maher went missing, it appears that the RCMP was the only agency of the Canadian government that initially knew his whereabouts.[35]

⊙ ⊙

Maher Arar's flight to New York arrived at 2:00 P.M. on September 26, 2002. He had a few hours to wait until his connecting flight to Montreal. At the immigration counter he was pulled aside and taken to another area. Two hours later his photograph and fingerprints were taken. He was told it was normal procedure, but like a Franz Kafka novel, things began to get stranger and stranger.

First his bags were searched, and then a team of people arrived to interrogate him. They told him that he had no right to a lawyer because he was not an American citizen. They did not allow him to make a phone call to anyone. They denied him consular rights. Maher was starting to get very worried. As he would later tell the Canadian public:

> They asked me where I worked and how much money I made. They swore at me, and insulted me. It was very humiliating. They wanted me to answer every question

quickly. They were consulting a report while they were questioning me, and the information they had was so private I thought this must be from Canada.

I told them everything I knew. They asked about my travel in the United States. I told them about my work permits and my business there.

They asked about information on my computer and whether I was willing to share it. I welcomed the idea, but I don't know if they did.

They asked me about different people, some I know, and most I do not.

They asked me about Abdullah Almalki, and I told them I worked with his brother at high tech firms in Ottawa, and that the Almalki family had come from Syria about the same time as mine. I told them I did not know Abdullah well, but had seen him a few times and I described the times I could remember, I told them I had a casual relationship with him.

They were so rude with me, yelling at me that I had a selective memory.

Then they pulled out a copy of my rental lease from 1997. I could not believe they had this. I was completely shocked. They pointed out that Abdullah had signed the lease as a witness. I had completely forgotten that he had signed it for me. When we moved to Ottawa in 1997, we needed someone to witness our lease, and I phoned Abdullah's brother, and he could not come, so he sent Abdullah.

But they thought I was hiding this. I told them the truth. I had nothing to hide. I had never had problems in the United States before, and I could not believe what was happening to me.[36]

The interrogation continued until midnight. Maher repeatedly asked for a lawyer, but U.S. officials ignored him. They put chains on his wrists and ankles and transported him to a holding center near the airport. They would not tell him what was happening. He was put in a room with metal benches in it, where he remained for the night.

The next morning the interrogation began again and lasted on and off for eight hours. Maher was exhausted and disoriented. He had not slept or eaten since he had been on the plane. U.S. interrogators tried to make him consent to be deported to Syria. They tried to coax him into signing a form without letting him read it.

About 8:00 P.M. that night, U.S. authorities chained and shackled Maher and transported him to the Metropolitan Detention Center in Brooklyn, New York. He was strip-searched and put into an orange suit like those worn by the detainees in Guantánamo Bay. They would not give him a toothbrush, toothpaste, or reading material. But on the fifth day he was allowed to make a phone call to his mother-in-law in Ottawa.

Although he was only allowed to talk for two minutes, that call may have saved his life. The Canadian Department of Foreign Affairs was alerted, and they arranged consular access and a lawyer. The outside world knew where he was.

But not for long.

At 9:00 P.M. on Sunday night, October 7, 2003, guards came to his cell to tell him his lawyer was there to see him. He thought it was a strange time. They took him into a room where seven or eight people were waiting for him. Maher asked where his lawyer was. They told him that the lawyer had refused to come (which was false) and started questioning him again. They pressed him again about going back to Syria. He told them he did not want to be deported to Syria, that he would be tortured there. He told them he had not done his military service, that he was a Sunni Muslim, that his mother's cousin had been accused of being a member of the Muslim Brotherhood and was put in prison for nine years. Over the last few days, he had plenty of time to remember the stories he had heard from his parents in the 1980s, about abuse in Syrian prisons.[37] They asked him to sign a document, and he refused.[38]

At 3:00 A.M. on October 8, 2002, a prison guard woke Maher and told him he was leaving. Two officials read something to him they said was a decision by the Immigration and Naturalization (INS) director. It accused him of being an Al Qaeda agent, even though, as it would later be revealed, the RCMP had repeatedly told American authorities while he was in custody in the United States that they had no evidence to link him to Al Qaeda.[39] The officials told Maher that, based on classified information that could not be revealed, he was being deported to Syria.

At that moment, Maher Arar began to cry. He was bundled into a van and then onto a private jet, chained and shackled. He was being cast into the abyss.

DETENTION IN SYRIA

The jet took him to Washington, D.C.; Portland, Maine; Rome, Italy; and Amman, Jordan, from where he was taken overland into Syria. In Syria, he was taken to what he would later learn was the notorious Far' Falestin (Palestine Branch) prison in Damascus. He arrived at the prison exhausted, hungry, and terrified. He had already been beaten by the men who had handled him in Jordan. Luggage that had been returned to him in Jordan was searched and gifts for his family, chocolate and perfume bought in Switzerland, were stolen. Three men came and took him into a room, and one of them started asking him questions. When he did not answer quickly enough, they threatened to "use" a metal chair in the corner of the room. At about one in the morning he was taken into the basement of the prison.

> We went into the basement, and they opened a door, and I looked in. I could not believe what I saw. I asked how long

> I would be kept in this place. He did not answer, but put me in and closed the door. It was like a grave. It had no light. It was three feet wide. It was six feet deep. It was seven feet high. . . . I spent ten months, and ten days inside that grave.[40]

On October 17, 2002, the RCMP faxed one set of questions for the Syrians to their liaison officer in Rome for the interrogation of Abdullah Almalki, along with another set for Maher Arar in case he decided to "voluntarily provide statements to law enforcement officials." On January 15, 2003, another set of RCMP questions for Abdullah Almalki, containing questions about Maher Arar, was hand delivered to the head of Syrian military intelligence by Canadian consul on the instructions of the Canadian Ambassador.[41] The RCMP and Canadian Ambassador ought to have known that providing questions increased the risk of the two Canadians being tortured by the Syrians. According to RCMP Superintendent Mike Cabana, the RCMP assumed that the Americans knew something about Arar that the RCMP did not know, because they had sent Arar to Syria. So the RCMP were looking to find out more too, hoping to build a case against Arar as well as their main target.[42]

⊙ ⊙

The ten months of torture to which Maher Arar were horrific. It is too much for most of us to bear witness to even one story of torture, too much to imagine ourselves or someone we love in their shoes for one day, or even one hour. In fact, Maher would later say that the most difficult thing he experienced during his detention was the screams of other people being tortured, especially the screams of women who had been brought to the prison with their infant children.

Like the "poor, bare, fork'd animal" in Shakespeare's *King Lear* and the victims in Nazi death camps or any number of other hells on earth, Maher Arar endured his fate. He told his torturers the truth and also what he thought they wanted to hear. Sometimes lying brought him respite, sometimes it made them angry. At times, he was "bombarded by memories" constantly thinking of his family and worrying about their finances and safety. At other times, he completely lost control and began to scream and bang his head against the wall. Over time, he found himself becoming "more selfish." After a few months he cared only about himself and his daily survival. This was the final degradation.[43]

Neither Canada, the United States, nor Syria ever had any evidence that Maher Arar was involved in terrorism or any other crime. Reportedly, CSIS told the Syrians in a November 2002 visit to Syria that they had "no interest" in Arar, that he was, in fact, just someone who knew other Muslims under surveillance.[44] And yet, when the Canadian government eventually drafted a letter to the Syrians calling for Maher Arar's return, CSIS vigorously objected to the inclusion of a sentence saying "the government of Canada has no evidence that Mr. Arar was involved in terrorist activity, nor is there any impediment to his return to Canada."[45] CSIS proposed the wording be changed to "Mr. Arar is currently the subject of a National Security Investigation in Canada. Although there is not sufficient evidence at this time to warrant *Criminal Code* charges, he remains a subject of interest" (emphasis added). The RCMP voiced similar concerns, and the letter that was ultimately sent under Prime Minister Jean Chretién's signature on July 11, 2003, said rather weakly, "I can assure you that there is no Canadian government impediment to [Mr. Arar's] return."[46]

Marlene Catterall, MP (Liberal–Ottawa West-Nepean), who traveled to Syria on the government's behalf to deliver an earlier letter from Foreign Affairs Minister Bill Graham—which similarly avoided clear statements that Maher Arar was not accused of any crime—asked, "[W]hy would a simple statement of fact be removed? It is that kind of fudging of Mr. Arar's status, based on no evidence, no charges, no opportunity to defend himself against anybody's suspicions, that I find so offensive.... This kind of thing should not happen in a democracy."[47]

On July 22, 2003, Canadian Senator Pierre De Bané traveled to Syria as the prime minister's special envoy. He met with the Syrian president, who, showing his frustration, told De Bané that it did not make sense that the Canadians request the Syrians to detain people, then blame the Syrians for doing what they were asked, and then accuse the Syrians of having mistreated the prisoners. As a result, the Syrian president told de Bané, the Syrians would not release any more Canadians from their prisons.

Then on July 25, 2003, as public pressure in Canada regarding Arar's case was reaching a fever pitch, the *National Post* and the *Ottawa Citizen* published a front-page report by Robert Fife asserting that "a network of Al Qaeda agents [had been] rounded up before it could carry out a plot to attack the American Embassy in Ottawa" and that the CIA had been "alerted to the ... conspiracy by the Syrian intelligence service."[48] The story of a planned attack against an American target in Ottawa had first been leaked to investigative reporter Seymour Hersh, presumably by American security agents. Hersh wrote an article in the *New Yorker* including the leaked information earlier in July. The article described how Syria had offered its intelligence services to the United States after 9/11 in a bid to improve relations with the United States and by early 2002 had evolved into "one of the C.I.A.'s most effective allies."[49]

On the same day the Robert Fife story ran in Canada, RCMP Inspector André Guertin told the media that there was never a plot to attack the U.S. Embassy and "if there were, we would know."[50] Canadian Foreign Affairs Minister Bill Graham and other officials echoed that if there were a plot, it was news to them.[51] The story was beginning to veer into the territory of a John le Carré novel.

At the end of July, Dr. Monia Mazigh received a report from the

London-based Syrian Human Rights Committee, which confirmed, based on "knowledgable" sources, that Maher was being tortured in Syria. Maher had not been seen by any Canadian official since April 22, 2003. Monia held a press conference on Parliament Hill along with the secretary general of Amnesty International Canada, and the former mayor of Ottawa to call on the prime minister to recall the Canadian ambassador to Syria. Days after, Foreign Affairs Minister Bill Graham stated that "the time [had] come for the Syrian authorities either to charge Mr. Arar with an offence and give him an opportunity in a free and open trial to defend himself, or to release him and allow him to return to Canada." Graham had telephoned his counterpart in Syria and had not received an answer to his call.[52]

The Canadian ambassador to Syria, Franco D. Pillarella, who had previously been receiving the interrogation reports on Arar and acting as a go-between for Canadian and Syrian agencies,[53] then met with the head of the Syrian military intelligence for two hours on the instruction of the Canadian government.

In mid-August, Monia was told by Foreign Affairs in Ottawa that the Syrians had confirmed they would try Maher in a civilian court and that the Canadian ambassador would attend the hearings. Foreign Affairs also confirmed to Monia that the Syrian president had not answered the Canadian prime minister's letter of July.[54]

In early September, Liberal MP Irwin Cotler (who would later become minister of justice) wrote an editiorial saying that Canada must make it unequivocally clear that it would not accept any outcome other than Arar's safe return to Canada and that Syria's prejudicial conduct would impact adversely on Canada's bilateral relationship with Syria.[55]

The prime minister wrote to Monia, telling her to "rest assured that the Government of Canada [would] do all in its power to gain consular access to [her] husband to determine his well being and to seek justice in his case."[56] The *Globe & Mail* published an editorial on the same day arguing that "publicly and privately, Canada needs to press the United States and Syria for answers, and a just end to Mr. Arar's captivity."[57]

By this time, Monia had been informed that Maher would be tried in the Syrian Supreme Security Court, that the process would be short, and that there would be no right of appeal. But Canadian officials still did not know what Maher would be charged with or what evidence would be presented against him. She was told Canada would not assist her with the cost of a lawyer for Maher.[58]

Maher's case was taken up by Syrian human rights lawyer, Haytham Al Maleh. On September 10, 2003, Al Maleh met with the general prosecutor in Syria and was told that he would not be able to see Maher before the hearing began. He was also denied access to the case file and any information about what Maher would be charged with.[59]

The next day, the secretary general of Amnesty International Canada, the executive director of the Council on American-Islamic Relations (Canada), and former Conservative cabinet minister Flora McDonald, representing more than thirty national organizations, met with officials at the U.S. Embassy in Ottawa. They were told that the United States could not help Maher Arar now, because the case was a matter between the Canadian and Syrian governments.[60]

◉ ◉

While all this activity was going on at home, Maher Arar was still cut off, adrift on his odyssey of torment, not knowing whether he would ever see his family again.

He noticed his skin was turning yellow. In nine months he had seen the sunlight three times. Still rotting in the grave, he felt as if he was descending into a nervous breakdown. He asked for a meeting with an investigator, and his request was eventually granted. He told the investigator that he had nothing to do with Al Qaeda. The Syrian investigator asked him why he was accused of this, why the

Canadians sent a delegation in April, and "why these people hate[d] him so much."[61]

On August 14, 2003, Arar received the first visit from the Canadian consul since February. As always, he was accompanied by Syrian officials and his Syrian interrogator. The head of Syrian military intelligence was also there. In past visits Arar had spent much of his time crying, unable to tell Canadian officials explicitly that he was being tortured for fear of what would happen to him if he did.

Evidence at the Canadian inquiry would later suggest that Canadian Foreign Affairs officials were willfully blind to, and maybe even complicit in, the torture he and others were being subjected to. As mentioned earlier, the Canadian ambassador to Syria, Franco D. Pillarella, had been acting since the beginning of Arar's detention as liaison between the Syrian military intelligence and the RCMP, receiving Syrian reports personally from the former about Maher Arar's interrogation and passing them on to the latter. He was a senior diplomat and former head of the Human Rights Legal Section of Canada's Foreign Affairs department and ought to have known of the extensive and well-documented human rights abuses committed by the Syrian military intelligence in Syrian prisons. His protestations at the subsequent inquiry that he had no reason to think Arar was being tortured were viewed generally with skepticism. "There is an indication that there are concerns that he [Arar] might be aggressively questioned," he said in response to a scathing cross examination by commission counsel. "Why should I jump to conclusions at that moment to say, 'Oh that means torture.' Why should I?"[62] In fact, it would later be revealed that a junior official at Foreign Affairs had raised a concern about torture in a meeting with Pillarella and the RCMP present. When the agencies were discussing the issue of whether to send questions to Syria for Almalki's interrogation, he had had the temerity to ask, "If you are going to send questions, would you ask them not to torture him?" Yet Pillarella arranged the delivery of the questions to the Syrians, and later testified that he had not been warned of the possibility of torture.[63]

At the August 14, 2003, consular visit Maher decided that he could not survive any longer in the hellhole of his "grave" and that it was worth risking anything to try to get out. He blurted out the conditions he was being held in—the dimensions of his grave-like cell, the fact that he was sleeping on the ground. He said he was mentally destroyed. The Canadian consul asked him about the treatment he was receiving, and Maher responded, that he was beaten a little at the beginning of his detention. The Syrians were visibly enraged, but they did not torture him afterward.[64]

At home, Foreign Affairs Minister Bill Graham would tell the media that Arar "totally rejects all allegations of torture" and was "interviewed independently" by Canadian consul.[65]

Within days of his interview with the Canadian consul, Maher was taken out of the Syrian hole to an interrogation room where he was forced to sit on the floor and write what was dictated to him. Among other things, he was told to write that he had attended a training camp in Afghanistan. When he objected, he was kicked and threatened with torture in the "tire." Finally he was forced to sign the document with his thumbprint at the bottom of the last page.[66]

The same day he was transferred to a different place, which he learned later was the Investigation Branch. He was stuffed into a

TORTURE WITH A TIRE: in which the victim's body is folded into the center hole of a tire, so that his exposed back and genitals can be beaten.

TORTURE WITH A CHAIR: in which the victim's back is bent backwards over the back of the chair until, in some cases, the back is broken.

twelve-by-twenty-foot cell with about fifty other prisoners. From there he was transferred the next day to Sednaya prison. Sednaya was "like heaven" for him. He could walk around and talk with other prisoners. He could buy food to eat. He was only beaten once.

About a month after he came to Sednaya, Maher heard that another Canadian had arrived there. As he would later say,

> I looked up, and saw a man, but I did not recognize him. His head was shaved, and he was very, very, thin and pale. He was very weak. When I looked closer, I recognized him. It was Abdullah Amalki. He told me he had also been at the Palestine [Far Falestin] Branch, and that he had also been in a grave like I had been except he had been in it longer.
>
> He told me he had been severely tortured with the tire, and the cable.
>
> He was also hanged upside down. He was tortured much worse than me. He had also been tortured when he was brought to Sednaya, so that was only two weeks before.
>
> I do not know why they have Abdullah there. What I can say for sure is that no human deserves to be treated the way he was, and I hope that Canada does all they can to help him.[67]

Then one day at the end of September 2003, Maher was blindfolded and taken away in a bus, back to the Far Falestin prison. His handlers would not tell him what was going on. He was terrified he would be thrown back into the grave. Instead, he was put in a waiting room where he languished for a week, listening, the entire time, to the screams of people being tortured. He was devastated. Once, he was taken out and asked what he would say if he returned to Canada, but no one told him he would be released.

Then on October 5, 2003, the gates of hell opened for Maher Arar, though he did not know it at first. He was told to wash his face. He was chained and driven to court and brought before a prosecutor. When he asked for a lawyer, the prosecutor told him he would not need one. The prosecutor read Maher's "confession" to him and Maher began to protest, saying that he had been beaten and forced to say he had gone to Afghanistan. But the prosecutor ignored him and told him to put his thumbprint on the document, which Maher did. He was not allowed to see it. Then the prosecutor told him he would be released.[68]

That night, Maher Arar was on a plane on his way home to Canada. Flying home, he was in a fragile state. He did not know whom to trust. It was a psychological condition that he would suffer from for many months.[69]

PATTERN EVIDENCE—"RENDITION LITE"

Despite the Syrians' complaints about the hypocrisy of Canadian officials and their threats not to release any more Canadians held in Syrian jails, three more Canadians—all of whom had been under investigation by the RCMP or CSIS and then detained when they were traveling to Syria—were released within months of Maher Arar. All of their interrogations were overseen by the same Syrian general, Hassan Kalil, with whom the Canadian ambassador to Syria, Franco D. Pillarella, liaised regularly.[70]

AHMAD ABOU EL MAATI

Ahmad Abou El Maati[71] was detained in Syria in November 2001, when he traveled there for his marriage to his Syrian bride. He was held in the same Far Falestin prison as Maher Arar, in cell number 5, until his transfer to an Egyptian prison and his eventual release on January 11, 2004.

Ahmad Abou El Maati was once a truck driver and is a big gentle bear of a man. His problems began with a map. In August 2001 he was driving a truck that his employer, Highland Transport, had assigned to him while his regular vehicle was being serviced at the garage. Returning from a delivery in the United States, he was stopped at the Buffalo border and the truck's glove compartment was searched. Border officials seized a copy of a map that was found in the compartment. It was a map of a government complex in Ottawa with nuclear facilities, a virus lab, and other government facilities.

Days later, Ahmad went with his father to Highland Transport to tell his manager what had happened at the border. Over the next few weeks the company looked into the matter of the map and found that the rig in which the map had been found had been driven previously by an Ottawa-based employee who made deliveries to the National Capital Region. The map was one the government regularly gave out to visitors to its Tunney Pasture complex. And, as it would be discovered later by journalist Jeff Sallot,[72] the map was, in fact, very outdated. The nuclear facilities and virus lab were long gone by the time Ahmad was stopped at the border.

On September 11, 2001, two CSIS agents came to visit Ahmad at his apartment. After about fifteen minutes of answering their questions, he said he would prefer to continue with a lawyer present. They threatened him, saying that if he did not cooperate, they would block his new wife from coming to Canada. Afterward, he noticed he was being followed everywhere.

On October 11, 2001, the *Los Angeles Times* published a front-page story about leads being followed by the FBI: "In Canada, U.S. agents were briefed on a thirty-six year-old Kuwaiti man in whose belongings were discovered documents that identified specific buildings in an Ottawa government complex—notably the atomic energy building and the virus and disease control labs."[73]

Ahmad heard news reports about himself on Canadian television and was flabbergasted. "Oh, my God," he thought, "that's about me! There is some mistake. We have to clear this up."[74] To compound matters, Ahmad had served as an ambulance and truck driver with the mujahideen in Afghanistan in the 1990s. He had taken flying lessons at the Buttonville Municipal Airport near Toronto before giving up because he was too frightened to handle the controls. And he had a brother, Amr, who may have been fighting in Afghanistan on the side of the Taliban, with whom the family had not spoken since 1999. But these circumstantial facts did not make Ahmad a terrorist. Ahmad and his father went to a lawyer, and the lawyer called CSIS to set up a meeting. CSIS did not answer his calls. Security intelligence officials were interested in him, but, as this and continuing failures to inquire would show, they were not very interested in investigating the source of the map or in talking to Ahmad further to sort things out. They had their man,[75] and, apparently, that was good enough for them.

In November 2001, Ahmad traveled to Syria with his mother to prepare for and celebrate his wedding. At Toronto Pearson International Airport, they were pulled aside by police who knew who Ahmad was and asked him where the map was. They let Ahmad and his mother board, but their seat assignments were changed so that Ahmad was sitting beside a talkative Lebanese man. The man might have been a government agent, since he ran to hurry them up so that they would catch their connecting flight in Frankfurt and was then seen by Ahmad standing beside two German agents who read details from Ahmad's passport into a cell phone. On the second leg of his journey another talkative Arab man sat down beside Ahmad, even though the plane was only half full.

Ahmad was detained by Syrian officials as soon as he landed in Damascus. They asked him about the map. When he told them the truth, they tortured him and threatened to bring his Syrian bride to the jail and rape her. Ahmad soon broke down and agreed to say what they wanted him to say. He said that he had seen both Arar and Amalki in Afghanistan, even though he had never seen Arar there, and had seen Amalki only in passing. (He barely knew Arar having met him once in Montreal. He was slightly acquainted with Amalki.)

They told him his brother Amr sent him instructions from Afghanistan to take flying lessons so he could recruit Ahmad into Al Qaeda. They told him that Amr wanted Ahmad to prepare for a suicide attack using an airplane. Ahmad said this did not make sense because he had quit the lessons. The Syrians eventually agreed that this did not make sense and said Amr wanted Ahmad to launch a suicide attack using a truck full of explosives.

When Ahmad agreed to falsely confess to this, they told him they wanted him to confess that Amr sent him a map of Ottawa, and said the target would be the U.S. Embassy in Ottawa. Ahmad did not want to be turned over to the United States, so he falsely confessed that he was supposed to pick his own target and had decided on the Canadian Parliament buildings.

Neither the Parliament buildings nor the U.S. Embassy were on the map that had made Ahmad a subject of interest in the first place. The confession that was proposed to Ahmad by his Syrian interrogators, was the "Ottawa plot," intelligence that would be leaked later, in July 2003, when public pressure over the Arar case was growing intense.

About January 25, 2002, Ahmad was transferred by airplane to Egypt and interrogated at the main intelligence headquarters in Cairo, the Mukhabarat Alama. For months Ahmad was transferred between different jails inside the country and tortured. He recanted the false confession and was tortured. He remade the false confession and was tortured. The torture was very severe, and the Egyptians were very skilled at it. They complained about the Syrians' ineptitude. A guard in one of the prisons where he was locked up for four and a half months was friendly with him and told Ahmad that information had come from Canada. Our countries, the guard said, referring to Syria and Egypt, "are like boots to do anything the West wants."

When at last Ahmad received his first Canadian consular visit, nine months after he had first been detained, he blurted out that he had been tortured in Syria and forced to sign a false confession, before the Egyptian officials present could stop him. He was too afraid to mention the treatment he was receiving in Egypt, however.

Ahmad was apparently a target of the Toronto side of Project A-O Canada, and back in Canada, project agents were informed of Ahmad's allegations of torture and of being forced to make a false confession. They began to worry that they might receive negative publicity about the case, and in August 2002, they discussed media lines on what they might say regarding Ahmad's allegations.[76] It is interesting to recall that within a year of the RCMP discussion about media lines, and when publicity really *was* getting hot because of the Arar affair, that American agencies leaked the story of Ahmad's map and the alleged plot to blow up the American Embassy in Ottawa. And, in Ottawa, neither the Department of Foreign Affairs, nor the Mounties, nor CSIS, admitted that the person who was being accused of this plot was a Canadian citizen who claimed he had been tortured into confessing it.

When media on the Arar case were just beginning to get traction, in November 2002, CSIS officers visited Ahmad's father in Canada and said they might go to Egypt to convince the Egyptians to release Ahmad if he would promise to stay in Egypt and not come back to Canada.

In late 2003, Egyptian officers at the State Security Headquarters in Nasr City told Ahmad that they knew that Canada had "done this" to him and that this was happening with many cases in the United States—people were being coerced into agreeing to be informants and to implicate others. They advised Ahmad to go back to Canada and fight back with a good lawyer. Around the same time, Ahmad learned that his bride's family had annulled his marriage. Her father had personally delivered the news to Ahmad's mother, who at this time, was staying in Cairo. The father told Ahmad's mother that he could not imagine a better husband for his daughter, but the family was afraid for their safety and had no choice but to ask for an annulment. Ahmad was overwhelmed on hearing the news, since his memories of his betrothed had helped him to survive.

Then, on January 11, 2004, Egypt's minister of the interior ordered Ahmad's release. He was interrogated one last time, and part of his beard was ripped out. Then he was left at the door of the Giza State Security Branch with his mother's address in Cairo.

A few days later the Canadian Embassy called and asked to see him. They gave him a travel document, but they refused to send someone to accompany him home to Canada. After one failed attempt to leave the country, Ahmad and his mother were able to get back on a plane together and make it home to Canada. He received treatment for the injuries he sustained from torture, including two operations.

On May 26, 2004, several months after Ahmad returned to Canada, FBI Director Robert S. Mueller III and Attorney General John Ashcroft warned the American people on prime time television of an impending "hard" attack on a U.S. target. They asked for help in tracking down seven suspects including Ahmad's brother, Amr El Maati. They said he was an "Al Qaeda member and a licensed pilot [who was] believed to have discussed hijacking a plane in Canada and flying it into a building in the United States." Canadian reporter Colin Freeze later reported that he could find no record of Amr having a pilot license. The warning came at a time when criticism over the United States' invasion of Iraq was becoming intense and this warning was regarded by many people with skepticism, especially since it did not result in a change in the national terror alert. During the preceding months, Unites States' agencies had been leaking news that Amr had been spotted in Toronto, Hamilton, and Nantucket, locations which Amr's family found highly improbable.

Around late December 2005, CSIS agents returned trucking logs and a will they had seized earlier from the El Maati home, saying they had no basis to lay charges against Ahmad. But they continued to try to speak to him without his lawyer's being present. Ahmad told them he had been through a lot because of CSIS and asked them to contact his lawyer.

ABDULLAH ALMALKI

Abdullah Almalki[77] was the main target of the Ottawa side of the Project A-O Canada investigation. He was detained about six months after Ahmad El Maati, while visiting Syria on May 3, 2002, and released on December 11, 2003. Before his ordeal in Syria, Abdullah Almalki was a sharp, ambitious young business man. While still a student, he became concerned about the plight of Afghani refugees in Pakistan and sponsored an Afghani orphan through Human Concern International. He traveled to Pakistan to see, and then work for, HCI projects in the region. In 1992 he spent two months working on a United Nations Development Program (UNDP) reconstruction of a village that HCI was administering near the Pakistani border, and he went back with his new wife to continue working on the project in the fall of 1993. Canadian citizen Ahmed Said Khadr was the regional director for HCI at the time. Abdullah did not agree with the way Khadr was managing the organization, and in April 1994 he and his wife returned to Canada earlier than they had planned.[78]

Khadr was later found to be a close associate of Osama bin Laden, but Abdullah says he did not know this at the time he worked with him, just as Prime Minister Jean Chretién did not know of the relationship in 1996, when he helped get Khadr released from a Pakistani prison. Khadr had emigrated to Canada from Egypt as a young engineer in the 1970s. In the 1980s he left a comfortable job to help Muslim refugees fleeing from the Soviet occupation in Afghanistan.[79] He built a camp for refugee orphans in Pakistan and frequently returned to

Canada to raise funds from the Muslim community, ostensibly for the project. In Canadian mosques, congregations are still trying to reconcile the "passionate Muslim who could bring himself to tears when he told harrowing stories about war-wounded widows and orphans" and the Al Qaeda henchman that he had since then become known to be.[80] Khadr was arrested in Pakistan in December 1995 with $30,000, accused of aiding and abetting terrorists in an attack on the Egyptian Embassy in Islamabad. On a trade visit to Pakistan a month later, Prime Minister Chretién raised his case with the Pakistani prime minister and met with the six Khadr children.[81] This intervention later became a big embarrassment to Canada after the bombing of the U.S. Embassy in Kenya in 1998 and the events of 9/11 and resulted in what some have called "the Khadr effect."[82] It contributed to the zeal with which the Project A-O Canada investigation and its earlier CSIS incarnation were conducted. Many of the Canadian terrorism suspects held abroad and the five Muslim immigrants held indefinitely in Canadian prisons on what are called security certificates, complain that they were wrongly targeted "after having only fleeting contact" with Khadr:[83] an early work experience with him like Abdullah's, a random encounter with him in Afghanistan, a shared car ride to Toronto, a stay at his in-laws' house.

On their return to Canada from Pakistan, Abdullah and his wife set up an electronic-components export business with her expertise in business and his in electrical engineering. He was still a student at the time. While in Pakistan he had researched the market thoroughly, and the fledgling company became a supplier to Pakistan's largest privately owned military and government manufacturer and supplier, Micro Electronics International. The company did well and soon branched out to serve more diverse clientele. According to Abdullah, none of the equipment the company exported was strategic or in any way related to weapons: it did not require military permits. Abdullah finished his degree in 1995 and traveled widely for his business in subsequent years.[84]

A CSIS agent first visited Abdullah in the summer of 1998, ostensibly to ask him about his view on Syria's opening an embassy in Canada. She said CSIS did these kinds of interviews randomly. He saw no reason not to talk with her. He told her about his work for HCI. The agent seemed surprised.

After the U.S. bombing of a pharmaceutical plant in the Sudan, the CSIS agent returned to talk with him, asking him questions about Khadr and Osama bin Laden. She asked if Abdullah sold equipment to the Taliban, and he said he did not.

Over the next three and a half years, Abdullah was subjected to intense surveillance. His company's shipment boxes appeared to have been opened regularly; a man in the Ottawa Muslim community told him that he had been asked to search Abdullah's house for bomb-making equipment, and others in the community were interviewed by CSIS about him. Abdullah himself was grilled at U.S. and Canadian customs. It appeared that a CSIS agent posing as a real-estate agent came to his house twice while he was away; that his bank accounts were being monitored; that his house was broken into; that his credit cards statements were mailed to someone impersonating him; that a camera was installed across the street from his house; and that his car was being followed. CSIS came several times to question him over this period. As it would later be revealed, CSIS had a theory about Abdullah. The theory was that he had sold equipment to a Pakistani company which dealt with the Pakistani army (likely Micro Electronics International, a legitimate customer of Abdullah's) and that equipment later turned up in Afghanistan. After three and a half years of close surveillance, however, they appeared to have no proof that Abdullah had any intentional involvement in such a transfer, and it is unclear whether they even had evidence about the equipment ending up in Afghanistan. Otherwise, they could certainly have charged Abdullah under the new Anti-terrorism Act in Canada.

As mentioned earlier, the RCMP initiated Project A-O Canada shortly after the September 11, 2001, attacks in the United States, taking over files from CSIS. Abdullah Almalki was a main target of CSIS, and it appears that he became the main target of the Ottawa side of the A-O Canada project from the start.

Abdullah and his wife were tired of being harassed and followed, and her mother in Malaysia was ill. In November 2001, they decided to take a vacation to visit her for several weeks. Their travel agent turned over their itinerary to the RCMP. In transit, their personal desktop computer was seized, apparently without a warrant. In Malaysia, Abdullah was questioned at the request of Canadian agencies about whether he would be returning to Canada. Malaysian officials apparently had also been asked by the Canadians to detain Abdullah while he was there, but they had refused since they had no evidence with which to justify detention.

While Abdullah was in Malaysia, his parents were in Syria, and the home where they lived together in Ottawa was searched and ransacked by Project A-O Canada. This was one of the seven warrants they executed in January 2002. The RCMP also visited Abdullah's three brothers and the homes of his extended family. They asked if Abdullah would be going to Syria.

Near the end of the family's stay in Malaysia, Abdullah decided to travel to Singapore and then Saudi Arabia for business. His parents had told him that his grandmother in Syria was ill, so he decided to travel there, too, to gather with the family.

According to Kerry Pither's *Abdullah Almalki Chronology*, as soon as Abdullah arrived, he was picked up and detained by Syrian agents.

> They questioned him while they beat him, asking if he sold equipment to al-Qaeda or the Taliban or others, and if he had ever met, communicated with or dealt with Osama Bin Laden or al-Qaeda. They asked him what computer equipment he had sold to them. Abdullah told them no, he had not sold to them or dealt with them in any way, and that he [did] not sell computers.

> ... the torture continued until Abdullah told them what he knew they wanted to hear—he lied and told them he knew Bin Laden. They asked him from when and where, and Abdullah said from when he worked on the UNDP project in Afghanistan.... A few minutes later they accused him of lying, and said Bin Laden had been in the Sudan when Abdullah was in Pakistan and Afghanistan. Abdullah told them that he had told them what they wanted to hear because he wanted them to stop torturing him. He told them he had never met Bin Laden.
>
> They started the beating again ...

Abdullah later learned that on his first day he had been beaten for seven hours and had received over one thousand lashes with a cable, though the maximum used on other prisoners was usually two hundred.

Like Maher Arar and Ahmad El Maati, Abdullah was kept for more than a year in a grave-like cell. The walls were dripping with condensation, and there was yellow and black mold and lice growing in his blanket. He suffered severe torture. He was asked about Khadr and Arar and about twenty other Canadians, some of whom he knew, some he didn't.

On the fortieth day of his detention, Abdullah was interrogated by George Saloum, the head of the investigation team. On more than one occasion, Saloum would order his underlings to beat Abdullah "until he needed to be hospitalized."

It appeared that the Canadians sent several reports to the Syrians about Abdullah during his incarceration. The first time, in July 2002, his interrogators beat him badly, calling him a liar. They told him they had planned to release him until they had received this new report. The second time, in August 2002, he was beaten, then taken to be interrogated with a Malaysian official present. From under his blindfold, he saw two reports on a table, one in English, another in Malay. On November 28, 2002, his interrogators seemed to have another report from Canada. When Abdullah said they should ask the Canadians for proof of their claims in the report, the Syrians told him he was not supposed to know this report had come from Canada.

> [Taking their direction from the report] the interrogators told him that the serial numbers on equipment found in Afghanistan proved that the equipment had come from him. Abdullah asked for a description of the equipment, and they did not know that information. He asked them to ask the Canadian government for the details, so that he could check to see who[m] he had sold it to.
>
> Abdullah also told them again that he had not sold equipment to anyone in Afghanistan.
>
> ... They also asked him repeatedly what he had shipped by sea ... [T]he report said that the U.S. navy was searching a ship in the Caucasian Sea for goods that he had sold to a terrorist organization, and that this would be proof of his guilt. Abdullah pointed out that he had been in detention for seven months now, and could not have shipped anything.
>
> Abdullah also said that if the report said that this would be proof, then it meant they had no proof yet.
>
> ... The interrogator closed the file and never questioned him about that again. Abdullah felt that the interrogators were beginning to lose confidence in the Canadians' credibility.

Later, in December 2002, he saw a document in Arabic, entitled, "Meeting with the Canadian delegation of November 24, 2002." It was addressed to the head of the prison and the head of military intelligence. On January 16, 2003, his interrogators had the biggest report he had seen yet, and they no longer tried to hide that the reports were coming from Canada. It included two long pages of questions. The RCMP liaison officer based in Rome had been in Damascus a few days earlier and had reported to his superiors, "in both cases, no new information was obtained."

After Maher Arar was released in October 2003, Abdullah continued to be held and tortured. But it seems that at some point, the Syrians sent the Canadians their interrogation reports, which cleared him of terrorist and other charges. That may have been before December 2003, when the RCMP agreed to write a letter for the lawyer the Almalki family had retained, stating that Almalki had no criminal record in Canada and was not the subject of a warrant of arrest in Canada.

On March 10, 2004, Abdullah was called up before the Syrian official in charge of his file, who told him that if the Canadians had sent a letter, it must have been after the Syrians sent them the interrogation reports that cleared him. On that same day, one year and seven months after he was detained, Abdullah was released on the conditions that he not speak to the media and would remain in Syria for at least one year.

Abdullah's parents were still in Syria, and as soon as he reached their house, he called his wife. They had not spoken since April 2002. She was already arranging to join him with the children. After a week, Abdullah went to the Canadian Embassy to get his passport renewed. The man he talked to through the thick glass window was Canadian consul Leo Martel. Abdullah had to ask to be let into the embassy. Martel seemed nervous with him, saying he was surprised to see him. He had been expecting Arwad Al Boushi, another Canadian held in Syria, to be released. He asked Abdullah how he had been treated, and Abdullah replied that he had been warned by the Syrians not to talk about his experience. "Martel told Abdullah that he must tell his wife not to speak to the media, because Foreign Affairs would be very upset if the media learned what had happened to him before he spoke with [Foreign Affairs] about it."[85]

Abdullah was terrified that he would be detained again while having to stay in Syria. Within a month of being released, he was called into questioning at Far' Falestin. His interrogators had a new report, and he wondered whether it was yet another one sent by the Canadians. The report claimed that Abdullah was the spiritual leader of a group called the "Prayers Group."

> He told them he had never heard of the group and that he only recognized one name on their list. The interrogators were frustrated, and threatened to bring the tire to torture him again. He told them that none of what was in the report was true. He reminded them that he had been in detention for almost two years and therefore could not be this group's spiritual leader. The interrogators let him leave.

Abdullah met Martel and another embassy person for lunch and told them about the report and his interrogation. During the conversation, Abdullah spoke about the need for the embassy to get access to Al Boushi and said that the head of the military intelligence interrogators, George Saloum, would be the person to contact. Martel said he was *good friends with Saloum.*

Abdullah's final departure from Syria was a harrowing experience. When his wife and children arrived in June, his youngest child did not recognize him. In July he was acquitted of all charges in a Syrian military court, but the judge said he should be handed over to the Syrian military police because, as a Syrian, he had not done his military service and he had not applied for a waiver while he was in detention. The judge released Abdullah for two days. Canadian Liberal MP Dan McTeague, who had been helping the family, contacted Abdullah's brothers in Ottawa to advise them that Abdullah should go to the Canadian Embassy or ambassador's residence until the issue of military service was cleared up. Abdullah went to the Canadian Embassy in Damascus as soon as he heard from his brothers. He told Martel he had been instructed by Dan McTeague to stay inside the embassy, but Martel said he could not, because Abdullah was a dual national and allowing him refuge would be disrespectful to Syria. Martel told Abdullah he had to leave the embassy building when it closed at the end of the day. At 4:30 P.M. he was forced out, despite calls made from the embassy to confirm McTeague's instructions and calls made to the embassy from media in Canada.

Abdullah stood outside the locked embassy, not knowing what to do. He was too afraid to return to where he was staying, and he walked the streets for hours. The next day he got in touch with people he knew in the Syrian government. They told him that if the judge had wanted to make him do military service, he would not have let him leave the court: Abdullah was supposed to leave the country so the Syrians could wash their hands of him. Abdullah was wary and went to immigration to see if his name was on any list and if he could get an exit visa. Then he called a travel agency to find out what was the first flight to Europe. It was from Beirut to Vienna. He drove fifteen minutes to the Lebanese border, made it through, and kept going all the way to Beirut, where he managed to catch the flight. From Vienna, he called his wife to tell her what had happened and urge her to leave Syria with the children before anyone discovered he had left. They made it out three days later.

MUAYYED NURREDIN

Muayyed Nurredin was the third Canadian to be detained in a Syrian prison and released after Maher Arar. He was detained in Syria on December 11, 2003, held and tortured in the Far' Falestin prison just as the other Canadians had been, and released January 14, 2004. Much less is publicly known about his story than the other men's. The fact finder in the Arar Inquiry described Nurredin as a "simple man"[86] but found him to be a credible witness who corroborated the details Maher Arar gave about his detention in Syria.

ARWAD AL BOUSHI

Arwad Al Boushi[87] was the last of the Canadian citizens held in Syria on terrorism suspicions to be released. He returned to Canada on December 23, 2005, after spending three and half years in a Syrian prison. Al Boushi was a member of the Muslim Brotherhood before he emigrated to Canada in the 1970s. He had not been back to Syria since he had left, but when his father grew ill, he asked Syrian authorities as to whether his membership in an opposition group would preclude him visiting the country. He was assured it would not be a problem.

Al Boushi says he did not know Maher Arar, Abdullah Almalki, Ahmad El Maati, or Muayyed Nureddin.

◎ ◎

Of course, all of the facts relating to the four cases described above are not yet known, but these stories, along with Maher Arar's, suggest a pattern of Canadian officials cooperating and even conniving at having Canadian suspects detained in third countries like Syria and Egypt, where they can be interrogated without any of the usual restrictions that interrogations are subject to in Canada.

Alex Neve, the secretary general of Amnesty International Canada, has suggested that Canada may, in fact, be practicing a form of rendition for which he has coined the name, "rendition lite." Kerry Pither, the author of the chronologies detailing the stories of Maher Arar, Abdullah Almaki, and Ahamd El Maati, and the coordinator of the intervenors in the Arar Inquiry, has said it might better be called "rendition on the cheap"—"rendition where the subject pays for his own plane ticket" and the only overhead for Canada is the cost of supplying questions to the foreign agencies doing the dirty work.

MAHER'S HOMECOMING

When Monia met Maher at the airport on his return from Syria, the first of the Canadians held in Syria or Egypt to be released, she was shocked to see a man who was submissive and without any light in his eyes. She said later that he looked "like a dog" and that he seemed "lost."[88] "He was preoccupied with his safety and was completely distrustful. Over the next few days, as the family spent time together in Montreal, [Maher] began to tell his story. He was completely disjointed, with random memories and continuous crying. He could not eat or sleep for two or three days.... [F]or many weeks [he] seemed 'confused.' He would pace back and forth, as if still in his cell, as he talked to his wife. He was always tired. He told [Monia] that he just wanted 'a normal life.'..."[89]

On November 4, 2003, Maher held a press conference. He said he was there to tell the people of Canada what had happened to him. He said he wanted to tell them who he was and who he was not. He was not a terrorist. He was not a member of Al Qaeda, and he did not know anyone who belonged to that group. He had never been to Afghanistan, and he had no desire to ever go to Afghanistan. Then he told his story.

But first, he talked about his wife, Monia. He said he knew that she was special when he married her, but he had no idea how special she would turn out to be. "If it were not for her I believe I would still be in prison."

Maher Arar was the first person to be "rendered" in the "war on terrorism" and come back alive to speak to the public fully about his experience. And to follow up on his passionate convictions that this should never happen to anyone again; that Canadians should know what had happened; and that he should have a the right to clear his name. As *Time* magazine would write in a feature article about him, "if Arar is a terrorist, he is unlike any other."[90]

Monia and Maher continued to call for a public inquiry. In this, they were supported by dozens of civil society organizations, government MPs, opposition parties, the media, and ordinary Canadians. The case fast became a cause célèbre, with all kinds of articles, editorials, and letters being written about it to demand answers from the government. It was Canada's "Dreyfus affair," but with less division over who the good guy was—and a determination to get to the bottom of who the bad guys were. The calls for a public inquiry were first turned down by Solicitor General Wayne Easter and then by the prime minister himself. In early November 2003, speaking to the House of Commons, Prime Minister Jean Chretién was adamant that he would not allow a public inquiry. But as the public demand continued to mount over the months, the government finally relented. By that time, there was a new Liberal leader and prime minister, Paul Martin, and he vowed that *he* would get to the bottom of the affair. But, when a Commission of Inquiry was set up in February 2004, its mandate was disappointing in that it was restricted to investigating the actions of Canadian officials in relation to Maher Arar and making recommendations concerning an independent, arm's-length review mechanism for the RCMP's national security activities. The Canadian government seemed to want to avoid any inquiry into whether there might be a pattern of Canadian complicity or connivance in having Canadian citizens detained abroad for terrorism interrogations. Nevertheless, Dennis O'Connor, Associate Chief Justice of Ontario, who was appointed commissioner of the Arar Inquiry, was a highly respected jurist in whom many placed their confidence.

After many months of hearing both public and secret testimony and many more months of negotiating with the government over what could be disclosed to the public, Justice O'Connor released his report on September 18, 2006. It confirmed Maher Arar's innocence. It exposed a political culture that led to the excesses and abuses I've described. And it called for a further probe into the cases of the other Canadians caught up in the grim net of a "prevention" mandate.

In February 2006, the United States District Court, Eastern District of New York, dismissed Maher Arar's civil lawsuit against the United States government, the federal judge saying, "One need not have much imagination to contemplate the negative effect on our relations with Canada if discovery were to proceed in this case and were it to turn out that certain high Canadian officials had, despite public denials, acquiesced in Arar's removal to Syria."[91] The decision is now on appeal, but, as I describe later, in September 2006 an unholy deal was struck between Congress and the Bush administration. If passed, it will strip Maher Arar and others who have been detained or rendered by the United States of any rights they have to challenge their treatment in U.S. courts.

⊙ ⊙

Monia rescued her husband, literally, from the grave. She was asked by two political parties to run for Parliament, lauded in magazine and newspaper articles and invited to speak in forums across the country. Maher was named newsmaker of 2004 by Canadian *Time* magazine, was invited to speak across Canada, and was sought out for his comments by the media. Both of them became widely respected for their modesty, grace, and determination. Ordinary Canadians would speak of them by the water cooler and over the dinner table, and would come up to them on the street to show their solidarity. It was along with these Canadians that Monia and Maher had forced the government to call a public inquiry.

But there would be no happy ending for them and their children.

The man Monia had married had been an energetic, focused, even driven person. After his return from Syria, he found it difficult to focus on anything. He would feel overwhelmed if he had more than two meetings in a day. Before, he was an easygoing person with strong family values. After his return, he was often emotionally distant from his family and preoccupied with his own concerns. This was a huge source of guilt for him. He was often impatient with the children and found it difficult to spend time with them on their own terms. He suffered for many months from headaches and pain in his back and neck. He was often stressed and ground his teeth. For a long time he was obsessed with having his story told, with the Commission of Inquiry, and with the fate of other people in detention. He would not accept any engagements that would require him to take an airplane, as he was terrified that his plane might be redirected and his nightmare started all over again. He could not read the Koran.[92]

When Canadian agencies "leaked" information after his return, apparently designed to smear his reputation and justify themselves, his sense of injustice dating from his detention and torture in Syria was compounded. Advisers described him as "devastated" by these leaks and sometimes "hysterical." "He simply could not control his emotions and it took many hours of constant conversation to calm him down each time new information surfaced in the press that he thought to be misleading and unfair."[93]

The fact finder appointed by the commissioner of the Arar Inquiry to determine whether Arar had been tortured and what the effects of it had been for him and his family eloquently described the ruined hopes and dreams of a talented couple that once had everything to look forward to:

> Although the psychological effects of Mr. Arar's detention and torture in Syria have been serious, the economic effects have been close to catastrophic, at least from the perspective of a middle class engineer who has had to rely on social assistance to feed, clothe and house his family. Every person I interviewed who knows Mr. Arar well stressed that his inability to find a job since returning to Canada has had a devastating effect upon both his psychological state and his family finances.
>
> Mr. Arar told me that his lack of employment was

> "destroying" him. Dr. Mazigh mentioned that it was a source of tension between her and her husband. She was encouraging him to look as widely as possible for any job, whereas he was still fixated upon finding a job in his field, computer engineering. . . . Failing to find a job has also encouraged Mr. Arar's sense of estrangement from the Muslim community: it is the most concrete example of a failure to help him when he needed help. Mr. Arar has sent out hundreds of email inquiries and letters, and has had few responses. When he was able to speak directly to prospective employers, some of his advisors told me that he has been dealt with abruptly and coldly.[94]

Indeed, it was not just the Muslim community and the high-tech sector that failed Maher Arar. None of the scores of organizations that supported his cause and respected him personally, in the labor movement, the human rights movement, or other areas of social justice offered him even a part-time contract when asked.

> To put Mr. Arar's inability to find a job in its proper context, it is important to note that Mr. Arar seems to find much of his self worth through his work. He is the most educated member of his family, the youngest child of a mother who pushed him to succeed in his studies. He is immensely proud of his engineering credentials, and has a strong self image as a successful and highly competent professional. He was pleased to be asked to travel for his work. As he described his past work experience and his commitment to various projects, a picture emerged of a man who might even be described as a workaholic. Mr. Arar took a job in Boston while leaving his wife behind in Canada with their first child while she completed her Ph.D. He did so because he was ambitious and thought this was the best job

> offer at the time, with the best prospects for the future. Mr. Arar cared deeply about his earning potential.
>
> In light of subsequent events, it is ironic that Mr. Arar seemed to harbour strongly positive feelings about American business culture. He told me, and this was confirmed by other observers, that he found American business people more professional, more competent and more committed than most Canadians he had dealt with. He seemed to believe that his future would lie in business contacts in the United States. He returned to Canada from the United States hoping to remain a consultant for his American employer. Boston was exciting professionally, but too expensive. He wanted to re-unite his family in the safe and relatively inexpensive environment of Ottawa where the family's standard of living would be best protected.
>
> That dream has collapsed utterly. The most recent information available to me is that Mr. Arar has finally been offered a small part-time position as a computer advisor in his daughter's school.[95]

Recently, a colleague of mine[96] said of Maher Arar, "That man is the most innocent person in Canada: of all the people in this country he is the one person of whom we can say 'he is truly innocent.' And yet the man will go to his grave without ever being fully embraced by us."

CHAPTER TWO

The Tip of an Iceberg: The U.S. President's Secret Spying

◎ ◎

A country is not only what it does—it is also what it puts up with, what it tolerates.
—Kurt Tucholsky

The executive shall never exercise the legislative and judicial powers, or either of them, to the end that it may be a government of laws and not of men.
—John Adams

The Arar affair became a cause célèbre because it is a cautionary tale of our times. However, it may never have had the impact it did without individuals like Monia Mazigh and Maher Arar as its protagonists. It took someone Canadians could relate to, individuals with the charisma, familiarity, and principle of Monia and Maher, so that we could see not just a "them" but a possible "us" in their situation. "There but for the grace of God . . ." was the thought. The story took the comfort out of the rationalization many Canadians had been lulled into accepting: that governments know best how to fight terrorism, that if there were a few broken eggs in making *that* omelet, at least it was better to be safe than sorry. *Better them than us.*

But for all the attention they got, the Arar story and those of other Canadians detained without charge and tortured in third countries are only the tip of a much bigger iceberg that, to date, has lain largely under the public's radar screen: an iceberg on which democracies and democratic movements may ultimately be shipwrecked in this century.

Another piece of that iceberg surfaced in December 2005 when the *New York Times* reported that the president of the United States had directly violated a congressional statute by secretly ordering the National Security Agency (NSA) to spy without warrants on the phone calls and e-mails of people *inside* the United States. The NSA's mission allows it to spy on foreign communications without warrants, but warrantless domestic spying is still officially illegal in the United States.

The Bush administration claimed that its warrantless eavesdropping program intruded only on international communications made and received in the United States. In other words,

> The National Security Agency was created by President Harry Truman in 1952 bringing military and civilian signal intelligence together under one roof. Jokingly referred to as "No Such Agency" or "Never Saying Anything," the very existence of the agency has been a matter of secrecy, since its inception. The mandate of the agency since the introduction of the Foreign Intelligence Surveillance Act, has been to spy on foreign and foreign agent communications, and the NSA has participated for many years in the Anglo-American signals intelligence effort, known as ECHELON. Now the largest government spy agency in the world, the NSA is located in Fort Meade, Maryland, and employs approximately 30,000 people. It shreds 40,000 pounds of documents a day and has a yearly electric bill of $21 million.
>
> Source: Susan Page, "NSA secret database triggers fierce debate in Washington," *USA Today*, May 11, 2006.

President Bush told the American people, "one end of the communication must be outside the United States."[97] The administration also asserted it was using a "probable cause" standard: that NSA access to communications was based on probable cause that a person in the United States was communicating with someone outside the United States who was linked to terrorist activities.[98] However, what the administration was not revealing, was that the NSA was in fact *trolling through vast troves of Americans' telephone and e-mail conversations with artificial intelligence, looking for key words and patterns.* The NSA was tapping into the "switches" that route communications in and out of the United States: it was vacuuming up enormous amounts of data in what some officials called a large data-mining operation.[99] This was, in fact, the normal way the NSA worked within its ordinary mandate of overseas electronic surveillance.

Communications that were flagged by computer programs as warranting human inspection were then viewed by NSA agents. However, news reports revealed that most of the communications that had been tagged in the warrantless domestic program had been rejected as having no intelligence value.[100] According to the *New York Times*, "[m]ore than a dozen current and former law enforcement and counterterrorism officials, including some in the small circle who knew of the secret program and how it played out at the FBI, said the torrent of tips [they received from the NSA about people in the United States] led them to few potential terrorists inside the country they did not know of from other sources and diverted agents from counterterrorism work they viewed as more productive."[101] Both U.S. and British counterterrorism officials questioned Bush administration assertions that the Canadian Communications Security Establishment (CSE) program "saved lives" in the alleged London fertilizer bomb plot and the alleged Brooklyn Bridge blowtorch plot. In both cases, officials said they had already learned of these plots through other means.[102]

Meanwhile, the scope of the intrusion under the NSA program into Americans' constitutionally protected privacy appeared to be vast. If the NSA was data mining without warrants at the main arteries of the American telephone system, the program potentially touched every person in the Unites States calling, e-mailing, or faxing internationally. The *New York Times* reported that the surveillance performed by human agents involved "up to 500 people in the United States at any given time," according to unnamed officials.[103] "The list change[d] as some names [were] added and others dropped, so the number monitored may have reached into the thousands since the program began. . . . Overseas, about 5,000 to 7,000 people . . . [were] monitored at one time."[104] According to the *Washington Post*, knowledgeable sources placed the total number of people in the United States who had their communications viewed by human agents between 2002 and 2006 at 5,000.[105]

In short, the idea that communications were being accessed by the NSA on the basis of "probable cause"—either by its data-mining programs or by its human agents—was pure fiction. To meet the legal standard of "probable cause" one government official has said that the NSA would have to be "right for [at least] one out of every two guys" whose communications it intercepted.[106]

There was "[p]alpable outrage" on the part of "Republicans as well as Democrats at the President's contempt for basic constitutional law" when the program was first revealed.[107] In December 2005, a bipartisan majority voted to block the reauthorization of parts of the USA PATRIOT Act, and some of them cited their anger over the program as a reason for their vote.[108] Senate Judiciary Committee Chairman Arlen Specter (R–Pennsylvania) called the president's domestic spying "inexcusable . . . clearly and categorically wrong" and vowed to hold hearings into it.[109] Senator Russ Fiengold (D–Wisconsin) called for a formal censure of the president for violation of federal surveillance laws. And a growing number of observers, including Elizabeth Holtzman,[110] a former member of the House Judiciary Committee during the Nixon Impeachment Proceedings, and Lewis H. Lapham,[111] editor of *Harper's Magazine*, called for the impeachment of President George W. Bush.

The law that the president's secret spying program directly violates is the Foreign Intelligence Surveillance Act (FISA).[112] It provides that law enforcement and intelligence agencies must apply to a court for warrants to spy on communications within the United States. In order to obtain a warrant they must show probable cause that the target of the surveillance in the United States is a "foreign power" or an "agent of a foreign power," and that the places at which surveillance is requested is used, or will be used, by that foreign power or its agent. FISA makes any electronic surveillance not authorized by statute a *criminal offense* and expressly provides that it and the Federal Criminal Code (which governs surveillance for criminal investigations) are the *"exclusive means by which electronic surveillance . . . may be conducted."*

FISA was enacted in the United States in 1978 to stem the widespread abuses of domestic surveillance that had been revealed in the U.S. Senate's Church Committee Report, officially entitled *The Final Report of the Select Committee to Study Governmental Operations with Respect to Intelligence Activities*, and in congressional hearings into the Watergate scandal. The revelations of domestic wiretapping abuses by the FBI and the president in those proceedings showed Americans how easily a national security rationale could be misused by those in power. Using the excuse of national security, the FBI had targeted the civil rights movement, the labor movement, and university campuses throughout the 1960s and into the 1970s. Among his many abuses of power, President Nixon had ordered the wiretapping of seventeen journalists and White House staffers. He had claimed the surveillance was for national security purposes, but it was politically motivated. Nixon began his wiretapping to counter opposition to the Vietnam War. The first wiretap he ordered was of a reporter who exposed the secret bombing of Cambodia in 1969. Nixon's abuse of domestic wiretapping formed one of the articles of his impeachment.[113]

The idea of warrantless domestic wiretapping evokes a strong bipartisan response in the political culture of the United States because of this history, as President Bush no doubt anticipated when he decided to keep his program secret. As Republican Senator Arlen Specter, observed, "The whole history of America is a history of balance.... I think [the Bush administration is] seeing concerns in a lot of directions from all segments: Democrats and Republicans in all shades of the political spectrum."[114] Republican Representative Heather Wilson and at least six other Republican lawmakers openly broke ranks to voice their concerns over the program.[115] In the middle of February 2006, Wilson became the first Republican on either the House or Senate Intelligence Committees to call for a congressional inquiry. Former President Jimmy Carter tacitly criticized the Bush administration program at the funeral of Coretta Scott King, commenting on the difficulties that she and her husband, Martin Luther King Jr., had endured as they became targets of abusive government wiretapping in the 1960s.

When the story of the program first came out, President Bush initially refused to confirm its existence. Asked on December 17, 2005, by Jim Lehrer of Public Broadcasting System (PBS) about the *New York Times* report of the previous evening, Bush called it "speculation" and said he did not "talk about ongoing intelligence operations."[116] But as the uproar over the story increased, the administration changed tactics and went on the attack.

Bush told Americans that the program was a "vital tool in our war against the terrorists," that he had reauthorized the program more than thirty times since the September 11, 2001, attacks, and that he would continue to do so "as long as our nation is facing a continuing threat from Al Qaeda and related groups."[117] He called the leak "a shameful act" and suggested that those who criticized the program were giving "aid and comfort" to the enemy—fighting words, since they match the constitutional definition for "treason."[118]

Speaking at a House Republican retreat in early February 2006, President Bush reached out to members who were uneasy about the program, saying, "You've got to understand something about me. September 11 changed the way I think. I told the people exactly what I felt at the time, and I still feel it, and that is we must do everything in our power to protect the country."[119]

The Bush administration explained that its warrantless surveillance program was necessary because FISA did not allow it to move quickly enough to counter potential attackers. This argument rang hollow, however, since FISA allows the president to start a wiretap without a warrant as long as he seeks approval from the FISA court within a three-day period. Moreover, between its enactment in 1978 and 2004, only five applications for warrants have been turned down by the FISA court, out of 18,748.[120] Thus, FISA is hardly a barrier to timely surveillance or to surveillance itself. The truth was that the Bush administration couldn't use FISA because they weren't wiretapping a few specific individuals, they were essentially wiretapping the majority of people in the country. As the *Washington Post* reported:

> Shortly after the warrantless eavesdropping program began, then–NSA Director Michael V. Hayden and Ashcroft made clear in private meetings that the president wanted to detect possible terrorist activity before another attack. They also made clear that, in such a broad hunt for suspicious patterns and activities, the government could never meet the FISA court's probable cause requirement.[121]

The Bush administration offered two legal justifications for its secret program. First, it said that Congress's 2001 Authorization for Use of Military Force (AUMF), which authorized the president "to use all necessary and appropriate force" against those connected with the September 11, 2001, attacks, implicitly authorized the president to conduct warrantless electronic surveillance in the United States since this was a necessary incident of the use of force in wartime. This was news to the members of Congress who had given the AUMF. In Senate Judiciary Committee hearings into the warrantless wiretap program, Republican Senator Lindsey Graham of South Carolina said he "never envisioned that he was giving to this president or any other president the ability to go around FISA carte blanche," adding that the argument was "very dangerous," since it would make it more difficult for future presidents to get a use of force resolution. Democrat Senator Patrick J. Leahy of Vermont told Bush's attorney general, Alberto Gonzales, "This is not a wiretap statute. We know what a wiretap statute looks like. This is not it." The former Senate majority leader who negotiated the 2001 resolution with the White House, Tom Daschle, said that the Bush administration had asked for explicit language enlarging the president's war making powers to include domestic activity, and the language had been rejected.[122]

When the program was first revealed, Gonzales himself told reporters that the administration had not tried to amend FISA to authorize its program, because "members of Congress" had "advised that that would be difficult if not impossible" to do.

If the first legal argument drew exclamations of incredulity from Congress and conjured up a spectacle of the Bush administration sucking and blowing at the same time, the second legal argument made by the administration to defend its program downright alarmed people.

The second argument was that the president, as commander in chief and supervisor of the "unitary Executive," had the constitutional power to suspend or break any U.S. law in wartime, on the grounds of national security. The nonpartisan Congressional Research Service rejected the commander in chief notion, noting that the Supreme Court had never granted the president a "monopoly over war-powers," nor recognized him as "Commander-in-Chief of the country," nor given him carte blanche in the area of wiretapping.[123] The doctrine of a unitary executive, moreover, is a highly doubtful one, not supported by most constitutional scholars in the United States or by the bulk of case law. It holds that all executive power is vested in the president, so that congressional power to divest the president of control over the functions, agencies, and officers of the executive branch is limited. Yet the very words of the Constitution of the United States contradict the theory, granting Congress the exclusive power to "make *all Laws* which shall be necessary and proper for carrying into Execution . . . *all* . . . *Powers* vested by this Constitution in the Government of the United States, or in *any Department or Officer* thereof" and obligating the president to "take Care that the *Laws* be faithfully executed" (emphasis added).[124]

This second argument made by the administration and its extreme interpretation of unitary executive theory is a dangerous one even to entertain. It puts the president above the law and fundamentally changes the structure of democratic government in the United States since it makes the executive branch of government dominant in power to the legislative and judicial branches of government, when each branch is intended to be coequal to, and a check on, the other. Many people began to wonder if the president could intercept international calls on the basis of national security, why not domestic calls? If he could break the FISA law, why not any law? Why bother to pass the PATRIOT Act; why bother to haggle over any law, any limit on government power, since the president was arrogating to himself what were essentially dictatorial powers?

They didn't need to wonder long. On April 7, 2006, Attorney General Alberto Gonzales suggested that the president *could* order the NSA to spy, without warrants, on purely domestic calls and e-mails made and received inside the United States.[125] And on May 11, 2006, *USA Today* broke the story that the NSA *was* spying on purely domestic telephone calls. Not only that, *it was storing the call records in a giant database.* "It's the largest database ever assembled in the world," the newspaper quoted an unnamed source saying. "[The agency's goal] is to create a database of every call ever made" within the nation's borders.[126] The administration, it was also revealed, had gained the cooperation of three out of four of the nation's telecom companies—AT&T, Verizon, and BellSouth—and was paying them for access to their call records.[127]

According to *USA Today*, the National Security Agency was only collecting the "external" or traffic data of telephone calls made within the United States, not the content, or the names and addresses of callers. It was analyzing calling patterns in order to detect terrorist activity.[128] But about a week after the *USA Today* story broke, veteran investigative reporter Seymour Hersh uncovered information that suggested the NSA was in fact looking at the content of communications.

> A security consultant working with a major telecommunications carrier told me that his client set up a top-secret high-speed circuit between its main computer and Quantico, Virginia, the site of a government-intelligence computer center. This link provided direct access to the carrier's network core—the critical area of its system, where all its data are stored. "What companies are doing is worse than turning over records," the consultant said. "They're providing total access to data."[129]

"This is not about getting a cardboard box of monthly phone bills in alphabetical order," Hersh quoted a former intelligence official as saying. The goal after 9/11 was to find suspected terrorists and capture or kill them. "The NSA is getting real-time actionable intelligence" the official said.[130]

Traffic pattern analysis inevitably led to looking at content.

> The N.S.A. also programmed computers to map the connections between telephone numbers in the United States and suspect numbers abroad, sometimes focusing in on a geographic area, rather than on a specific person—for example, a region of Pakistan. Such calls often triggerd a process, known as "chaining," in which subsequent calls to and from the American number were monitored and linked. The way it worked, one high-level Bush Administration intelligence official told me, was for the agency "to take the first number out to two, three, or more levels of separation, and see if one of them comes back"—if, say, someone down the chain was also calling the original, suspect number. As the chain grew longer, more and more Americans inevitably were drawn in.[131]

An administration intelligence official told Hersh that at that stage there was no need to get a warrant, because "there's no personal identifier involved, other than the metadata from a call being placed."[132] Whether this is a correct legal view or not, what "chaining" led to certainly did require a warrant.

"After you hit something, you have to figure out what to do with it," the administration intelligence official told Hersh. The lawful thing would have been to get a suspect's name and go to the FISA court for a warrant to listen to the content of his or her communications. But the quality, ambiguity, and sheer volume of the information that had been generated were a major stumbling block. "There's too many calls and not enough judges in the world" a former senior intelligence official" told Hersh.[133]

> The agency would also have had to reveal how far it had gone, and how many Americans were involved. And there was a risk that the court could shut down the program.... Instead, the N.S.A. began, in some cases, to eavesdrop on

callers (often using computers to listen for key words) or to investigate them using traditional police methods. A government consultant told me that tens of thousands of Americans had had their calls monitored in one way or another. "In the old days, you needed probable cause to listen in," the consultant said. "But you could not listen in to generate probable cause. What they're doing is a violation of the spirit of the law."[134]

CHAPTER THREE

The New Mantra: Preemption of Risk

◎ ◎

Evil is whatever distracts.
—Franz Kafka

The iceberg of which President Bush's secret eavesdropping program and Maher Arar's story are but the tip is the new way surveillance is being used by governments since 9/11. To understand the scope and genesis of this new use of surveillance, it is useful to begin by examining the context from which this new use has emerged.

After 9/11 the mantra of the Bush administration was that of "preempting" or "disrupting" terrorist plots before they happened, drying up the sources of terrorist financing, and draining the swamps of "failed" and "rogue" states that harbored terrorists. In part, the administration was responding to the extreme feelings of insecurity Americans had after 9/11. Though statistics showed the number of people killed in car crashes in the United States each year outnumbered, many times over, those killed globally by terrorism each year, people felt vulnerable.[135] But the new mantra also served other agendas beyond merely reassuring the public.

First, it led to a profound policy shift in law enforcement and security intelligence. The Unites States' government was no longer focused on ordinary law enforcement and intelligence gathering about specific risks in which specific leads on specific suspects are followed up and developed. Rather, it had begun to focus on the *preemption of risk*, and this allowed the administration to put into effect a whole wish list that law enforcement and intelligence agenicies had been wanting for years. This was preventative policing and secret service work on steroids. Canadians caught a glimpse of it in the testimony of RCMP Superintendent Mike Cabana at the Arar Commission of Inquiry, when he spoke about having a mandate of prevention and a zero-tolerance approach to the risk of future attacks. Americans got a good dose of it when they heard the revelations and justifications concerning President Bush's secret spying program.

The mantra of preemption and the crisis mentality that the Bush administration whipped into a frenzy to justify it also served to keep the administration in office and helped to consolidate power into its executive hands. And the mantra was very useful in outflanking opponents, manipulating the general public, and putting pressure on dissenting individuals and organizations. But above all, the mantra served the foreign policy agenda of neoconservatives in the Bush administration.

With the fall of the Communist regime in the Soviet Union between 1989 and 1991, and the end of the Cold War, a popular myth took root in the United States. It held that the large defense spending of the Reagan administration (1981–89) and the "irresistible appeal of American political values" had brought about the downfall.[136] And from this conviction, some extrapolated that "the United States should and could use these same assets to remake the whole world in its own image—a transformation that would, in the eyes of most Americans, simultaneously do everybody else a favor and make the world a safer place for Americans."[137]

In the spring of 1992, two former members of the Reagan administration, Paul Wolfowitz and I. Lewis Libby, circulated a "Defense Planning Guidance" inside the George H. W. Bush (Bush senior) administration (1989–1993), that proposed a strategy for the twenty-first century in which unchallengeable American military power would "establish and protect a new order." Dick Cheney, another former Reagan official, was secretary of defense at the time. The draft called for "deterring potential competitors" like Japan and Germany "from even aspiring to a larger regional or global role." It predicted that American military intervention would be a "constant feature" of the future and that the United States must be willing to use preemptive force against other states developing capacities for mass destruction and to act alone if necessary. This was a radical, unilateral strategy that eschewed international law and a reliance on the exercise of "soft" power and multilateral institutions, while ignoring the very real limits of American military power when it came to the tolerance of the citizenry for high death tolls among American troops. It was rejected by senior Republicans like Secretary of State James Baker and National Security Adviser Brent Scowcroft, who insisted the Wolfowitz / Libby document be revised.[138]

After Bill Clinton won the 1992 national election and took office in 1993, Dick Cheney, Paul Wolfowitz, Lewis Libby, and others who believed the United States should seize the "unipolar" moment to secure its predominance into the foreseeable future were left out in the political wilderness. They used their years out of office to mount "a well-coordinated ideological campaign" that would "sharply radicalize defence and foreign policy in the upper ranks of the Republican party."[139] Known as neoconservatives, "neo" owing to the fact that many of them had started their political careers as Democrats, they banded together in 1997 to sign a Statement of Principles,[140] calling their agenda, the Project for the New American Century (PNAC). The Statement of Principles ends with the admonition, "A Reaganite policy of military strength and moral clarity may not be fashionable today. But it is necessary if the U.S. is to build on the success of this past century and ensure our greatness in the next."

PNAC advocated preemptive military strikes on "rogue states" like Iran, Syria, Libya, and North Korea and fixated particularly on the removal of Saddam Hussein from Iraq. As Gwynne Dyer has observed, all of these had "been under the same management for between ten and forty years at this point, and their regimes had all been much more hostile towards the United States in their early years than they were by the early 1990s, but suddenly, for want of anything better, they were promoted to the first rank of global threats."[141] A number of the PNAC members, including Paul Wolfowitz (who later became George W. Bush's deputy secretary of defense), Richard Perle (who served as chair of the Defense Policy Board until 2003), Douglas Feith (a top official in George W. Bush's Pentagon) and Elliott Abrams (George W. Bush's chief adviser on the Middle East) had long-standing ties with the hard-line Likud Party in Israel.[142] Perle and Feith wrote a study in 1996 called *A Clean Break* for the newly elected Likud prime minister, Binyamin Netanyahu, in which they urged him to militarily attack and overthrow Saddam Hussein's regime as part of a "peace through strength" strategy that would allow Israel to reject the constraints of the Oslo Accords.[143] They and others had been gnashing their teeth in 1991 when Bush senior stopped short of "taking Saddam out." In a 1998 letter to President Clinton, PNAC urged Clinton to remove Saddam Hussein from power, since Hussein's regime endangered "the safety of American troops in the region, of our friends and allies like Israel and the moderate Arab states, and a significant portion of the world's supply of oil." The signatories to the letter included Donald Rumsfeld, Paul Wolfowitz, Richard Perle, William Kristol, Richard Armitage, John Bolton and others who later became members of George W. Bush's administration.

There was a fixation on the removal of Saddam Hussein, but the overarching agenda of the neoconservatives in the Middle East was to remake the political landscape of the region in a way that was more advantageous to American and Israeli interests. For PNAC, this included establishing a military presence in the Gulf region and reforming or replacing by military force what the neoconservatives saw as corrupt, despotic Arab regimes that bred fanaticism and, depending on whether they were a client state of the United States or not, overtly or covertly encouraged anti-Semitism and tolerated clerics who preached jihad against the West.[144] Iraq was the obvious place to start: it was "already in trouble with the United Nations, had little international standing and was reviled even by some Arab nations."[145] In its September 2000 report entitled, *Rebuilding America's Defenses: Strategy, Forces and Resources for a New Century*, PNAC bluntly stated, "[T]he United States has for decades sought to play a more permanent role in Gulf regional security. While the unresolved conflict with Iraq provides the immediate justification, the need for a substantial American force presence in the Gulf transcends the issue of the regime of Saddam Hussein." PNAC's stated goal was the democratization of the Middle East, but, as events in Afghanistan and Iraq and later the Palestine election of Hamas demonstrate, the neoconservatives were not prepared to accept *any* kind of democratically elected government; they wanted to retain enough control to ensure that pro-Western governments were installed.

The *Rebuilding America's Defenses* report called for a *Pax Americana* in which the United States would be the hegemonic military power and bring democracy to the rest of the world. It was a kind of Wilsonian vision on steroids, with a military twist.[146] In the introduction of the report, the authors state: "At present the United States faces no global rival. America's grand strategy should aim to preserve and extend this advantageous position as far into the future as possible."

The way to do this, according to the report, was to establish unchallengeable nuclear superiority by developing a new family of smaller, more usable nuclear weapons; to turn the airforce into a "Global First-Strike Force"; to revolutionize the military; and to deploy a global missile defense (Star Wars) system that would give the United States nuclear first strike capability and ensure "U.S power projection around the world." The report proposed that U.S. troops perform "constabulary" duties around the world, which "demand American political leadership rather than that of the United Nations." To fulfill these duties and ensure a "visible expression of the extent of America's status as a superpower" the report called for a much larger military presence spread across more of the globe, in addition to the already 130 nations in which American troops were then deployed. The report called for permanent military bases in the Middle East, in southeastern Europe, in Latin America, and in Southeast Asia, where they did not then exist. But the report was less than optimistic that this ambitious and radical plan could actually be implemented: "[T]he process of transformation, even if it brings revolutionary change, is likely to be a long one, absent some catastrophic and catalyzing event—like a new Pearl Harbor."

9/11 became that catalyzing event. Not quite one year into the war on terrorism, when the public had largely adapted to the idea of preemptions being an essential strategy for security, and when most political opponents had either been co-opted or cowed into cooperating with the Bush administration's aggressive antiterrorism agenda, it was a relatively easy thing for the administration to take the antiterrorism mantra of preemption and, like pulling a rabbit out of a hat, turn it into a new doctrine for the use of force: the doctrine of preemptive war that the neoconservatives had been advocating for a decade.

In the first few months of George W. Bush's first term (2001–5), the less aggressive, more multilateral views held by Republicans like Secretary of State Colin Powell held sway. On the afternoon of the September 11, 2001, attacks, however, with "smoke still rising from the Pentagon's western facade," Secretary of Defense Donald Rumsfeld told his staff "to fetch briefings ('the best info fast . . . go massive; sweep it all up; things related or not') that will justify an attack on Iraq."[147] Days later, Paul Wolfowitz was announcing that the government's aim was not just to get the terrorists connected to Osama bin Laden, but to fight a "global war and end states who sponsor[ed] terrorism."[148] By January 2002, George W. Bush signaled his firm embrace of the neocon agenda in his State of the Union Address in which he declared Iraq, Iran, North Korea, and "their terrorist allies . . . an axis of evil" and indicated that he would use preemptive force against them. "[T]ime is not on our side. I will not wait on events, while dangers gather. I will not stand by, as peril draws closer and closer."[149]

In June 2002, speaking at a graduation ceremony at the United States Military Academy at West Point, Bush explicitly announced a doctrine of preemptive action: "Our security will require all Americans to be forward-looking and resolute, to be ready for preemptive action when necessary to defend our liberty and to defend our lives." He also called for American hegemony in the world. "America has, and intends to keep, military strengths beyond challenge." Both of these strategic aims were echoes of the recommendations made by Paul Wolfowitz and Lewis Libby in their controversial 1992 Defense Planning Guidance draft.[150]

Then, in September 2002, the Bush administration released its National Security Strategy. It was the first time that the various elements of what became known as the Bush Doctrine were formally articulated in one document. It stated: "America will act against . . . emerging threats before they are fully formed. . . . [W]e will not hesitate to act alone, if necessary. . . . The greater the threat, the greater the risk of inaction—and the more compelling the case for taking anticipatory action to defend ourselves, even if uncertainty remains as to the time and place of the enemy's attack."[151]

On March 20, 2003, the United States attacked Iraq.

For the neoconservatives and their British ally, Prime Minister Tony Blair, whether or not Saddam Hussein had weapons of mass destruction was less important than his intention to get them. Intelligence showed his capability to do so was at best remote.

"Once the nuclear materials are there, you're screwed," Gary Schmitt, the executive director of the Project for the New American Century was quoted as saying in 2003. "When you can really do preemption is when it's early."[152] Speaking after the invasion to justify his country's participation in the aggression, Tony Blair echoed this view, stating that the new threats posed by terrorism and rogue states "[force] us to act even when so many comforts seem unaffected, and the threat so far off, if not illusory."[153] While the White House and Downing Street made tortuous legal arguments to assert that the invasion of Iraq was legal in international law, Pentagon adviser and neocon Richard Perle frankly told an audience in London that the invasion had been illegal: "I think in this case, international law stood in the way of doing the right thing."[154]

The new doctrine of preemptive war is a profound contradiction of existing normative restraints on the use of military force which were enshrined in the U.N. Charter after the horrors of World War II. These restraints prohibit wars of aggression and permit states to use force only in self-defense or under authorization from the Security Council.[155] By customary law, the use of force for self-defense in anticipation of an attack is authorized only in the narrowest circumstances, when the threat of armed attack is "instant, overwhelming and leaving no choice of means, and no moment for deliberation."[156] The United States and other countries have often used force in circumstances that have not resembled self-defense or met the requirements for the anticipatory use of force. However, they have always sought to cloak those aggressions in the mantle of the law and have never before put forward such a *bald* doctrine to excuse their wars of aggression.[157]

While completely illegal, the doctrine of preemptive war was what the neoconservatives needed to make an example of Iraq to the rest of the Middle East and the world. In February 2003, "Undersecretary of State John Bolton reportedly told Israeli officials that after defeating Iraq, the United States would 'deal' with

Iran, Syria and North Korea."[158] "To these states," Richard Perle suggested, "we could deliver . . . a two-word message: You're next."[159] Donald Kagan, an original member of PNAC and Yale professor, likened the United States' new role in the world to Gary Cooper's in the movie *High Noon*. "People worry a lot about how the Arab street is going to react. Well, I see that the Arab street has gotten very, very quiet since we started blowing things up."[160] That was in the fall of 2002—before the Iraq insurgency.

On March 16, 2006, the Bush administration reaffirmed its continuing commitment to the doctrine of preemptive strike, calling it "sound" and threatening Iran this time.[161] In the National Security Strategy (NSS) of 2006 released on the same day, the Bush administration attempted to soften the edges of its doctrine, trying to situate it "under long-standing principles of self defense" and stating that diplomacy was the administration's "strong preference" in tackling the threat of weapons of mass destruction. But, the doctrine remained a central part of the administration's foreign policy.

The hijacking of American foreign policy was not a conspiracy. The neoconservatives had articulated their policy in the past, though they had never dared to discuss it honestly with the American electorate before or after they came to power. It was not a conspiracy, but a "lucky" confluence of events and deft opportunism, giving rein to immense hubris.

CHAPTER FOUR

Preemption and Globalized, Mass Surveillance

◎ ◎

The more opaque the affairs of State, the more transparent an individual's affairs must be . . .
—Milan Kundera

The rationale of preemption, whether applied to foreign policy, security intelligence, law enforcement, or the exercise of executive power, is extremely dangerous because it justifies *almost anything.*

In the fields of law enforcement and security intelligence, it produced the draconian USA PATRIOT Act,[162] and many other acts cast from the same mold in other countries. It produced Security Council Resolution 1373, which in broad terms, backs the antiterrorism template of the United States with Security Council sanctions. It has been used to justify turning aid into security assistance, enabling and strengthening repressive regimes, and diverting development assistance to bolster security apparatuses. It has led to a shocking increase in the use of arbitrary detention, extraordinary rendition, and extrajudicial killing by the United States and other Western democracies. And it has been used to justify the idea that surveillance should be ever more pervasive and that everyone should be watched all the time.

Led and sometimes pushed by the United States, governments—largely in the Group of Eight countries (the G-8 consists of Canada, France, Germany, Italy, Japan, Russia, the United Kingdom, and the

ARBITRARY DETENTION. There is no clear definition of *arbitrary detention* in international law. However the UN Working Group on Arbitrary Detention set up by the UN Commission on Human Rights has defined three categories of arbitrary detention:

1. Where there is no legal basis for the deprivation of liberty
2. When a person is deprived of their liberty because he or she has exercised the rights and freedoms guaranteed in the Universal Declaration of Human Rights (UDHR) and the International Covenant on Civil and Political Rights (ICCPR)
3. When a person has been deprived of his or her liberty after a trial that did not comply with the standards for a fair trial set out in the UDHR and other relevant international instruments

Source: The UN Commission on Human Rights Working Group on Arbitrary Detention: http://www.frontlinedefenders.org/manual/en/wgad_m.htm

EXTRAORDINARY RENDITION. This term, considered by critics to be a euphemism for what is in actuality torture by proxy, is an extrajudicial procedure believed to be used by the government of the United States and other Western countries whereby untried suspects are sent to another country for interrogation under less humane conditions. Although it is known that torture is likely to occur, the dispatching country hopes to avoid being viewed as in default of its humanitarian commitments.

Source: en.wikipedia.org/wiki/Extraordinary_rendition

EXTRAJUDICIAL KILLING. The U.S. Torture Victim Protection Act defines extrajudicial killing as "a deliberated killing not authorized by a previous judgment pronounced by a regularly constituted court affording all the judicial guarantees which are recognized as indispensable by civilized peoples. Such term, however, does not include any such killing that, under international law, is lawfully carried out under the authority of a foreign nation."

Source: U.S. Torture Vicitim Protection Act of 1991, Pub. L. No. 102–256, 106 Stat. 73, sec. 3(a) (Mar. 12, 1992).

United States) and Europe, but also in Asia and elsewhere—have embraced the justification of preemption and have quietly set about constructing something that is quantitatively and qualitatively new in the world of security intelligence and law enforcement. It is an infrastructure to facilitate the mass registration and surveillance of populations.

The infrastructure consists of numerous initiatives, some of them domestic in focus, others of which have global reach. In many cases, the global systems feed into the domestic ones and the domestic into the global. Although some of these initiatives have been reported in the media, it is difficult to grasp their significance by looking at each one in isolation, as they are often presented by journalists. Viewed together, it can be seen that they aim to ensure that almost everyone on the planet is "registered," that all travel is tracked globally, that all electronic communications and transactions are monitored or accessible to to the state, and that all information collected about individuals in public and private sector databases is stored, linked, data-mined, and made available to state agents.

Governments are not just collecting individuals' personal information and checking it against information about known terrorists, or those suspected of terrorism on "reasonable grounds" as they cross borders, send e-mails, or conduct transactions. They are using the information to assess and *preemptively eliminate* the risk that any of us might pose to the state. The basic idea behind the project is that governments can register each of us using biometric identifiers, link information to our unique identifiers from as many sources as possible, and use the resulting dossiers of personal information to *continually* assess the degree of risk each of us poses to the state. And, using Radio Frequency Identification (RFID) chips, they may soon be able to track us wherever we go and scan us wherever we meet together.

Governments are acquiring and storing information not just about their own citizens but also about every alien who crosses their borders and even aliens who do not. And governments are sharing information about their own populations with each other, often with little or no control over how other countries will ultimately use the information.

Surveillance in a world of risk preemption requires that *everyone* be evaluated as a potential suspect in order to eliminate risk to the furthest degree possible. In this paradigm, the criminal law and due process protections that have been developed over centuries in democratic societies—such as the presumption of innocence; habeas corpus and rights against arbitrary, indefinite detention; attorney-client privilege; public trials; the right to know the evidence against one and to respond; the right against

HABEAS CORPUS: In common law countries, habeas corpus is the name of a legal instrument or writ by means of which detainees can seek release from unlawful imprisonment. A writ of habeas corpus is a court order addressed to a prison official (or other custodian) ordering that a detainee be brought to the court so it can be determined whether or not that person is imprisoned lawfully and whether or not he or she should be released from custody. The writ of habeas corpus in common law countries is an important instrument for the safeguarding of individual freedom against arbitrary state action.

. . . The right of habeas corpus—or rather, the right to petition for the writ—has long been celebrated as the most efficient safeguard of the liberty of the subject. Dicey wrote that the Habeas Corpus Acts "declare no principle and define no rights, but they are for practical purposes worth a hundred constitutional articles guaranteeing individual liberty."

Blackstone cites the first recorded usage of habeas corpus in 1305.

Source: Wikipedia, http://en.wikipedia.org/wiki/Habeas_corpus

unreasonable search and seizure; and the right to remain silent—are viewed as intolerable risks. Judicial oversight over law enforcement agents and public officials is viewed as an intolerable risk. Statutory privacy and data-protection rights are intolerable risks. Constitutional guarantees, basic human rights norms, and the rule of law itself are now seen as compromising and intolerably risky. For the risk screeners, what matters is the avoidance of risk from the point of view of the state.[163] Guilt, innocence, and even the true identity of individuals are secondary concerns. The screeners' function is to separate "the risky from the safe on the basis of the best information available from all sources."[164] Whether the "best information" is complete or even accurate is not really their concern.

In a risk preemption model, the information appetite of states is infinitely expandable,[165] as they increasingly orient themselves to the future and concern themselves with the predictive power of the information gathered.[166]

There are, of course, historical antecedents of this kind of system—the witch hunts of the McCarthy era in the United States, the registration of the Jews in Nazi Germany, the secret files of the Stasi in Communist East Germany. But the system that is currently being constructed is unlike anything that has come before, for two reasons. First, its technological capacity dwarfs any previous system. Second, its global reach ensures that one has to worry, not just about what one's own state might do with one's personal information, but about what any other state might do.

It is now evident that the United States and other countries are acting aggressively on information they gather and share, seizing and detaining people without reasonable grounds, and in some cases, "rendering" them to third countries or extraterritorial camps run by the United States, where they face torture and indefinite detention. The Arar story was not an isolated incident but a glimpse of a global gulag in which unknown numbers of people are languishing.[167] That gulag runs alongside the global system for mass registration and surveillance. It is part of the world of risk preemption.

In implementing the initiatives that make up the infrastructure for globalized, mass surveillance, governments often anticipate that normal democratic processes are too risk-posing to put their stock in as well. Many of the initiatives governments are embracing have already been "floated" in the past and defeated in courts and legislatures because they violate existing laws, democratic values, or international treaty obligations. Since 9/11, where governments have not co-opted opponents afraid of being seen as "soft on security" to achieve their ends, they have done so by introducing measures incrementally and by stealth. Initiatives are often put in place in stages, in secret, or "policy laundered" through administrative agreements, international joint working groups, regulations and the use of international forums such as the International Civil Aviation Organization (ICAO) and the G-8. In many instances, there is an arrogation of power into the hands of the executive branch of government at the expense of the power constitutionally owed to the legislative and judicial branches. In this way, leaders of the executive part of governments avoid exposing their initiatives before their democratic houses of government (legislatures) and so avoid the public debate and democratic accountability that go along with that process. In the cases where democratic institutions and civic organizations catch up and put the kibosh on their governments' secret programs, the programs are often repackaged or are continued in secret.

When the existence of the United States' National Security Agency program was revealed in the media, we saw many of the features described above. The program involved the mass surveillance of a population; the cooperation of the private sector; the evasion of democratic institutions and existing laws; and the arrogation of power by the executive branch—all of which characterize the new surveillance regime. In the Arar story, we see the global reach of surveillance, the tracking of travel, the cooperation of the private sector, the manner in which personal dossiers are being assessed for risk, and the human consequences of a negative assessment. In both we see secrecy, lack of democratic accountability, and the jettisoning of criminal law protections, due process, and the rule of law itself.

Again, this is not conspiracy but policy based on a mixture of expediency and opportunism. Governments justify their various initiatives as technical solutions to the threat of terrorism . . . and it may be that governments believe that these initiatives will do something to prevent terrorism. Certainly, governments believe that they must be seen to be doing something to prevent attacks. Some governments are acting on some initiatives merely to appease the United States for economic reasons. Some are being driven by the interests of their security establishments, linked to the interests of corporate profit.

But for most governments, the excuse of fighting terrorism has given them, like the Bush administration, new license to embrace initiatives that did not succeed nor did they dare to adopt in earlier periods. And these initiatives serve agendas that go far beyond security from terrorism; namely, the suppression of dissent, harsh immigration and refugee policies, increased law enforcement power, increased control over access to state benefits, the concentration of power in the executive branch of government, reelection, political advantage over one's opponents, and the securing of greater control generally over one's population.

So far, governments have been fairly successful at either selling or eluding public accountability for their surveillance initiatives, which have been presented piecemeal, and when necessary, the public has been told that it should be willing to sacrifice a little privacy and convenience in the interests of greater security. Those who have nothing to hide, we are told, have nothing to fear. The sacrifice seems minor—why should we care? What can we do about it anyway? But what is really at stake in this new world order is far more than privacy, and we should, in fact, be deeply concerned about it.

CHAPTER FIVE

Biometric Registration of Alien Populations

◎ ◎

The logic of our times is: never mind the evidence, just focus on the possibility.
—Bill Durodié, Director, International Centre for Security Analysis, King's College

In 1930s Germany, the Holocaust began with the simple registration of people of Jewish descent. First, they were registered, and then the State began an incremental stripping-away of their civil rights. In the countries invaded by the Nazis, the death rate of Jews was directly related to the census information available. In Norway, which had a population register, fifty percent of Jews were killed—compared with only fifteen percent in Denmark and 0.5 percent in Finland.[168] Moreover, technology greatly increased the efficiency of the registration of those who were to be singled out. A punch card sorting system, developed and leased by IBM to the Nazis, allowed them to register the population's characteristics and later target groups within that population.[169] First, the punch cards were used "to enforce the bar on Jews working in certain academic, professional and government jobs and later to carry out the mass evictions from their homes and into the ghettoes."[170]

I do not need to draw a full analogy to current circumstances to make the point that the registration of populations by ethnic origin, race, religion, political belief, or similar personal characteristics—while used for benign purposes in some countries—can also be a dangerous thing, easily abused by those in power. And where technological means are used for registering and sorting people, the malevolent effects are amplified. One needs only to recall further examples—the internment of Japanese citizens that took place in North America during World War Two, the 1994 genocide that took place in Rwanda,[171] and the Pass Laws of apartheid South Africa—to know this is true. Registration is the tool by which those in power can easily single out and target specific groups of people—not for what they have done, but for who they are.

MASS DETENTION AND REGISTRATION OF IMMIGRANTS THROUGH THE NATIONAL SECURITY ENTRY-EXIT REGISTRATION SYSTEM

One of the U.S. government's first responses to 9/11 was to ethnically profile and round up hundreds of Arab and South Asian noncitizens. In a systematic campaign, FBI and INS officers, sometimes assisted by the New York [City] Police Department (NYPD), swept through immigrant neighborhoods in New York's outer boroughs picking up hundreds of men.[172] This was happening in other cities as well, though when community organizers and lawyers tried to verify the numbers and identities of people being held, they were told that no such arrests were occurring or that there was no information on individuals inquired about.[173] The families of the men detained were often left in desperate straits, without any income and not knowing for weeks or months what had happened to their husbands, fathers, sons, and brothers.

The mass arrests had been authorized days after September 11, 2001, by John Ashcroft, who instructed all U.S. attorneys general to use "every available law enforcement tool" to round up individuals who might be connected to terrorism.[174] The government also encouraged ordinary citizens to report on their co-workers, customers, friends, and neighbors. Grassroots organizers and civil liberties activists estimate that some two thousand people were swept up in the dragnet.[175] They were held in deplorable conditions for prolonged and indefinite periods, and the U.S. government denied them their legal rights to habeas corpus and speedy charges, impeded their right to counsel, denied them contact with the outside world, and overrode judicial orders to release them on bond.[176]

The Department of Justice's Inspector General's Report that was later written on the detentions said that "little effort was made to distinguish between legitimate terrorism suspects and people picked up by chance."[177] One man, who had paid for a purchase a short time before 9/11 with an air miles card and in an idle conversation said he'd like to learn to fly one day, was reported by the other person in the conversation after the attacks and arrested. Another man who owned a grocery store and closed it the day after the attacks, was reported by one of his customers and arrested.[178]

The investigation by the Office of the Inspector General also revealed that systematic abuse took place in some of the centers where detainees were held. At the Metropolitan Detention Center (MDC) in Brooklyn, New York, in which Maher Arar spent his first days of detention, "almost all the detainees were slammed against walls . . . one officer always twisted detainees hands," and some officers stepped on detainees' leg chains "whenever they were stopped." Many detainees complained that when they were first brought to the center guards pushed their faces up against a T-shirt pinned to the wall in the entrance: the T-shirt had a picture of the American flag on it with the caption, "these colors don't run."[179]

Ehab Elmaghraby, an Egyptian who used to run a restaurant in Manhattan's Times Square, and Javaid Iqbal, a Pakistani immigrant to the United States, are among a number of the detained who subsequently pursued lawsuits against U.S. officials for their detentions. They claimed that while shackled in the MDC, they were kicked and punched until they bled, cursed as terrorists, and subjected to multiple body-cavity searches, including one in which a flashlight was forced into Elmaghraby's rectum, causing him to bleed. The federal government settled Elmaghraby's suit for $300,000.[180]

In the end, not one immigrant who was detained in these sweeps "was charged with any criminal offense relating to the attacks and not one was confirmed to have links to al Qaeda."[181]

When the first roundups and mass arrests had been executed, the U.S. government went on to systematically register and create dossiers on nearly every male over the age of sixteen with ties to a list of designated (mostly Muslim) countries who was living as a visitor inside the United States or traveling to or through the country.[182] This was done under a program called the National Security Entry-Exit Registration System (NSEERS). In addition to registering on arrival to the United States, visitors were required to leave and report on departure at designated ports; to submit to being interviewed and digitally fingerprinted every time they entered the United States; to report to Bureau of Citizenship and Immigration offices if remaining in the United States for more than thirty days and/or for more than one year; and to notify the bureau within ten days of any changes regarding place of residence, employment, or educational institution. Failure to comply with any of the requirements of the program could result in denial of future entry to the United States.

Many stories of harassment, insult, and rough treatment have been told by the more than *80,000 people* registered under NSEERS in its first years of operation.[183] Thousands of men who reported to offices within the United States never returned home. They were shackled and locked up on presenting themselves at the registration offices. The United States had not seen anything like it since the mass roundup of Americans and immigrants of Japanese descent during World War II.

Mohamed Hassan Mohamed was a young Canadian professor of Sudanese origin.[184] His was one of the first stories to emerge about Canadians with origins in Muslim countries having trouble in the United States, and it was a foreshadowing of Maher Arar's story which would hit the news soon after. Mohamed lived in Saint Catharines, Ontario, with his family and commuted weekly across the border to work in an American university. In September 2002, he arrived at the Peace Bridge crossing where he usually entered the United States and was told that he would have to be fingerprinted, photographed and interrogated. According to Mohamed, "I told them that I'm traveling on a Canadian passport, on the basis of a NAFTA visa, and I didn't see why I should be treated as a citizen of Sudan, when I was a Canadian. They told me that because I was a dual citizen, I would be treated as a citizen of Sudan."

Mohamed did not want to be fingerprinted because he was afraid he would somehow be registered as a Sudanese citizen and lose his United States visa. Mohamed reported, I didn't understand the whole thing. They told me I'm not going anywhere, until I comply with INS regulations. They took me to a small room in the back and told me to wait there until I was ready to comply. I asked them, 'Am I under detention?' They said yes. I suggested that I might need some kind of help, either from the Canadian consulate or a lawyer. I asked if I could use the telephone to call for help."

The answer was *no*. An INS officer told him he could contact the Canadian consulate after six hours had passed, but when they had and Mohamed asked for the consulate to be notified, he was told that he "was in legal limbo, and as such, had no rights, that I could be held indefinitely." By this time it was after 10:00 P.M. and he had been detained since 4:00 P.M. He asked for water and food, and the INS officers refused. Finally at about 1:00 A.M., after a new shift of officers came on, a taxi was called and instructed to let Mohamed off on the Canadian side of the bridge, where Mohamed spent a cold and troubled night.

Faramarz Farahani[185] was a Canadian citizen of Iranian origin who had been lured south to the United States by a six-figure salary with a large software firm. He decided on his own to see if he needed to register under the NSEERS program. He was not sure whether, as a Canadian, the new program applied to him. Farahani stopped in at a U.S. Immigration and Naturalization office in San Jose, California, one day on his way to work. When he arrived, he learned that he was two days late for the deadline. He was handcuffed and shackled in leg irons and flown to a prison in San Diego. There, he was held with about twelve other prisoners, crowded in a tiny cell, hardly fed, and not allowed to sleep. When his wife finally received a call from him, she couldn't believe what had happened. Later she told a reporter: "I have seen this kind of thing happen in repressive regimes in other places twenty years ago. So this is very shocking for me."

Farahani's lawyers were able to get him released five days later, and the INS brought deportation proceedings against him for his failure to register by the deadline. In Southern California, several hundred men and boys were handcuffed and detained as Farahani had been and were accused of immigration violations. Many of them were applying for permanent residence status and had a right to be in the United States.[186]

In its first years of operation, NSEERS resulted in more than *13,000* people being detained and put into deportation hearings, many of them for minor infractions of the U.S. immigration code.[187] Thousands more left the country in fear, destroying communities.[188] In Brooklyn, a thriving, 120,000-strong Pakistani community—the largest in the country—was halved as people fled in fear or were deported.[189] In Chicago, where roughly 20,000 Pakistanis typically jammed along either side of Devon Avenue each August to mark the independence of Pakistan, no more than 8,000 showed up in 2003. Similarly, where hundreds of Bangladeshis lined up on the same avenue for their homeland's independence day, in 2003 only a few dozen showed up.[190] All over the United States, immigrant families from Arab, African, and South Asian countries left "all they had built in America—selling medical practices, gas stations, restaurants, homes and furniture for whatever they could get."[191]

"Many returned to the countries from which they came. Many others, desperate not to return to their homelands, packed their worldly possessions into cars and vans and made their way to Canada."[192] But after December 2002 when Canada signed a so-called "Safe Third Country" agreement with the United States that recognized it as a safe place for refugees to file claims, all of these people were turned back to the United States to face their fates in the U.S. immigration system. It was almost a kind of ethnic cleansing of Muslim immigrants from the North American continent—all those who could be deported were.

The NSEERS program is an ongoing one. At the time of writing, the countries on the "special registration" list are Afghanistan, Algeria, Bahrain, Bangladesh, Egypt, Eritrea, Indonesia, Iran, Iraq, Jordan, Kuwait, Lebanon, Libya, Morocco, North Korea, Oman, Pakistan, Qatar, Saudi Arabia, Somalia, Sudan, Syria, Tunisia, United Arab Emirates, and Yemen.[193] In many states, local police have been deputized to stop and check the status of immigrants, so that, presumably, the deportations will be ongoing.[194]

BIOMETRIC VISAS: US-VISIT AND THE EUROPEAN UNION'S VISA INFORMATION SYSTEM

Under the U.S. Visitor and Immigrant Status Indicator Technology (US-VISIT) program, which went into operation in January 2004, the registration that has been occurring through NSEERS is being expanded to most visitors to the United States.[195] People applying for a visa for travel to the United States are now being registered by having their photographs and digital fingerscans taken at "virtual borders" outside the country, and citizens of visa waiver countries are being photographed and fingerscanned on entry. Photo and fingerscan data is being stored in a central U.S. database and inside a computer chip in each visitor's visa.[196] The technology being used to do this is known as "biometrics": it records and encodes the physical characteristics of a person—such as facial dimensions, fingerprints, iris patterns, or voice patterns—into a computer chip or database, so that the identity of the person presenting himself or herself can be verified against the information in the chip and/or a database.

As of September 2006, a similar program in the European Union (EU) called the Visa Information System was being developed following a binding Framework Decision by the European Council of June 2004. It will capture and store all of the information, including biometric data, from visa applications to the twenty-five EU member states—about 15 million per year.[197]

BIOMETRIC VISAS WITH RFID CHIPS

Within the US-VISIT program, the Department of Homeland Security has been testing and implementing a plan to insert RFID chips in entry documents since July 2005.[198] RFID chips are tiny computer chips with tiny antennae that can be put into physical objects. When an RFID reader emits a signal, nearby RFID chips transmit their stored data to the reader. "Passive" chips do not contain batteries and can be read from a distance varying from an inch to sixty-nine feet.[199] "Active" or self-powered chips can be read from a much greater distance. Among the ideas being tested by the Department of Homeland Security is a technology that would allow the scanning of up to fifty-five passengers on a bus passing through a border point at about fifty mph.[200]

Of course, anyone with a reader could, secretly if they wished, read the chip through a wallet, pocket, or backpack. So, not only will the customs officials of the United States have access to the information in individuals' visas, but retail companies, identity thieves, and the agents of other governments could have access, too. Government agents could use this kind of technology to sweep the identities of every visa holder in a public place. RFID chips can also be "written into" so that secret "security clearance" information could be inserted into them by government agencies.

LINKAGE OF BIOMETRIC INFORMATION TO A GLOBAL WEB OF DATABASES

The plan in the US-VISIT program[201] is not merely to verify that people carrying visas are who she and he say they are, or even to check their photographs and fingerscans against those of known terrorists or of persons suspected of terrorism on "reasonable grounds."

The *plan* is to create information dossiers on all persons entering the United States, to store these dossiers for one hundred years,[202] and to link individuals' biometric data to a web of databases, encompassing more than twenty U.S. federal government databases as well as U.S. commercial databases.[203] Moreover, there is evidence that US-VISIT will eventually be linked to other programs—so that the web of databases that dossiers are compiled from could be even wider and have a global reach. A Federal Register Notice published by the Transportation Security Administration's (TSA) on August 1, 2003, for example, stated that the TSA anticipated linking the US VISIT program with a program discussed in chapter 10 of this book—CAPPS II—when both programs became "fully operational."[204] CAPPS II is the acronym for a controversial passenger profiling system that envisioned linking a virtually unlimited number of public and private sector databases together. It was replaced by a slightly modified program, Secure Flight, but the aim of the project appeared to remain the same: networking as many databases as possible to more fully monitor and assess the level of risk individuals pose to the United States.

Potentially, the data accessed by the United States under US-VISIT and other programs described in this book could include information about individuals' medical histories, social benefits, driving records, immigration status, passport applications, criminal records, security intelligence files, census responses, tax returns, employment histories, address histories, banking records, credit card purchases, air travel patterns, as well as their e-mails, e-mail correspondents, Internet use, online purchases and Internet music selections, cell phone calls, Internet phone calls, and library, bookstore, and video selections.

Insiders are calling the database that is being built by the United States the *black box*, as no one knows the extent of what it will eventually contain,[205] only that it will be as comprehensive as possible.

Of course, some convergence of databases was taking place before September 11, 2001, but since that date there has been a radical acceleration of this trend. In the post-9/11 world, the public can no longer rely on the existence of firewalls between databases that to some extent previously protected privacy. Whereas in the past one could be relatively confident that no business or government agency could know everything about one, now, this is simply no longer true.

U.S. ACQUISITION OF DOMESTIC AND FOREIGN DATABASES

One shocking aspect of the increasing convergence of databases since 9/11 is the U.S. government's aggressive acquisition of foreign and domestic databases.

Some of this access has been obtained under the USA PATRIOT Act, which gives the FBI a procedure to access any business records held by American-based companies and their subsidiaries, whether the data pertains to American residents or to residents of other countries.[206] These records could include the archives of personal information held by credit card companies, computer and Internet companies, bookstore and video companies, and others. It could include employment information about the people who work for these companies. And, as governments outside the United States contract out more of their services to U.S. companies and their subsidiaries, it could also include public-sector information on citizens in countries outside the United States.

The Canadian federal government, for example, has contracted out part of the 2006 national census to Lockheed Martin Canada—a unit of the U.S.-based Lockheed Martin Corporation.[207] The provincial government of British Columbia has contracted out the operation of its Medical Services Plan and PharmaCare to Maximus B.C., which is owned by the Canadian subsidiary of the U.S.-based company, Maximus.[208] A number of BC Hydro services—such as customer relationship management, human resources, financial procurement services, and information technology—are handled by a Canadian subsidiary of Accenture, a Bermudan company with its main office in the United States.[209] Under the USA PATRIOT Act, the FBI need only ask for seizure of the business records of these companies in order to obtain them. As I mentioned earlier in the context of President Bush's secret NSA program, between its enactment in 1978 and 2004, the special court set up under the Foreign Intelligence Surveillance Act has turned down only 5 applications for warrants out 18,748.[210] When seizure is granted, a gag order is placed on the business involved, preventing that business from telling anyone about it.

Access to private-sector information has also been obtained by the United States under the Enhanced Border Security and Visa Entry Reform Act of 2002. Pursuant to this act, the United States has demanded that all airlines traveling to or through the United States provide U.S. authorities with access to their passenger databases.

In addition to statutory access, U.S. government agencies are *voluntarily* being given access to individuals' personal information by the private sector. As mentioned earlier, in Maher Arar's case, the real estate company that held his lease gave it voluntarily to the RCMP, and in the NSA program, American telecom companies appear to have given the agency direct access to their systems. Many other companies, institutions, and organizations have shown themselves equally willing to simply hand over private information about their customers and members. Some believe it is the patriotic thing to do; others may be afraid or eager to please the government. Examples include the following:

- In 2001, 195 U.S. universities and colleges voluntarily turned over personal information about their students to government agencies—172 of them did not wait for a subpoena.[211]

- In 2001, 64 percent of U.S. travel and transportation companies voluntarily turned over information about their customers and employees.[212]

- In 2002 the Professional Association of Diving Instructors voluntarily gave the FBI a disk with the personal information on about 2 million people.[213]

- Under a program called InfraGard, more than 10,000 private companies in the United States voluntarily exchange information with the government,[214] checking out security alerts and monitoring the computer activity of customers and employees.[215]

- The airline JetBlue voluntarily gave the Transportation Security Administration more than 5 million passenger itineraries, which were then given to the Pentagon and combined with data profiles on each passenger obtained from Acxiom, a large data aggregator company.[216]

- Northwest Airlines denied sharing passenger records with the government when the JetBlue story broke, but later it was discovered that it had voluntarily given millions of passenger records to the National Aeronautics and Space Administration (NASA).[217]

- In April 2004, American Airlines admitted to sharing 1.2 million records with the Transportation Security Administration and four research companies that were bidding for a government data-mining contract.[218]

- In May 2004, the biggest airline companies in the United States—including American, United, and Northwest—admitted to voluntarily handing over millions of passenger records to the FBI after the 9/11 attacks.[219]

All of the above incidents occurred without the consent of the individuals whose records were involved and, for the most part, in direct violation of the privacy policies of the organizations providing the information.

Alarmingly, the U.S. government has also been *buying* personal data on Americans and the citizens of other countries from commercial data aggregators. Inside the United States, companies like DoubleClick boast that their data include information from more than 1,500 companies, adding up to information on 90 million households and records of 4.4 billion transactions.[220] Outside the United States, the company ChoicePoint Inc. has collected information on hundreds of millions of residents in Latin America, without their consent or knowledge, and sold them to U.S. government officials in three dozen agencies.[221]

In Mexico, ChoicePoint bought the driving records of 6 million Mexico City residents and the country's entire voter registry and sold them to the U.S. government. In Colombia, ChoicePoint bought the country's entire citizen ID database, including each resident's date and place of birth, passport, and national ID number, parentage, and physical description. It bought personal data from Venezuela, Costa Rica, Guatemala, Honduras, El Salvador, Nicaragua,[222] and Argentina as well. The company will not reveal who sells it the information, but privacy experts say that government data are often sold clandestinely to companies like ChoicePoint by government employees.[223]

THE TEMPLATE FOR THE GLOBAL SYSTEM OF MASS REGISTRATION AND SURVEILLANCE

In many ways, an examination of the US-VISIT program and the data acquisition that the United States has embarked on reveals the template for the project of globalized, mass surveillance. Driven and designed largely by the United States, the project's goal, as I have suggested earlier, is to register individuals using biometric identifiers and to link that biometric data, embedded in an RFID-readable identity document and/or stored in a database, with a web of databases—so that information dossiers can be compiled for each individual and each individual can be screened for "risk," on the spot in some circumstances.

In this "brave new world,"[224] the U.S. government and other governments will compile information dossiers on as many people as possible and create, as much as possible, an information infrastructure that is not merely domestic in scope but global in its reach.

CHAPTER SIX

The Creation of a Global Registration System

◎ ◎

BIOMETRIC PASSPORTS

In recent years, many countries in Asia have started or intensified efforts to implement biometric national ID cards, notably, India, China, Hong Kong (China's special administrative region), Bhutan, Malaysia, South Korea, Thailand, the Philippines, Indonesia, and Vietnam.[225] In the Western Hemisphere, Mexico is planning to introduce a national ID card, and Chile and Peru already have them. In the EU most countries also have national identification cards, but in most of these systems, the kind of information linked to the card is limited, and access is restricted to domestic officials for specific purposes.[226] In the democracies that use the common law system, however, the idea of a national identity card is anathema—associated with police states and politically unacceptable because of its potentially corrosive effect on civil liberties.

An internationally mandated biometric passport is a politically palatable way of imposing a de facto identity document on citizens in countries that do not already have them and of making the information linked to such a document globally available.

"POLICY LAUNDERING"

Like many other global surveillance initiatives, biometric passports have been the subject of discussion among states for some time. The International Civil Aviation Organization (ICAO), the organization that governs international civil aviation, has been researching biometric passports since 1995, but national and regional laws protecting privacy and civil liberties were barriers to the adoption of most models for their deployment until recently. The U.S.-led "war on terror" breathed new life into these efforts.

The USA PATRIOT Act, passed in 2001, required the U.S. president to certify, within two years, a biometric standard for identifying foreigners entering the United States. The U.S. Enhanced Border Security and Visa Entry Reform Act of 2002 required all countries wishing to retain their visa-waiver status with the United States to implement the technology necessary to meet the standard by October 2004[227] and designated ICAO as the standard setter. Handing the matter over to ICAO ensured that the organization would finally produce biometric passport specifications and that all countries, including the United States itself, would ultimately be obliged to adopt a biometric passport.

With the prospect of "international standards" being imposed on them by ICAO to relieve them of political responsibility, governments likely felt freer to dispense with their earlier concerns about biometric passports. In May 2003, Canada, the United Kingdom, France, Japan, Italy, Russia, and Germany jumped on the biometric bandwagon that their G-8 partner, the United States, was driving and agreed to implement a biometric passport system.[228]

The standards that ICAO subsequently set for biometric passports were minimum requirements, giving governments leeway to adopt just about any model of deployment they choose.

THE MODEL: CARTE BLANCHE

At its spring 2004 meeting in Cairo, the ICAO adopted globally interoperable and machine-readable specifications for biometric passports with facial recognition as the mandatory biometric standard and fingerprints and iris scans as optional additional standards.

The ICAO specifications only require countries to implement systems that can verify the identity of passport holders against the biometric information stored in the computer chip in their passports and that can check that information against the biometric information of other individuals "of interest"—on a terrorist suspect list, for example.

But ICAO standards leave states with full discretion to use biometric passports for other purposes.[229] States have free rein to create central databases of all travelers' biometric information, to store information other than biometrics on chips, to use biometric passports as "keys" to multiple state and private databases, and to use biometric passports for purposes beyond antiterrorism. In the EU, where a centralized database is already being set up to store visa applicants' fingerprints, the European Commission has also proposed a central database for the fingerprints of passport applicants, that is, of citizens,[230] though as of September 2006, it had yet to be set up. If the US-VISIT program for biometric visas and U.S. data acquisition are anything to go by, the United States will be storing biometric passport information of citizens and travelers and linking it with every available database around the world to create dossiers on them. In fact, every country could be keeping the biometric and personal information they collect from travelers and citizens, keeping it for as long as they want, and using it for any number of purposes.

RADIO FREQUENCY IDENTIFICATION CHIPS (RFID)

The likelihood that states will store, link, and use biometric passport data for purposes other than antiterrorism once they implement the ICAO-mandated biometric passport is not the only reason to be concerned about this new global initiative. Under the ICAO specifications, states are obligated to insert "contact-less integrated circuits"—a technology similar to RFID and sometimes called by the same name—into their biometric passport.[231]

Like RFID chips, contactless chips allow for identification at a distance. Although at the present time, the ICAO standard only requires identification within ten centimeters (about four inches), this does not prevent states from adopting technology that allows scanning from longer distances, and reader technology is always developing. As with RFID chips, contactless chips are always broadcasting a person's identity to anyone with a reader. In August 2006, a German security consultant, Lukas Grunwald, told a security conference in Las Vegas that it took him just two weeks to figure out how to copy the passport chip onto a blank chip. Although he said he could not figure out how to change the information on the chip, he told a journalist, "The whole passport design is totally brain damaged. From my point of view all of these RFID passports are a huge waste of money. They're not increasing security at all."[232]

Grunwald's experiment shows that with these chips in passports, terrorists could easily use information from passports to forge identity documents. As well, with their own scanners to read the information on others' passports, terrorists could easily pick out Americans to target. In August 2006, the U.S. government started issuing contactless chips in new American passports.[233] It has said that the passports will contain a protective foil so that they cannot be read while closed or without being scanned up close.[234] If they are planning up close reading, however, one wonders why they would not use contact chips—unless, as one commentator has speculated, the government wants the option of surreptitious access itself.[235] Like RFID chips, contactless integrated chips are also capable of being "written into" and could hold "security clearance" types of information inserted by government agencies, which any country's customs and security officials may be able to read.

If we are required to carry identity documents at all times, which is possible if biometric identity checkpoints are expanded from foreign air travel to domestic air travel and other forms of cross-border and domestic transportation, we will be extremely vulnerable to the surreptitious reading of our identities. In the future, government agents could use this kind of technology to sweep the identities of everyone at, say, a political meeting, protest march, or Islamic prayer service, or even to set up a network of automated readers on sidewalks and roads in order to track the locations of individuals.

BIOMETRIC PASSPORTS, IDENTITY CARDS, AND THE DEMOCRATIC DEFICIT

The way in which biometric passports are being introduced around the world—and how they have paved the way in common-law countries for the introduction of long-resisted national ID cards—are prime examples of how governments have been acting in stealth, outside democratic processes, to build a surveillance infrastructure.

In Canada, a proposal for a biometric national ID card was floated in the fall of 2002 and soundly rejected in a parliamentary committee[236] and the forum of public opinion by the fall of 2003.[237] The proposal was officially dropped. However, after government restructuring in 2004, the committee examining the idea was relieved of its duties before its final report could be released, and the deployment of a biometric passport (starting in 2005) was announced.[238] These developments came as a complete surprise to most of the institutions and organizations engaged in the earlier debate about a biometric identity document. They had not heard about Canada's agreement at the G-8 summit to implement a biometric passport system, and there had been no public debate before that undertaking had been made. When the plan was announced, the government claimed it had no choice in the matter; if Canadians wished to enjoy global travel, they would have to go along with the measure.[239]

In the United States, the idea of a national ID card has historically always been rejected. When the Social Security Number was initiated in 1936, it was only to be used for the administration of the social security system. Efforts to make it or any other document a universal identifier were consistently opposed. The Electronic Privacy Information Center has chronicled relevant events:

> In 1971, the Carter Administration reiterated that the SSN was not to become an identifier, and in 1981 the Reagan Administration stated that it was "explicitly opposed" to the creation of a national ID card. The Clinton Administration advocated a "Health Security Card" in 1993 and assured the public that the card, issued to every American, would have "full protection for privacy and confidentiality." Still, the idea was rejected and the health security card was never created. In 1999 Congress repealed a controversial provision in the Illegal Immigration Reform and Immigrant Responsibility Act which gave authorization to include Social Security Numbers on driver's licenses.[240]

Moreover, when Congress created the Department of Homeland Security it made clear in the enabling legislation that the agency was not to create a national ID system. Department of Homeland Security Director Tom Ridge emphasized at the time, "The legislation that created the Department of Homeland Security was very specific on the question of a national ID card. They said there will be no national ID card."[241] Yet the federal government *mandated* a biometric passport for Americans through an international forum without many of them even being aware of it.[242] And after doing this, it managed to ram through the REAL ID Act in May 2005, which creates a de facto national ID card by mandating national standards for state drivers' licenses and forcing states to link their DMV databases. The bill had been voted down in the fall of 2004 but was reintroduced and attached to legislation requesting money for military actions in Iraq. As "must pass" legislation, the REAL ID Act was passed with no hearings, no debates in committees, and no debates on the floor of the House or Senate.[243]

The Intelligence Reform and Terrorism Prevention Act passed in October 2004 had already implemented the security measures for drivers' licenses recommended by the 9/11 Commission. The REAL ID Act went further by requiring the linkage of databases and the verification that applicants for licenses were in the country legally. It appears, also, that the government has plans to demand that states insert RFID chips into drivers' licenses: the government specification for RFID chips embedded in biometric passports included details about embedding them in drivers' licenses.[244] The Real ID Act is proving to be a headache for state authorities to implement. The new database-sharing provision, in particular, was described by one Illinois administrator as "a nightmare of nightmares." "Can we go home now?," she wrote.[245]

There is a real concern that this new universal ID drivers' license will bring with it a new level of "show-me-your papers" checks by government agents, especially since the U.S. Supreme Court ruled in 2004 that police can demand to see ID without reasonable grounds, from law-abiding citizens.[246]

In the United Kingdom, there was hot debate over a proposal to introduce a national ID card. Under criticism, the idea was shelved by the government in October 2003.[247] However, several months earlier, in May 2003 in the G-8 forum, the UK government had already agreed to develop a biometric passport system.[248] Then, in December 2004, the EU announced that mandatory biometric passports would be introduced with facial scans required from 2006 onward and fingerprints required from 2007 onward.

The UK government subsequently introduced an ID Cards bill proposing that the same biometric data be included in a new national identity card issued to everyone renewing their passport and to all immigrants and refugees. Under the bill, cards would become mandatory once three-quarters of the population had them. A new national population database is being developed as well. Among the data the government is planning to collect are previous addresses, records of travel abroad, and records of the occasions on which various personal information was provided to government agencies. Such information, reaching indefinitely into the past, could provide a "detailed picture of a life" and violate the European Convention on Human Rights' privacy protections, according to a joint parliamentary committee examining the bill.[249]

The ID Cards bill was passed by the UK's House of Commons on February 10, 2005, with 224 votes in favor and 64 against. More MPs abstained than voted.[250] The House of Lords then rejected the bill as it was written, inserting provisions that would have made the cards strictly voluntary. But the House of Commons then rejected the amendment, provoking what threatened to turn into a constitutional stalemate: under the original bill both Houses had to approve the legislation.[251] In the final back-and-forth rally in March 2006, the Lords approved a compromise bill that will delay the implementation of ID cards until 2010, after the next general election. This will allow a Conservative government, if it comes to power, to scrap the cards.[252] If national ID cards are implemented in Britain, they also will likely have RFID chips in them. In January 2006, a government plan for this was leaked from the Home Office.[253]

While Canadians escaped the imposition of a national ID card the first time the idea was floated, it is possible that such a card is not far down the road. Until very recently, Canada was exempt from U.S. requirements that visitors carry either a biometric visa or a biometric passport when entering the United States. That loophole, however, was closed by the Intelligence Reform and Terrorism Prevention Act. It requires Canadians to present a biometric passport or some other approved biometric document at the U.S. border. Negotiations over what the other approved document should be, might be the "opener" to a resurrection of the idea of a national ID card in Canada. The United States is developing a biometric card for U.S. travelers reentering the United States from Canada[254] and would prefer that Canada go the same route.[255] There is also talk of shared databases linked to a harmonized card.[256] The U.S.–Canada Smart Border Declaration and Action Plan, negotiated shortly after 9/11, were meant to implement many of the initiatives described in this book. One of the Action Plan's items requires biometric identity cards with common standards to be used across different modes of travel. With all these pressures, one wonders how Canadians will avoid having a new biometric national identity card imposed on them.

FLAWED TECHNOLOGY AND ASSUMPTIONS

By the time biometric passports are fully implemented, they could be used to monitor over one billion people worldwide.[257]

While biometric technology is being touted as the only way to ensure secure identity documents, it is also known to be seriously flawed. Facial recognition, in particular, has a high rate of "false negatives" (where the technology fails to recognize individuals) and "false positives" (where the technology matches an individual to someone else, incorrectly). U.S. government tests have shown that even when the identity of a document holder is being compared only to the biometric information contained in the document (a "one-to-one" comparison as opposed to a "one-to-many" comparison) using recent photographs, there is a 5 percent rate of false negatives and 1 percent rate of false positives. The reliability rates quickly deteriorate as photographs become dated, rising to 15 percent after only three years for the best systems tested.[258]

Fifteen percent of a billion people could mean 150,000,000 people misidentified! Even the people who invented biometric technology admit that it is dangerously flawed. George Tomko, regarded as one of the fathers of the technology, says that even a 99.99 percent accuracy rate—which doesn't exist for any of the identifiers—could leave millions of people vulnerable to mistaken identity.[259]

Moreover, determined enemies of the state could use false identities to obtain biometric identity documents. A security breach like the one suffered by the data aggregating company ChoicePoint recently—which allowed thieves access to personal data on 145,000 people—could help terrorists forge false documents.[260] Enemies of the state can also be successful using their own identities. All but two of the known 9/11 hijackers traveled in and out of the United States using their real identities.[261] Spain had a national identity card system at the time of the March 2004 Madrid train bombing, but identity cards did not assist authorities in preventing the attack.

EXPANSION TO OTHER TRANSPORTATION SYSTEMS

Governments, in fact, have recently been talking about expanding the security measures that are being implemented for air travel to other transportation systems.[262] If this happens, the use of biometric identity documents would expand exponentially, and transport systems could become the kind of internal checkpoints generally associated with police states.

INSTITUTIONALIZING "NONPERSONHOOD"

Of course, in a global identity system predicated on the avoidance of risk, *not* being registered or having a personal profile amounts to being a "nonperson." By creating inclusion, the system also creates exclusion.[263] For practical purposes, a person without a mandatory identity document will not exist—or will exist only as a risk to the state.

If one doesn't have an identity document (because it has been lost or stolen or withheld through a bureaucratic mistake) or a data profile (because one is poor, or a conscientious objector, or doesn't participate in the kinds of activities by which data are collected)—one will be, by definition, a risk. And one will be *at* risk, since the state will deal with one aggressively, granting one few, if any legal safeguards.

CHAPTER SEVEN

The Creation of an Infrastructure for the Global Surveillance of Movement

◎ ◎

Freedom of movement is basic in our scheme of values.
—Justice William O. Douglas, U.S. Supreme Court

The biometric passport and the biometric visa are components of a more extensive infrastructure that is being set up to monitor people and their movements worldwide. This infrastructure includes another initiative: the sharing of advanced passenger information (API) and passenger name record (PNR) information. It is likely that Maher Arar was flagged and then detained in the United States because his air carrier shared its API and PNR with U.S. officials before landing.

API is the list of passengers on an airplane's manifest. PNR information is the data kept in air travel reservation systems. PNR can include more than sixty fields of information, including the name and address of the traveler, the address of the person with whom the traveler will stay, the trip itinerary, the date the ticket was purchased, credit card information, seat number, meal choices (which can reveal religious or ethnic affiliation), medical information, behavioral information, and linked frequent-flyer information.

U.S. DEMANDS FOR SHARING PASSENGER NAME RECORDS

In its Aviation and Transportation Security Act, the U.S. required foreign air carriers to make PNR information available to its customs agency on request and provided that this information could be shared with other agencies. The Bush administration then passed an interim rule in June 2002, which interpreted the legislative requirement broadly. The rule required

- that carriers give U.S. Customs *direct* access to their computer systems;
- that data be available for *all* flights, not just those destined for the United States;
- that once transferred, data be made available to federal agencies other than Customs for national security purposes or as authorized by law; and
- that the United States be permitted to store transferred data for *50 years*.[264]

Airlines, faced with fines and the possible denial of landing rights in the United States, began giving the United States what it wanted, even though they were violating core principles of the privacy laws in their home countries. These principles generally require

- restriction on the disclosure of personal information to third parties;
- limits on the use of data to the purpose for which it is collected;
- retention of data only as strictly required for a declared use;

- legal redress for individuals to correct inaccurate data or challenge misuse of data; and
- the maintenance of data security by the data holder.[265]

National governments in the countries where these air carriers were based were then left with the question of whether to enforce their privacy laws against the airlines or to allow the information transfers. At the same time, the U.S. government was approaching them to negotiate formal bilateral agreements for the sharing of PNR.

THE DEALS MADE

In Canada, where the government was planning its own PNR system—and, in December 2001, had agreed to share PNR information in some way with the United States under the Smart Border Action Plan[266]—an exemption to the Canadian Personal Information Protection and Electronic Documents Act was quietly pushed through Parliament. It allowed Canadian carriers to disclose any passenger information in their possession to a foreign state if required by the law of that foreign state.[267]

In Europe, the European Commission reached an agreement on PNR sharing with the United States in December 2003.[268] To do so, the commission made a highly contested ruling about the "adequacy" of U.S. undertakings to protect the privacy of European information in conformity with the EU's data protection directive.[269] In fact, the deal breaches many of the core principles in the directive.[270] Data are being collected for multiple, undeclared purposes and will be shared widely among the numerous entities that make up the U.S. Department of Homeland Security.[271] Once stored in the United States, there are no guarantees that information will not be shared or even transferred wholesale to third countries.[272] There is no clear right of access for individuals, no judicial right of redress,[273] and no requirement that the data be stored for the shortest possible time.[274] Tellingly, the deal left open the question of whether the personal data of European citizens would be used in the U.S. Computer Assisted Passenger Pre-Screening System (CAPPS II), even though it was known at the time of negotiations that the United States was *already* using European data to test the program.[275] The aim of CAPPS II was to use PNR and other information to "risk score" all airline passengers.

PNR AND THE DEMOCRATIC DEFICIT—ANOTHER REFERRAL TO ICAO

Usual democratic processes were circumvented in order to conclude the EU-U.S. arrangement. The deal was voted down three times by the European Parliament, the only directly elected body in the European Union, which referred the question of "adequacy" to the European Court of Justice.[276] Both the European Parliament and the European Court of Justice were overridden when the Council of the European Union (the legislative body made up of representatives of the national governments in the EU) reverted to its treaty powers to rubber-stamp the deal.[277]

At the end of May 2006, the European Court of Justice ruled that the European Commission and the Council of the EU lacked authority to make the deal.[278] The ruling is a Pyrrhic victory for the European Parliament, however. It does not address the data protection issue and will allow the United States to replace the original agreement with either bilateral agreements or a "Third Pillar" instrument, over which the European Parliament has no power of approval. These new agreements could be even worse in terms of data protection than the original one.[279]

The Council of the EU, it seems, had its own ambitions to create a system for the collection and use of PNR data.[280] The Justice and

Home Affairs ministers approved a European PNR sharing scheme in April 2004, just in time to avoid a new "co-decision" procedure that came into force on May 1, 2004, that would have required approval by the European Parliament. National parliaments were also bypassed—the right of the UK Parliament to scrutinize the document was, for example, overridden by the UK government.[281]

Moreover, the Council of the EU, in order to avoid further controversy, had the matter of PNR sharing referred to ICAO, asking it to develop global standards.[282] As with biometric passports, a global system will be established by an unelected, international body, and governments will be given an excuse for doing what their laws and citizens might otherwise have prevented. To date, the United States, the EU, the UK, Canada, and Australia have passed legislation to set up PNR-sharing systems,[283] and others will surely follow once ICAO standards are adopted.

EXPANSION TO OTHER TRANSPORTATION SYSTEMS

As mentioned earlier, government officials are talking about expanding the security measures that are being implemented for international air travel to other transportation systems. Canada, for example, indicated its intention to expand its PNR system to different modes of transportation in a submission made to the ICAO in spring 2004,[284] and it has already expanded the system to include domestic air travel.[285] The Department of Homeland Security has made similar suggestions with respect to the planned air passenger screening system in the United States.[286] The United Kingdom has said that its "e-Border" PNR system will "roll out incrementally to all air, sea and rail carriers operating internationally to/from all major UK ports."[287]

Again, if this happens, the transportation systems in our countries could become the kind of internal checkpoints generally associated with police states. And with the many fields of information that PNR provides, the state could glean a highly detailed picture of our personal lives, tracking and recording our movements inside and outside the country. As a British colleague of mine once quipped, PNR-sharing schemes should carry the warning: "Buy a ticket, get a record."[288] One might equally say, "Got a record? don't buy a ticket!" since governments have already started to use PNR systems for ordinary law-enforcement purposes. In 2003, U.S. Customs and Border Protection caught 4,555 American citizens wanted by the police for various criminal offenses, and in 2004 the number rose to 6,189.[289] Behind this dragnet is the FBI's National Crime Information Center, "a repository of 40 million records covering everything from terrorists to stolen boats."[290] At the same time, authorities have begun to use API/PNR screening routinely to apprehend noncitizens for immigration offenses, using immigration databases to make checks.[291]

Or, the warning might well be, "Buy a ticket, take your chances." As I will discuss later, in countries that currently have legislation permitting PNR data sharing, PNR data are being stored and used to create data profiles on individuals so that these can be "data-mined" using computer algorithms to "identify risk." There is no due process for individuals before they are listed as "risks" to the state: the criteria for listing are not even disclosed. And there are few, if any, legal avenues of redress to challenge one's risk "score" after one is flagged as a risk. Those who are singled out and detained as moderate or "unknown" risks will miss flights. Those who are flagged as high risk will be prevented from traveling on transportation systems altogether.

These might not seem like very serious consequences at first impression, but as U.S. Supreme Court Justice William O. Douglas observed, the right to travel, to move from one place to another, is a critical freedom:

> The right to travel is a part of the "liberty" of which the citizen cannot be deprived without due process of law under

> the Fifth Amendment. . . . Freedom of movement across frontiers in either direction, and inside frontiers as well, was part of our heritage. Travel abroad, like travel within the country, may be necessary for a livelihood. It may be as close to the heart of the individual as the choice of what he eats, or wears, or reads. Freedom of movement is basic in our scheme of values. "Our nation," wrote Chafee, "has thrived on the principle that, outside areas of plainly harmful conduct, every American is left to shape his own life as he thinks best, do what he pleases, go where he pleases."[292]

For some, the consequences of being flagged as a risk will be dire. Like Maher Arar, who was probably flagged on a passenger manifest list, they will be abducted by state authorities and rendered to prisons in third countries or extraterritorial camps run directly by the United States, where they will be indefinitely held, tortured, and perhaps even killed. Like Maher Arar, many of these people will be innocent of any links to terrorism; a handful will be guilty, but none will deserve the lawless brutality to which they are subjected.

CHAPTER EIGHT

Global Surveillance of Electronic Communications, Records, and Financial Transactions

◎ ◎

> *It was even conceivable that they watched everybody all the time. But at any rate they could plug in your wire whenever they wanted to. You had to live—did live, from the habit that became instinct—in the assumption that every sound you made was overheard. . . .*
>
> —George Orwell, *Nineteen Eighty-Four*

Along with the creation of a global registration and identification system and global infrastructure for the surveillance of movement, governments are now working to substantially enlarge their powers to intercept and monitor electronic communications and financial transactions, both within and across their borders. President Bush's secret, criminal eavesdropping on Americans under his NSA program is one of the best-known manifestations of this trend, but many more examples exist, which I will describe shortly.

It is the historical tendency of law-enforcement agencies and governments concerned with law enforcement to push for ever-greater surveillance powers. In democratic countries, civil liberties laws and traditions have acted as a brake to their overreaching, insisting that governments balance the law-enforcement interests of the state against the rights of the individual to be left alone and to be free from unreasonable search and seizure. However, these counterweights have been overridden as countries have adopted antiterrorism measures that expand their interception and search-and-seizure powers while weakening or removing judicial oversight over those powers.[293]

But something else is happening, too. As I illustrate throughout this chapter, the private sector is being pressed into service as the state's eyes and ears. Just as it has done with the acquisition of private-sector databases and airline passenger record systems, the state is using the private sector to exponentially increase its surveillance capacity in the realm of electronic communications and financial transactions. And, instead of relying on the inconsistent practices of businesses, governments are starting to tell businesses how to design their information systems, what information to gather, how long it must be stored, what must be checked and reported, and what must be given directly to state officials.

ACCESS TO ELECTRONIC RECORDS IN THE UNITED STATES

The United States is driving a lot of the international efforts to expand electronic and financial surveillance, and it is also a case study in the domestic expansion of this kind of surveillance. I have already described President Bush's secret NSA eavesdropping program.The USA PATRIOT Act authorizes many more snooping powers for state agents, and laws that existed before the events of 9/11 are being interpreted in aggressive ways to provide further access. I begin with an example of the latter trend before moving on to describe some of the most troubling provisions in the USA PATRIOT Act.

Access to Cell Phone Location Data under the Stored Communications Act

There are more than 195 million cell-phone subscribers in the United States, and most of them do not know that the government could be tracking their every move through electronic signals radiating from those phones.[294] When a cell phone is turned on, cellular operators like Rogers or Verizon Wireless can determine within 300 yards the location of one of their subscribers. Even when a cell phone is off, it emits signals to cellular towers allowing the operating company to record the subscriber's position as she or he travels.[295]

Department of Justice prosecutors in the United States have been arguing that the standard for accessing this extremely revealing information is that contained in a 1994 amendment to the 1986 Stored Communications Act.[296] That standard is much lower than the usual "probable cause" standard, in that it only requires the government to show that the records it seeks are "relevant and material to an ongoing investigation." And it seems, courts have regularly been granting warrants for historical and real-time cell-phone location data on this basis.[297] Clifford S. Fishman, a former prosecutor in the Manhattan District Attorney's Office, told the *New York Times* that in his experience, the requests for these kinds of warrants had become more and more prevalent since 2003.[298]

In the last part of 2005, three federal magistrate judges denied requests for cell-phone location data on the "relevancy" standard, saying that cell-phone tracking was just as intrusive as home searches and should, therefore, be subject to the same probable cause standard as warrants for home searches.[299] But, whether this judicial trend will defeat easy government access to cell-phone location data is yet to be seen.

National Security Letters

One summer's day in 2005, across from the tennis courts on Matianuk Avenue in Windsor, Connecticut, George Christian was accosted by FBI agents. Christian was the executive director of Library Connection Inc. and managed the digital records of three dozen Connecticut libraries. The letter the agents handed him, "crested with the shield and stars of the FBI," directed him to hand over "all subscriber information, billing information and access logs of any person" who used a particular computer in a library some miles away.[300] The letter said the material was being sought as part of an investigation "to protect against internal terrorism or clandestine intelligence activities," and it prohibited Christian from "disclosing to any person that the FBI ha[d] sought or obtained access to information or records under [the PATRIOT Act]."[301] Christian refused to surrender the records, and his employer, along with the American Civil Liberties Union, filed suit against the gag order. The *Washington Post* was able to piece together the identity of Christian and his employer by comparing unsealed portions of the court file with public records and "information gleaned from people with no knowledge of the FBI demand."[302]

As the *Washington Post* noted, the case afforded "a rare glimpse of an exponentially growing practice of domestic surveillance under the USA PATRIOT Act": the use of National Security Letters (NSLs). National Security Letters are a form of administrative subpoenas that are used by a number of United States government agencies.[303] But in the law-enforcement area, their use has always been tightly restricted. Created in the 1970s, FBI National Security Letters began as a narrow exception in consumer privacy law, allowing the FBI—without a court order—to look in secret at the communications and financial and credit records of suspected foreign agents. With Section 505 of the PATRIOT Act and new guidelines for their use, the Bush administration has seriously widened the use of FBI

National Security Letters in the same way it widened the NSA's mandate. Now the FBI can use National Security Letters against law-abiding citizens and residents for whom there are no reasonable grounds to believe they are linked to a foreign agent or terrorist organization. The "reason to believe" standard in earlier legislation has been replaced with a mere requirement that the FBI certify the information it is seeking is "relevant" to an investigation "to protect against international terrorism or clandestine intelligence activities."

National Security Letters cannot be used by the FBI to read the content of communications. But, as former FBI lawyer Michael J. Woods has said, "The composite picture of a person which emerges from transactional information is more telling than the direct content of your speech."[304] It allows agents to see what you buy and where, what videos you rent, what Web sites you surf, what subjects you Google, whom you send e-mail to, where you make your money, what you pawn and borrow, what you gamble, where you travel and with whom, and who telephones you and where. Anyone who receives a National Security Letter is gagged, forever, from telling anyone about the fact that they received it.

According to the *Washington Post*, the FBI has issued more than 30,000 National Security Letters each year in the recent past, compared with the approximately 3,000 a year it used to issue. The agency does not report to the Department of Justice or Congress on its use of the NSLs, and the executive branch keeps only incomplete statistics, which are found only in classified reports.[305]

It is no wonder that the FBI's use of National Security Letters is burgeoning, given the new guidelines Attorney General John Ashcroft issued to the agency on May 30, 2002, and October 31, 2003. In them, he "gave overriding priority to preventing attacks by any means possible."[306] And so we see the effect of the doctrine of pre-emption at work again. As the NSA is doing with its secret program, the FBI is using National Security Letters to *generate* leads as well as to pursue them.[307]

To Joseph Billy Jr., the FBI's deputy assistant director for counterterrorism, "It's all chicken and egg. We're trying to determine if someone warrants scrutiny or doesn't," although he acknowledges that innocent people will have their records swept up and understands that "merely being in a government or FBI database . . . gives everybody, you know, neck hair standing up."[308]

To Michael Mason, a Washington, D.C., FBI field office chief with authority to issue the NSLs, there is no valid argument that can be made against them: "I don't necessarily want somebody to know what videos I rent or the fact I like cartoons." But if those records "are never used against a person, if they're never used to put him in jail, or deprive him of a vote, et cetera, then what is the argument?"[309]

At the same time, the FBI has offered no example of a terrorism case in which a National Security Letter helped them.[310] "I'd love to have a made-for-Hollywood story," Mason said, "but I don't have one. I am not even sure such an example exists."[311]

In 2004, the American Civil Liberties Union (ACLU) challenged the constitutionality of the new National Security Letter provision in a case involving a New York Internet company. Department of Justice lawyers tried to conceal the existence of the case, objecting to its entry into the public docket of the court.[312] The ACLU won the lawsuit on the grounds that the FBI's present power to issue National Security Letters violated the Fourth Amendment (unreasonable searches and seizures) and the First Amendment (freedom of speech and association).[313] In August 2005, ACLU brought the Library Connection's civil suit to federal court, and U.S. District Judge Janet Hall ruled that the gag provision violated the First Amendment. During oral argument in open court, Justice Hall said that one government explanation for the NSL that was served on George Christian was so vague that "if I were to say it out loud, I would get quite a laugh here."[314] Both decisions were appealed by the government; however, in April 2006 the government dropped its claim to enforce the gag order against the librarians from Connecticut.[315]

Access to Any Tangible Thing

The FBI could just as well have gone after Library Connection's records under Section 215 of the PATRIOT Act. It is known as the "Libraries clause" or the "Business Records" provision, but its scope is much broader than these names suggest. Section 215 amends the Foreign Intelligence Surveillance Act, discussed earlier, to allow the FBI to seek an order from the FISA court to compel the production of "any tangible things (including books, records, papers, documents, and other items)." Under Section 215, the government need only show that the thing it seeks access to may be related to an ongoing investigation into terrorism or foreign intelligence activities. As with National Security Letters, persons served with a FISA warrant cannot disclose the existence of the warrant or the fact that items were provided to the government. The content of business customer and employee records, library records, medical records, credit records, telecommunications records, educational records, and objects like computers, Blackberry devices, and PalmPilots and handhelds can all be seized under this provision.

As mentioned earlier, U.S. companies and their subsidiaries holding the personal information of citizens of other countries, could be compelled under Section 215 of the PATRIOT Act to hand over to the FBI that information, in violation of those countries' laws. This is a particularly acute concern in Canada where most credit card companies are American-based and the federal and provincial governments have contracted out medical plans, parts of the national census, and the student loan program to American companies.

Librarians, those supposedly mild-mannered professionals, have been the ones leading the charge against Section 215. In a determined revolt, many have posted signs in their libraries like the one posted at the sign-out desk in the Santa Cruz public library: "*Warning: Although Santa Cruz Library makes every effort to protect your privacy, under the federal* USA PATRIOT Act . . . *records of books you obtain from this library may be obtained by federal agents.*" The American Library Association, which has lobbied hard against Section 215 of the PATRIOT Act, released a survey of its members in June 2005, which showed that law-enforcement agents had contacted libraries, with formal and informal requests about their records, at least 200 times since 2001.[316]

Sneak-and-Peek Searches

The Fourth Amendment of the U.S. Constitution guarantees people the right to be secure in their persons, houses, papers, and effects against unreasonable searches and seizures.

It used to be that when law-enforcement officials searched your home in the United States, they had to knock at the door and give you notice before they entered. Under the law, delayed notice of entry was permitted only under a "very small number of circumstances,"[317] for example, when agents were setting up surreptitious electronic surveillance.

Now, under Section 213 of the PATRIOT Act, government agents can enter your house secretly to conduct a search and seizure of your documents, computers and other electronic communications devices, where a court "finds reasonable cause to believe that providing immediate notification of the execution of the warrant may have an adverse effect." Notice need only be given within a "reasonable period" and can be extended by a court for "good cause."

Lower Standard for Foreign Intelligence Surveillance under FISA

Recall that since FISA's enactment in 1978 up until 2004, the special FISA court has turned down only five applications for warrants *out of 18,748*.[318] Then consider that these extraordinary warrants used to be permitted only where the collection of intelligence on foreign governments or agents was the primary purpose of an investigation.

Section 218 of the PATRIOT Act, expands the use of FISA warrants to situations where foreign intelligence gathering is only a "significant" purpose of an investigation, opening up the use of these easily obtainable warrants (including the so-called "business records" warrants described above and several more described below) for ordinary criminal investigations and against citizens and residents inside the United States. This amounts to a serious erosion of the constitutional rationale underpinning FISA: the idea that laxer standards in respect of foreign intelligence are justifiable since the executive branch should not be unduly restrained when it comes to the protecting national security against foreign interests.[319]

Roving Wiretap Authority under FISA

The Fourth Amendment of the Constitution of the United States requires government agents to obtain a warrant to search premises and to particularly describe in the warrant the place to be searched and the persons or things to be seized.

Section 206 of the PATRIOT Act ignores this requirement, allowing government agents to apply under FISA for multipoint or "roving wiretap" warrants. This means authorities can intercept any communication made by or to the person targeted by a warrant without having to specify the computer or telephone to be monitored. So that if the target were a user of a university computer lab, a cybercafé, or a public library computer, all of the other users of those facilities would also be monitored.

Expanded Use of Pen Register and Trap and Trace Devices under FISA

Section 214 of the PATRIOT Act removes an earlier requirement in FISA that government agents prove their target is "an agent of a foreign power" before obtaining a pen register/trap and trace order from the FISA court.

Pen Register and Trap and Trace Devices and "Carnivore"

Pen registers are devices which record the numbers of outgoing calls made on a telephone. Trap and trace devices record the numbers of incoming calls. Under the Pen Register and Trap and Trace statute of the Electronic Communications Privacy Act (ECPA), pen register and trap and trace devices were those that provided real-time interception of "numbers dialed or otherwise transmitted on the telephone line to which such device [was] attached."[320] State agents could obtain a pen register or trap and trace order from a court merely by certifying that the information likely to be obtained was "relevant to an ongoing criminal investigation."[321]

Section 216 of the PATRIOT Act expanded the definition of these devices to cover devices or processes that decode or identify "dialing, routing, addressing or signaling information" transmitted by any wire or wireless communication. This makes pen register/trap and trace orders, whether obtained under FISA or the ECPA, much more intrusive than they formerly were, since the information that can be gleaned from routing and other information in respect to e-mail, Web surfing and other forms of wireless communication, as discussed earlier, can be extremely revealing.

Section 216 might also justify the use of technology like "Carnivore," a system reportedly used by the FBI to monitor all the traffic handled by an Internet service provider (ISP) in order to filter out and deliver to investigators those "packets" that they have legal authorization to view. Of course, the controversy with such systems is that their details remain secret and the public is left to trust that government agents do not abuse them.[322] A system like Carnivore (a version of which has been renamed DCS 1000) could potentially be used in the same way the NSA's technology is used—to screen huge masses of communications for key words, traffic patterns, phrases, and other putative "indicia" of terrorist activity.

Nationwide Surveillance Orders and Search Warrants

Before the enactment of the PATRIOT Act, surveillance orders and search warrants could only be obtained within the geographic jurisdiction of the court to which government agents applied. Sections 216 and 220 of the PATRIOT Act permit courts to issue nationwide surveillance orders and search warrants. This places a significant obstacle in front of businesses and individuals, who may not be able to travel to the place where an order or warrant is being applied for, in order to challenge it.

Voice-Mail Messages

Section 209 of the PATRIOT Act amends Title III (which requires that law enforcement show probable cause to access the content of communications) and the Stored Communications Act to make stored voice-mail communications accessible through a search warrant instead of through a more difficult to obtain wiretap order.

Sunset Provisions and Renewal of the PATRIOT Act

The USA PATRIOT Act's Sections 206, 209, 214, 215, 218, and 220 described above, along with a number of other surveillance provisions, were due to expire on December 13, 2005, under a "sunset clause" (Section 224) in the PATRIOT Act. In December 2005, U.S. senators, expressing their anger over the revelation of President Bush's secret and illegal NSA program, almost scuttled legislation reauthorizing these sections of the PATRIOT Act. But hopes that the provisions would not be renewed were snuffed out when both the Senate and the House voted for the renewal of all sixteen provisions at issue in March 2006. Fourteen of the sixteen were made permanent by the USA PATRIOT Improvements and Reauthorization Act, signed into law on March 9, 2006. Only the roving wiretaps and the "business records" provisions will expire in four years. Section 215 has been modified to require the FBI director or deputy director to approve requests for library and medical records and to permit those who receive production orders to disclose them to lawyers so that they can be challenged in court. The legislation also contains provisions requiring the FBI to report to Congress about how often they used certain powers and in what type of situations.

When President Bush signed the reauthorization legislation in March 2006, however, he again asserted that he could disregard Congress's laws when he chose to. Using the same theory of a unitary executive government that he used when defending his right to disobey the FISA statute and set up the secret NSA domestic spying program, he added the following reservation along with his signature when signing the legislation: "The executive branch shall construe the provisions . . . that call for furnishing information to entities outside the executive branch . . . in a manner consistent with the president's constitutional authority to supervise the unitary executive branch and to withhold information."[323]

This drew some heated words from Democratic Senator Patrick J. Leahy, but the issue went largely unnoticed in the media. Leahy said that Bush's assertion that he could ignore Congress's law—and a law that had been the subject of intense debate to boot—"[was] nothing short of a radical effort to manipulate the constitutional separation of powers and evade accountability and responsibility for following the law. The president's signing statements are not the law, and Congress should not allow them to be the last word. The president's constitutional duty is to faithfully execute the law as written by Congress, not cherry-pick the laws he decides he wants to follow. It is our duty to ensure, by means of Congressional oversight, that he does so."[324]

ACCESS TO ELECTRONIC RECORDS IN THE UK AND CANADA

Space does not permit a full inventory of access laws in all countries, but a sketch of the laws that have been or are about to be enacted in the UK and Canada, two of the United States' closest allies, is worthwhile.

In the UK, the Regulation of Investigatory Powers Act (RIPA) creates a mechanism similar to the FBI's National Security Letters. It allows inspectors and superintendents of police to authorize access to the electronic records of service providers without a judicial warrant. Under RIPA, there is also a process by which police can gain authorization to access data directly where this is technically possible. Like the National Security Letter provisions of the USA PATRIOT Act, RIPA does not apply to the content of electronic communications but does apply to subscription data, records of phone calls made and received, the routing of e-mail, Web sites visited, and cell-phone location data.[325] And since there is no national security limitation, police and intelligence officers can access data for a multitude of purposes, including the prosecution of minor offenses. In June 2002, Home Office plans to give a host of other public authorities access to electronic records without judicial warrant were revealed, and an ensuing outcry forced the government to put the measure on hold.[326]

In Canada, a bill providing for police access to the subscriber records of telecommunications service providers without judicial warrant was tabled before the defeat of the Liberal government in January 2006. Another bill was being developed by the Department of Justice that included lower standards for police access to traffic data and cell-phone location data. With a new Conservative government in place, and one determined to forge closer relations with the Bush administration, moreover, it is likely that these bills will be brought forward in the same or some strengthened form in future parliamentary sessions.

In Canada there are also provisions in the Anti-Terrorism Act[327] that allow the minister of defense to authorize *the same kind of program* in Canada as President Bush's secret, unlegislated NSA program in the United States. In other words, the Canadian government has legislated what the Bush administration dared not legislate. Curiously, the provision has attracted little attention in Canada, despite media about the outcry in the United States over the NSA program.

DATA RETENTION

Of course, what state authorities can access depends both on what data they and the private sector store or retain, as well as on their technical capacity to access systems, whether for stored or real-time data.

I have already described how the secret NSA program authorized by U.S. President Bush is amassing one of the largest databases in the world. Other state agencies are increasingly storing the data they obtain. The FBI is a case in point.

FBI Retention

There used to be an FBI guideline that required the agency to destroy all information obtained about a U.S. citizen or resident if it were "not relevant to the purposes for which it was collected" or when an investigation was closed. In late 2003, Attorney General Ashcroft rescinded the guideline and replaced it with one that requires the FBI to retain all the records it collects and to share the information widely within the federal government, and with state, local, and tribal governments and "appropriate private sector entities."[328]

Ashcroft's new guidelines also permitted the FBI to add to their databases, for the first time, the commercial databases of aggregating companies like ChoicePoint and LexisNexis. Ashcroft's predecessors had never dared to do this, having determined that it would violate the Privacy Act.[329] The same guidelines instructed the FBI to develop data-mining technology—the use of computer models to scrutinize masses of data for patterns or criteria—to find links between people, places, and events in its "growing cache of electronic files."[330] Heeding the guidelines, the FBI set up a new system called "Investigative Data Warehouse" in January 2004 based on the Oracle technology that the CIA uses.[331] This kind of retention and data mining of records allows the personal data of Americans to be scrutinized again and again as new data are added.

A glimpse of how electronic data acquisition, data storage, and data mining work in the hands of law enforcement can be seen in the FBI's handling of a suspected terrorist attack in Las Vegas in December 2003, as reported by the *Washington Post*.[332] The Department of Homeland Security had raised the threat level to "orange":[333] there was intelligence about a possible New Year's Eve attack and the chief of the FBI's Proactive Data Exploitation Unit was called in. Almost 300,000 tourists visit Las Vegas every day, staying an average of four days each, and the Proactive Unit was going to keep track of all of them over a two-week period. That meant almost a million suspects:

> An interagency task force began pulling together the records of every hotel guest, everyone who rented a car or truck, every lease on a storage space, and every airplane passenger who landed in the city. [The] unit filtered that population for leads. Any link to the known terrorist universe—a shared address or utility account, a check

deposited, a telephone call—could give investigators a start.

. . . Investigators began with emergency requests for help from the city's sprawling hospitality industry. "A lot of it was done voluntary at first," said Billy, the deputy assistant FBI director.

According to others directly involved, investigators turned to national security letters and grand jury subpoenas when friendly persuasion did not work.

Early in the operation, according to participants, the FBI gathered casino executives and asked for guest lists. The MGM company, followed by others, balked.

"Some casinos were saying no to consent [and said], 'You have to produce a piece of paper,'" said Jeff Jonas, chief scientist at IBM Entity Analytics, who previously built data management systems for casino surveillance. "They don't just market 'What happens in Vegas stays in Vegas'. They want it to be true."

The operation remained secret for about a week. Then casino sources told Ron Smith, gaming editor of the *Las Vegas Review Journal*, that the FBI had served national security letters on them . . .

What happened in Vegas stayed in the federal data banks. Under Ashcroft's revised policy, none of the information has been purged. For every visitor, [a representative for the Justice Department said], "the record of the Las Vegas hotel room would still exist."

The operation was a bust. No terrorist was found, and the orange alert was lifted on January 10, 2004.

Mandatory Data Retention in Europe and the United States

In addition to asking state agencies to store the information they acquire, states are asking the private sector to retain the data they have in their possession for mandatory periods of time. Mandatory data retention statutorily obliges the private sector to save and store data it would otherwise erase, for example, when the data were no longer needed, or as required by privacy laws. Even more than agency retention, mandatory data retention in the private sector exponentially expands the amount of information that can be tapped into by state authorities.

In a letter dated October 16, 2001, the Bush administration made a number of demands to the EU, asking for cooperation in its "war on terror."[334] One of these demands was for the EU to require mandatory, routine data retention by communication service providers. The demand was made despite the lack of mandatory data retention laws in the United States at the time and the absence of data retention provisions in the Convention on Cybercrime (see pp. 131–132).

In 2002, the EU data protection directive was amended to allow member states to pass domestic laws on mandatory data retention of traffic data for all communications. (Previously, data could only be stored for billing purposes.) By the end of 2003, eleven of the member states had set up or planned to introduce data retention regimes with retention periods ranging from one to five years. In the UK, where the government had been lobbying hard for mandatory data retention across the EU, a voluntary scheme for data retention exists under the Anti-terrorism, Crime and Security Act 2001 (ACTSA), which allows the home secretary to enter into formal agreements with service providers for the routine retention of data. But Section 140 of ACTSA allows the home secretary to introduce a compulsory scheme, and the recent adoption of mandatory data retention at the EU level will justify its adoption in the UK.[335]

Mandatory data retention had been floated before in the EU under a proposal known as "ENFOPOL 98." But widespread criticism from civil society groups and the public killed it. With the new request from the United States and subsequent terrorist attacks in Madrid and London, the European Council became the main driver of a new data retention initiative aimed at telecommunications providers. This initiative fell under the treaty establishing the European Community and as such, was subject to a co-decision procedure in which both the European Council and the European Parliament have to agree on a text for what is called a "directive."

Under intense pressure from the European Council, the European Parliament agreed to a text for a directive on mandatory data retention on December 14, 2005.[336] An EU directive allows each member nation to draft its own laws, as long as the results comply with the directive. The directive of December 2005 calls for the harmonization of mandatory data retention laws across the EU, and requires "the providers of publicly available electronic communications services or of public communications networks" to retain data which are generated or processed by them "for the purpose of investigation, detection and prosecution of serious crime, as defined by each Member State in its national law."[337] The directive does not apply to the content of communications but does apply to what, again, is often more revealing: traffic, location and subscriber data.[338] Under Article 6, the various categories of data are to be retained for periods of not less than six months and not more than two years from the date of the communication, though member states "facing particular circumstances" may apply to the EU Commission for an extension of the maximum period.[339] Finally, under the directive, member states must ensure that retained data "can be transmitted upon request to the competent authorities without delay," opening up the possibility of authorities having direct access to stored data.[340]

In a high-level meeting between the United States and the

European Union on "Freedom, Security and Justice" held in March 2006 in Vienna, the U.S. contingent indicated that the United States might seek bilateral treaties with each member of the EU to ensure that the data collected on the basis of the recently adopted directive on mandatory data retention will be available to U.S. agencies.[341]

Up until the time the European Parliament approved mandatory data retention, the Bush Adminstration had "explicitly opposed" adopting it, saying it had "serious reservations" about such an initiative.[342] But, in another example of "policy laundering," Bush adminsitration officials began speaking more favorably about mandatory retention after it was passed in the EU,[343] until the idea became quite popular on Capitol Hill.[344] Then in May 2006, U.S. Attorney General Alberto R. Gonzales and FBI Director Robert S. Mueller III met privately with industry representatives to urge them to retain subscriber and network data for two years,[345] citing the need for such retention in child pornography and terrorism cases. Only weeks later, a Republican bill was introduced in the House of Representatives, providing for mandatory data retention in respect of all criminal investigations. Moreover, while the EU requirements do not compel the storage of content data, the U.S. bill gave the attorney general wide discretion to prescribe what was to be stored.[346] The Republican Congressman, F. James Sensenbrenner, (R-WI), who introduced the bill, later backed away from it. But soon after, a Democratic representative, Diana DeGette, (D-CO) began working on a new bill with Republican representatives Joe Barton and Ed Whitfield. The new bill, expected to be introduced at the end of September 2006, is said to require Internet providers to store traffic data for one year.[347]

"BUILDING-IN SURVEILLANCE"[348] AND THE CONVENTION ON CYBERCRIME

The legal access that state agents have to electronic records and communications is limited by their technical capacity to access service providers' systems and by their budgets to install interception devices where it is possible. Since the events of 9/11 law enforcement agencies in the United States and other countries have been pushing to make service providers responsible for removing technical barriers, calling on them to, in effect, reengineer their systems to give state agents a permanent "back door" through which they can monitor electronic communications. In other words, the private sector is being asked to "build" surveillance capacity "into" their systems and to bear the cost of that reengineering.

Since 1994, landline telephone companies in the United States have been required by the Communications Assistance for Law Enforcement Act (CALEA) to design their equipment according to the FBI's specifications in order to give law-enforcement officials a "back door" through which they can wiretap communications. In October 2005 the Federal Communications Commission (FCC), bowing to pressure from the FBI, the U.S. Department of Justice, and the U.S. Drug Enforcement Administration adopted a new rule that expanded CALEA requirements to "build in" surveillance capacity to cover "providers of facilities-based broadband Internet access services and providers of interconnected voice over Internet Protocol."[349] In expanding CALEA to the Internet, FCC Commissioner Michael J. Copps admitted that the FCC was reaching beyond Congress's intention: "[the] statute is undeniably stretched," he said.[350] Fellow commissioner Kathleen Q. Abernathy, "issued a plea" to Congress asking it to reconsider its decision to exempt the Internet from CALEA: "the application of [the statute] to these new services could be stymied for years" by litigation, she said.[351]

Compelling service providers to "build in" surveillance capacity to their systems means that within minutes of receiving a warrant from a court, real-time interception of a person's Internet or voice over Internet use can be implemented with just a few computer strokes, making a connection between the computerized listening stations of law enforcement and the service provider's system. At the same time, tools like the FBI's "Carnivore" software, mentioned earlier, can be used to search masses of information within a system for key words.[352] The access to personal information that could be gained in this way is virtually limitless, since there will be few technical impediments and little cost to the state.

The United States is pressing other countries to follow its lead and implement more intrusive interception and search-and-seizure laws, like those just described. As part of this effort, it is pushing for the global adoption of the Council of Europe's Convention on Cybercrime, which would toughen and harmonize all countries' cybersecurity laws and allow countries to carry out investigations across borders.[353]

Negotiations for the convention were difficult and prolonged and were apparently sliding toward deadlock because of barriers in countries' various domestic laws, when the events of September 2001 galvanized the parties to conclude the agreement. In November 2001, the United States and twenty-nine other countries signed the document, and as of August 2006, fifteen countries had ratified the Convention.[354] The convention's purpose is not limited to antiterrorism, but includes ordinary law enforcement as well.

In order to ratify the Convention, signatories must first implement the legislative changes necessary to comply with it. One obligation is to require "service providers" to provide law enforcement with real-time or direct access to the content data and traffic data in their systems.[355] Gag orders on service providers whose systems have been accessed are another of the Convention's requirements.[356] Mandatory preservation orders (orders directed at service providers requiring them to preserve information in their systems) are another.[357] Alarmingly, another aspect of the Convention is the requirement, in some circumstances, to provide mutual assistance to co-signatories even where the activity to be investigated is considered a crime only in the requesting country.[358] Governments of each of the signatory states are now drawing up legislation to implement these measures.

As with the ICAO guidelines for biometric passports, citizens would do well to carefully study the exact requirements of the Convention on Cybercrime. It appears that the Convention requires less draconian measures than governments claim it does. The Convention does not require service providers to design their systems to provide direct, real-time access, for example, as the U.S., Canada,[359] and the E.U.[360] are asking them to do, but only to provide such access "within existing capabilities."[361] The Convention does not require the use of powerful word-searching software like the Carnivore (DCS 1000) system developed by the FBI, which can scan millions of e-mails per second. Nor does it require warrantless access, such as Colombia's new Anti-terrorism Act and China's "Golden Shield" project provide, and such as state agencies in Russia and Ukraine have sought in the past.[362]

Similarly, the Convention for Cybercrime does not require mandatory, routine storage of data by communication service providers, a practice the European Union has embraced. A proposal for mandatory storage[363] was defeated in convention negotiations because of national concerns about privacy laws.

ECHELON AND ACCESS TO COMMUNICATIONS CONTENT

If the officials whom investigative reporter Seymour Hersh interviewed are right,[364] and the NSA is, in fact, looking or listening to the content as well as the traffic data of domestic communications, this would be truly shocking. In the United States and most other countries, access to the content of domestic communications requires judicial authorization, and access to domestic communications on a *mass* scale was unheard of previously. However, on the international stage, in respect of foreign communications abroad, this kind of access is routine for the United States and a number of its Commonwealth allies.

In 1948, the United States, the UK, Canada, Australia, and New

Zealand created a program under which they trawled the world's telephone communications in order to spy on other countries and on occasion, it is believed, to share information on each others' citizens that could not be obtained by their own officials under domestic laws. Since the early 1980s, this program has been called ECHELON and has been expanded to intercept e-mails, faxes, telexes, electronic transactions, and international telephone calls carried via satellites. The five agencies participating in ECHELON are the National Security Agency in the United States, the Government Communications Headquarters in the UK, the Defence Signals Directorate in Australia, the Government Communications Security Bureau in New Zealand, and the Communications Security Establishment in Canada.

Under the ECHELON program, millions of messages and conversations are analyzed daily for key words and traffic patterns.[365] Each of the five centers supplies dictionaries to the other four of key words, phrases, people, and places to "tag." The tagged intercepts are forwarded straight to the requesting country.[366] While ECHELON was previously used as a foreign espionage tool, in the current political climate it is likely to also be used domestically for counterterrorism purposes, just as the NSA is being used, and perhaps for other law-enforcement purposes, as well. The number of countries participating in ECHELON may also expand.

MANDATORY REPORTING ON AND ACCESS TO FINANCIAL TRANSACTIONS

Reporting

UN Security Council Resolution 1373, passed shortly after September 11, 2001, required states to, among other things, "prevent and suppress the financing of terrorism, as well as criminalize the willful provision or collection of funds for such acts ... [and] ... to prohibit their nationals or persons or entities in their territories from making funds, financial assets, economic resources, financial or other related services available to persons who commit or attempt to commit, facilitate or participate in the commission of terrorist acts."[367] Under the Resolution, states *must* report on their implementation of these measures, and states failing to implement them face UN Security Council sanctions.

The UN Security Council resolution and pressure from the United States and the international financial institutions promoting "harmonized standards"[368] have led to new national laws around the world that enlist financial institutions and ordinary businesses into the surveillance infrastructure.[369] Many of these laws require banks and businesses to do more than simply "build" surveillance capacity "into" their information systems. They also require them to actively *gather* information about their customers that they would not otherwise gather, to *report* to government on certain kinds of transactions, and to *check* their customers against government watch lists.

Again, the United States is both a driver and case study of these trends. Terrorist money has been difficult to identify, much less seize, in part because terrorist operations are conducted on relative shoestring budgets. Planning and operations for the attacks on September 11, 2001, were believed to have cost Al Qaeda $400,000 to $500,000, with no unusual transactions found, according to the 9/11 Commission, and the 1998 embassy bombings in East Africa only $10,000."[370]

Nevertheless, the Bush administration has repeatedly stated that it wants the financial sector to be a full partner in its efforts to block terrorist financing.[371] The USA PATRIOT Act has dramatically expanded existing requirements for banks and credit unions to report deposits by customers, lowering the threshold to $10,000.[372] Now, "any person engaged in a trade or business" is required under Section 365 to file a "Suspicious Activity" report when he or she receives that amount or more in cash. This means that every plumber, shop owner, general contractor, car salesperson and real-estate agent will be inducted into the financial transactions surveillance infrastructure.

Section 326 of the USA PATRIOT Act requires financial companies to check customers against government watch lists. Executive Order No. 13224, issued September 24, 2001, requires businesses involved in helping individuals buy or sell various kinds of property (such as pawn brokers, real-estate companies, and jewelers) also to check customers against government watch lists.

Regulations stemming from Section 314 of the USA PATRIOT Act require financial institutions to search through their records for any transactions made by individuals suspected of money laundering by any arm of the U.S. government with a law enforcement function. Money laundering is a broad offense encompassing any attempt to disguise illicit profits in pursuit of more than two hundred different crimes. In other words, under USA PATRIOT Act regulations, agencies like the U.S. Agriculture Department and the U.S. Postal Service have the power to conduct a cross-country search for financial records matching someone they suspect of illicit dealings, whether these dealings are related to terrorism or not.[373]

Around the world, charities are also being monitored. In Canada, for example, the Anti-Terrorism Act imposes significant liability on charities accused of having links with terrorist organizations, including the deregistration of their charitable status and the seizure of their assets. Laws like these are having an enormous effect on humanitarian organizations operating in the conflict zones of the world, where it is often impossible to avoid direct or indirect contact with entities that are rightly or wrongly labeled as "terrorist."[374]

ACCESS TO BANK RECORDS

The Mutual Legal Assistance Agreement signed by the EU and the United States in June 2003 gives "U.S. law enforcement authorities access to bank accounts throughout the E.U. for investigations into serious crimes, including terrorism, organized crime and financial crime."[375] The extent of the access gained by U.S. authorities through this treaty was only revealed in June 2006, when the *New York Times* and *Washington Post* broke the story of "operation" SWIFT. SWIFT, or the Society for Worldwide Interbank Financial Telecommunication, is the name of the Belgian-based banking consortium that operates the nerve center of the global banking system. It routes $6 trillion a day between stock exchanges, banks, brokerages, and other financial institutions. Most of its records involve international transfers rather than purely domestic transactions, but these include transactions made by Americans inside the United States.[376]

Like the NSA program, the operation began as a temporary, emergency measure right after the events of 9/11 and became permanent nearly five years later without debate by or authorization from Congress. The information gleaned about it by the *New York Times* came from current and former government officials and industry executives, on condition of anonymity, since the program is still classified. It is run out of the CIA with supervision from the Treasury Department and is said to be based in part on the president's emergency economic powers. Like the NSA, the program does not seek individual warrants or subpoenas from the courts to access records of Americans' specific financial transactions, but in a radical departure from accepted practice, it relies on broad administrative subpoenas to access millions of records at a time. Treasury department officials have said that American laws restricting government access to personal financial records do not apply because SWIFT is a messaging service, not a financial institution.[377]

"The capability here is awesome or, depending on where you're sitting, troubling," a former senior counterterrorism official told the *New York Times*. "The potential for abuse is enormous." According to the officials interviewed, SWIFT is "the biggest and most far reaching of several secret efforts to trace terrorist financing." Smaller agreements with other financial companies have provided access to ATM machine records, Western Union wires, and credit card records.[378]

In addition to the SWIFT program and these other smaller operations, the use of Natonal Security Letters in the financial sector has been expanded significantly. In December 2003, when news was focused on the capture of Saddam Hussein in Iraq, President Bush signed into force a little noticed bill called the Intelligence Authorization Act for the Fiscal Year 2004. Tucked away in it was a new definition of "financial institution" for the legislation governing FBI National Security Letters, which previously only referred to banks. It expanded the reach of the NSLs to stockbrokers, car dealerships, casinos, insurance agencies, jewelers, airlines, the U.S. Post Office, and any other business "whose cash transactions have a high degree of usefulness in criminal, tax, or regulatory matters."[379]

◎ ◎

Orwell wrote about state agents "plugging in" the wire of individuals they wanted to eavesdrop on. In the wired world of the twenty-first century, most people in the developed world and many in the developing world as well have their "wires" permanently plugged in to the many surveilled networks that they must engage with in their daily lives. Thus, the information we leave behind creates an ever-accumulating, virtual picture of us, which state agents can call up to scrutinize again and again.

CHAPTER NINE

The Linkage of National and International Databases

◎ ◎

RADICAL ACCELERATION OF LINKAGE SINCE 9/11

The collection of new information has been accompanied by a new and rapid convergence of information—a linking together or sharing of multiple sources of information so that larger and larger pools of information are accessible to state officials. Certainly linkage has been a trend in the last couple of decades, a notable example being the Schengen Information System (SIS) in Europe, which was set up to compensate for the abolition of internal border controls and which provided for the sharing of criminal and immigration information between signatory countries.[380]

But there has been a radical acceleration of linking and sharing of information since September 2001. UN Security Council Resolution 1373 calls on states to intensify and accelerate the exchange of information regarding terrorist actions and movements, and governments have been taking steps nationally and internationally to heed the call.

Some of the convergence that has been taking place since 9/11 has already been described:

- the aggregation of companies' telecommunications records in the NSA's giant database

- The convergence of private and public databases under the US-VISIT program
- The access to domestic and foreign databases the United States has gained through purchase from "for profit" data aggregators
- The voluntary sharing of data by the private sector in the United States at the request of U.S. government agencies
- The access the FBI has gained under the USA PATRIOT Act to the business records of U.S.-based companies and organizations operating at home and in other countries
- The creation in the United States, the EU, Canada, the UK and Australia of central databases for PNR data
- Plans for the creation of a Europe-wide fingerprint register piggybacking on the biometric passport initiative
- The addition of information obtained through the 30,000 National Security Letters served each year to the FBI's permanent files
- The United States plan to seek bilateral treaties with each member of the EU to give U.S. agencies access to the data that is mandatorily retained by service providers under the new EU directive
- Private-sector reporting of financial transactions to government
- The access gained by the United States to international banking data through the SWIFT program

Many more examples of convergence could be added to the list.

Maher Arar was the victim of indiscriminate information sharing between law enforcement and security intelligence agencies participating in a joint effort across the U.S.-Canada border. The Toronto, or "O" side of that A-O Canada investigation, was an Integrated National Security Enforcement Team (INSET) set up pursuant to the Smart Border Action Plan,[381] and the Ottawa or "A" side of it later became an INSET, too. The United States is also setting up joint investigation teams with the EU under a new "mutual legal assistance" agreement signed in June 2003. These teams can include customs, police, and immigration agents, as well as agents from organizations like the UK Security Service (MI5), the Canadian Security Intelligence Service (CSIS), the FBI, and the CIA. They share information without the formal state-to-state requests ordinarily required under mutual assistance agreements. Members of the teams are also able to directly request their counterparts to facilitate interceptions, searches and seizures, arrests, and detentions, and may not be legally accountable for their actions on foreign soil.[382]

As mentioned earlier, the new EU-U.S. agreement on mutual legal assistance also provides for cooperation in the exchange of banking information in relation to any criminal matter.[383] There are no effective data protection provisions in respect of information shared under the agreement, either by joint investigation teams or by banks. The state providing the information can choose whether it puts conditions on the information's use or not. There are no rights of access, correction, or deletion for individuals and no prohibition on passing on uncorroborated information, or information that implicates innocent people without reasonable grounds as was done by Canadian authorities in the Arar case. There are no prohibitions on the receiving state's passing information to third parties.[384]

In November 2004, the German publication *Der Speigel* revealed the existence of an intelligence operation called "Camolin" involving agencies from the United States, Germany, Canada, the UK, and Australia. The operation was set up in February 2003 with a headquarters in Paris, where regular meetings of the participating agencies take place. Reportedly, the role of the European agencies is to supply dossiers on suspects for the CIA to act on.[385]

In Europe, a Supplemental Agreement on the Exchange of Personal Data and Related Information was signed on December 20, 2002, between the United States and the European Police, or Europol.[386] It gives an unlimited number of U.S. agencies access to Europol information—including sensitive information on the race, political opinions, religious beliefs, health, and sexual lives of individuals,[387] for the *the prevention*, detection, suppression, investigation, and prosecution of any specific criminal offenses and for any specific analysis.[388]

In Europe, in the name of combating terrorism, a second generation Schengen Information System, called SIS II, is being developed. It will cover twenty-seven European countries, will share a technical platform with the EU Visa Information System, and will exist alongside the EU population database being developed as part of the biometric passport proposals.

After the Madrid attacks of March 2004, the Council of the European Union agreed to a set of principles known as the Hague Programme. One of these was the principle of availability, which the program said should govern the exchange of information within the EU from January 2008 onward. Under this principle, a law-enforcement officer in one member state who needed information in order to perform his or her duties would be able to obtain it from law-enforcement officers in another member state.[389]

In May 2005, seven countries—Germany, Spain, France, Luxembourg, the Netherlands, Austria, and Belgium—signed a treaty known as Schengen III or the Prüm Treaty. The Prüm Treaty embraces the principle of availability, setting up the exchange of DNA data for purposes of criminal prosecution, and the exchange of fingerprints and vehicle information for criminal prosecution *and prevention.* It also provides for the exchange of information on political demonstrators for events like G-8 summits and WTO talks.[390]

An unpublished overview report on the principle of availability, obtained by the NGO Statewatch, suggests that "the endgame"[391] is not just for all EU law-enforcement agencies to have access to the personal data held by each other for law-and-order purposes, but that they should also have "direct access to the national administrative systems of all Member States (e.g., registers on persons, including legal persons, vehicles, firearms, identity documents and drivers' licenses as well as aviation and maritime registers)."[392]

In the United States, the FBI has direct access to US-VISIT databases and to the databases of a similar program named the Student and Exchange Visitor Information System (SEVIS), which tracks foreign students.[393] Attorney General John Ashcroft's new guidelines for the FBI also allow the FBI to add consumer data from commercial aggregators like LexisNexis and ChoicePoint to its government files. Attorneys general in the past had not authorized this because they believed it violated the Privacy Act. FBI agents in many field offices now have access to ChoicePoint in their squad rooms.[394]

Under a U.S. program called Multistate Anti-Terrorism Information Exchange or MATRIX, government databases from participating states of the United States are being combined with a private database that claims to have "20+ million records from hundreds of sources."[395] Government information that feeds into MATRIX includes records on property ownership, FAA pilot licenses and aircraft ownership, Coast Guard–registered vessels, sexual offenders lists, federal terrorist watch lists, corporation filings, bankruptcy filings, Uniform Commercial Code filings, and professional licenses.[396] Authorities using MATRIX could identify all black-haired, blue-eyed divorced male residents of Miami driving a silver Mazda and owning a boat, for example. They can then display the data on "social networking charts," suggesting links between people, photo lineups, and "target maps." While MATRIX currently only operates in a handful of states, the private company that runs it has driver's license information for fifteen states, motor vehicle registration for twelve states, department of corrections information from thirty-three states, and sexual offender information from twenty-seven states. In some cases, states have sold their data to the company.[397]

The U.S.-Canada Smart Border Action plan calls for increased information sharing and interoperability of databases between the two countries. "Our data should be your data," said George Tenet, the former director of the CIA, to Canadian security professionals gathered at a counterterrorism conference in San Francisco in late 2004.[398] He might have added, "Your data should be our data." In her 2003–4 report, the privacy commissioner of Canada noted that "[p]ersonal information about Canadians continued to be gathered, stored, sorted and shared in alarming amounts on the basis of the idea—however unproven—that more information about individuals equals greater security against terrorists and other threats."[399]

In Canada, a Public Safety Information Network is being constructed that links together key justice records and possibly criminal investigation information, passport information, and travel information. It is accessible to numerous Canadian agencies that formerly did not routinely share information and will reportedly be interoperable with systems in the United States and other countries.[400]

In Colombia, the new Anti-terrorism Act envisions the creation of a new registry containing private information on all Colombians, to which military authorities will have access.[401]

Information sharing and an integration of security function with the United States has been occurring most frequently in countries known for their oppressive regimes. Since 9/11 countries like Georgia, Indonesia, Egypt, Malaysia, and Uzbekistan have been sharing information, suspects, and in some cases, intelligence and military operations with the United States in an unprecedented manner.

THE "BLACK BOX" OF INFORMATION

The "black box" of information that was described in the context of the US-VISIT program—the database of databases that some say the United States is currently amassing with the help of the convergences just described—could contain all of the information described above and more. And if it does, it will be a global web of databases, encompassing domestic and foreign, and public and private sector sources.

CHAPTER TEN

The Dangers of a Risk-Assessment Model—A World That Is Orwellian and Kafkaesque

⊙ ⊙

My guiding principle is this: Guilt is never to be doubted.
—Franz Kafka

DATA MINING—THE HIGH-TECH "SOLUTION" TO RISK ASSESSMENT

A veritable ocean of information about our private lives is being collected, stored, linked and shared. No country has the capacity to analyze it using people power alone. The high-tech solution that some governments are pursuing with fervor is data mining.

As explained earlier, data mining is the use of computer models, or algorithms, to scrutinize masses of data for selected patterns or criteria. In the post-9/11 world, data mining is being used to identify patterns of behavior that are supposedly indicative of terrorist activity, in order to assess the level of risk that individuals pose to the state.

George Orwell's famous book *Nineteen Eighty-Four* presents us with a dystopic vision of what living in a surveillance society could be like, but the methods it describes are quaint in that they require human beings to spy on each other using auditory or visual devices. In the Orwellian society of the twenty-first century, we will be watched and assessed by computers. And the assessment will be based, not on our actual observed involvement in illegal, criminal, or even suspicious activity, but on the *probability* that we might be engaged in such activity.

Lee Tien, a staff attorney at the Electronic Frontier Foundation, has observed, "[W]e don't realize that, as we live our lives and make little choices, like buying groceries, buying on Amazon, Googling, we're leaving traces everywhere. We have an attitude that no one will connect all those dots. But these [data-mining] programs are about connecting those dots—analyzing and aggregating them—in a way that we haven't thought about. It's one of the underlying fundamental issues we have yet to come to grips with."[402]

In the Cold War/McCarthy period in the United States of the 1950s, the maxim was that if any doubt existed as to the reliability or loyalty of an individual, such doubts should be resolved in favor of the state.[403] As Reg Whitaker, a historian of the period has said, "Anyway, there was little or no interest in individuals, as such. Individuals were messy, unfathomable in their complexity and idiosyncrasy to bureaucrats who had to deal with large numbers of cases and in universal categories. Dossiers were neat, simple and serviceable for the specific purposes required. . . . Of course, it was possible that mistakes could be made, that information might prove faulty in some particulars, that innocence might be mistaken for something else. . . ."[404]

An example of the many mistakes that were made in that era was the naming of academic Owen Lattimore as the Soviet Union's top spy in the United States. He was later fully cleared of the charges. In his account of the affair he noted that the FBI and other agencies had "built up on him a dossier of '*a man who might have existed.*'"[405] Again, as a historian of the period has observed, "that phrase catches the very essence of the creation of the *national inse-*

curity state: a data world that shadows, mimics, and caricatures the real world."[406]

We may think that anyone looking at our personal data with the proper explanation would conclude that we do not pose security risks, but, in fact, in the data world we have no control over our "virtual identities" or the interpretations that others make of them.

TIA, ADVISE, and MATRIX

The forerunner of many post-9/11 data-mining projects was a program known as Total Information Awareness (TIA), run by Iran-Contragate's John Poindexter out of the U.S. Department of Defense's Defense Advanced Research Projects Agency (DARPA). The goal of the program, as described by Poindexter, was to mine "the transaction space" to find "signatures" of terrorist activity. According to the program's Web site, the transactions mined would include individuals' financial, medical, travel, "place/event entry," transportation, education, housing, and communications transactions. The description lends credence to the idea that the United States *is* constructing a "black box" of information and that risk assessment through data mining is one of the goals of that project.

Poindexter envisioned his program as developing software that could quickly analyze "multiple petabytes" of data. The eighteen million books in the Library of Congress could fit into one petabyte fifty times over; one petabyte, the equivalent of one million gigabytes, could hold forty pages of information on each of the 6.2 + billion persons on earth.[407] As the manager of the project described it, the task was "much harder than simply finding needles in a haystack. Our task is akin to finding dangerous groups of needles hidden in stacks of needle pieces. We must track all the needles all of the time."[408]

One of the researchers for the TIA project, David D. Jensen at the University of Massachusetts, acknowledged that the program could generate "high numbers of false positives. . . ."[409]

Because the concept of "total information awareness" on the part of government repulsed Americans so much, the program's name was later changed to "Terrorism Information Awareness." Nevertheless, Congress terminated its funding in autumn 2003.

TIA lives on, however, in hidden research projects and other programs. As Steve Aftergood of the American Federation of Scientists (an organization that tracks work done by U.S. intelligence agencies) has written, "the whole congressional action looks like a shell game. There may be enough of a difference for them to claim TIA was terminated while for all practical purposes the identical work is continuing."[410]

The U.S. Congress has transferred some TIA funding to the National Intelligence Program, which, it says, can only use its research against persons overseas or against non-Americans within the United States. But there is nothing to stop the government from expanding this program to American citizens at a later date. Some say parts of the original TIA program live on in the Pentagon's secret "black budget."[411] People with direct knowledge have told the press that the surviving TIA programs include some of the eighteen data-mining projects collectively known as "Evidence Extraction and Link Discovery."[412]

In its May 2004 report on federal data-mining efforts,[413] the U.S. General Accounting Office (now known as the Government Accountability Office or GAO) revealed that at least fourteen projects focused on counterterrorism. One of these, run by the Defense Intelligence Agency, mines data "to identify foreign terrorists or U.S. citizens connected to foreign terrorism activities." The National Security Agency has a program called "Novel Intelligence from Massive Data," which is supposed to extract information from databases including text, audio, video, graphs, images, maps, equations, and chemical formulae. The CIA reportedly has a data-mining program, in addition to its Oracle program, called "Quantum Leap." Quantum Leap "enables an analyst to get quick access to all the information available—classified and unclassified—about virtually anyone." The deputy chief information officer of the CIA told a reporter that the program's technology "is so powerful it's scary."[414]

A new program that was recently revealed by the *Christian Science Monitor*[415] looks very much like the original TIA project, as described by John Poindexter.

According to the *Monitor*, "[T]he U.S. government is developing a massive computer system that can collect huge amounts of data and, by linking far-flung information from blogs and e-mail to government records and intelligence reports, search for patterns of terrorist activity." The "core of this effort" is something called Analysis, Dissemination, Visualization, Insight, and Semantic Enhancement, or ADVISE. It is a program situated within the Department of Homeland Security's "Threat and Vulnerability Testing and Assessement" portfolio, which was set up in 2003 and received nearly $50 million in funding in 2006.

ADVISE is meant to collect both corporate and public online information, "from financial records to CNN news stories," and "cross-reference" it against law enforcement and intelligence records: "The system would then store it as 'entities'—linked data about people, places, things, organizations, and events, according to a report summarizing a 2004 DHS conference in Alexandria, Va. The storage requirements alone are huge—enough to retain information about 1 quadrillion entities, the report estimated. If each entity were a penny, they would collectively form a cube a half-mile high—roughly double the height of the Empire State Building."

Joseph Kielman, the manager of ADVISE, wrote a conference paper that he delivered in Richland, Washington. In it, he stated that the object of the program was not merely to identify terrorists, or search for key words, but to find patterns in data that illuminated motives and intentions. According to him, understanding the relationships between things, using social behaviour and other techniques, is key to going beyond mere data mining and arriving at comprehensive "knowledge discovery." Among the parts of ADVISE that are already operational is a tool called Starlight, which can provide a graphic view of data.

The report from the 2004 conference reveals that the Department of Homeland Security envisions all security agencies in the United States using ADVISE: "All federal, state, local and private-sector security entities will be able to share and collaborate in real time with distributed data warehouses that will provide full support for analysis and action."

The Multi-State Anti-Terrorism Information Exchange, or MATRIX, program was another data-mining initiative of the U.S. government. The database company, Seisint Inc., won the contract for MATRIX in May 2003 largely based on a "high terrorism factor" scoring system it had developed shortly after the events of September 11, 2001. The idea for the scoring system had come to Hank Asher, the man who started the company, while sipping a martini on September 13, 2001, in his $8 million home.[416] In its sales pitch to win the MATRIX contract, Seisint boasted that it had given the Immigration and Naturalization Service (INS), the FBI, the Secret Service, and the Florida Department of Law Enforcement the names of 120,000 people who, in 2001, had a statistical likelihood of being terrorists, and that this list had sparked a number of investigations and arrests.[417]

In awarding the MATRIX contract to Seisint, the Department of Justice cited the company's "technical qualifications," including the software "applying the 'terrorism quotient' in all cases." While Seisint and law-enforcement officials insist that the scoring system was ultimately left out of the MATRIX project, the Associated Press could not find one document in the thousands it requested that confirmed this was true.[418] And the ACLU found many documents that suggested that data mining has always been one of the most important components of MATRIX.[419]

MATRIX was criticized by groups on both sides of the political spectrum and, like TIA, it was terminated in May 2005.[420] Before that, at least eleven of the sixteen states that went through the pilot program for MATRIX pulled out of it.[421]

CAPPS II and Secure Flight

The data-mining program to which US-VISIT was supposed to be linked, CAPPS II, or the second-generation Computer Assisted Passenger Prescreening System, was designed to use algorithms to sort through PNR and other information in order to "risk score" all airline passengers as "green," "amber," or "red." "Green" stood for minimal risk, "amber" for an unknown or intermediate risk requiring heightened security measures, and "red" for high risk, requiring grounding of the passenger and reference to law enforcement for detention. The criteria for assigning the scores were undisclosed.

According to a notice published in the U.S. *Federal Register* in January 2003, the intent of the Transportation Security Administration (TSA), the agency developing CAPPS II, was to create a screening database that would be linked to virtually unlimited amounts of data from private and public sources, including "financial and transactional data." Also, numerous public and private entities were to have access to the system.[422] The TSA told the press, the GAO, and Congress that it had not used any real-world data in the testing of CAPPS II, but this later turned out to be patently false.[423]

According to the TSA, about 5 percent of the traveling public would be rated "amber" or "red" under the CAPPS II program.[424] The program contained no mechanism by which a passenger could challenge her or his score. The Association of Corporate Travel Executives estimated in a study that if only 2 percent of travelers were rated "red," there would be up to 8 million passengers detained or denied boarding every year under CAPPS II.[425]

The GAO issued a report in February 2004[426] in which it said the TSA had failed to show that CAPPS II was effective in identifying possible terrorists and had failed to resolve crucial privacy issues of oversight and passenger redress.

In July 2004, the U.S. government finally bowed to pressure from the GAO, civil libertarians, and airlines and decided to kill the CAPPS II program.[427] However, it soon became clear that the program was only being modified and postponed.[428] A Homeland Security spokesperson said that a new screening program would rise from the ashes of CAPPS II and that it would cover all passengers traveling to, through, or within the country.[429] In August 2004, a new passenger-screening program called "Secure Flight" was announced.[430]

Congress dictated that Secure Flight was to forgo the use of private sector data and risk scoring its predecessor had employed, and the TSA made assurances to this effect. However, reports in July 2005 revealed that the TSA did, in fact, link passenger information to commercial databases under the program, after it instructed a contractor to secretly collect 100 million records on at least 250,000 people.[431] In addition, the manager of Secure Flight announced that the TSA had planned to test whether commercial data could be used to detect terrorist "sleeper cells" under the program.[432] Bruce Schneier, a security expert who served on the TSA-appointed oversight panel for Secure Flight, wrote, "The TSA has been operating with complete disregard for the law and Congress. It has lied to pretty much everyone. And it is turning Secure Flight from a simple program to match passengers against terrorist watch lists into a complex program that compiles dossiers on passengers in order to give them some kind of score indicating the likelihood that they are a terrorist."[433]

In February 2006, after spending nearly four years and $150 million, the TSA found that the Secure Flight database was accessible to hackers and suspended the program. Since the Intelligence Reform and Terrorism Prevention Act requires the TSA to create and implement a passenger screening program, however, Secure Flight, like CAPPS II before it, is likely to rise from its own ashes with yet another name attached to it.[434]

Passenger Protect

The likelihood that the new U.S. passenger screening system will include a risk-scoring mechanism is corroborated by developments in Canada.

The U.S.-Canada Smart Border Action Plan called on both countries "to explore means to identify risks posed by passengers on international flights arriving in each other's country" and pursuant to these commitments, Canadian documents show that Canada and the United States have agreed to implement a "jointly developed" and therefore *interoperable* "risk scoring mechanism."[435]

According to a Smart Border Action Plan Status Report dated December 17, 2004, on Canada's Department of Foreign Affairs Web site, the first phase of this goal was implemented on August 10, 2004. The Canadian side of the risk-scoring project is currently located in the Canadian Risk Assessment Centre, under the auspices of the Department of Public Safety and Emergency Preparedness. It is not known what criteria are being used or tested, only that the program, like the American CAPPS II program, is a data-mining one: it uses computer algorithms to sort through personal information and identify the risk posed by travelers.[436] An early news report of January 2004[437] established that the program was going to score passengers as red, amber and green risks as did the CAPPS II program; however, whether this scoring code will be retained or not in a new passenger screening program in the United States is not known. Early news reports also stated that the information the Canadian risk-scoring project was going to use included PNR data on air passengers on incoming, outgoing, and domestic flights[438] and that the federal government intended to eventually expand the program to border-crossing passengers using all modes of transportation.[439]

In August 2005, the Canadian risk-scoring project was recast as the second phase of a new program called Passenger Protect.[440]

The UK E-Borders Initiative

The UK e-Borders initiative also has a risk-scoring component to it, like the American CAPPS II, Secure Flight, and Canadian Passenger Protect programs. E-Borders documents talk of analyzing "bulk" passenger data to assess "in advance of arrival, the immigration and security threats posed by passengers." Documents say that "[t]he Border Agencies will make use of profiling which involves running a series of pre-defined profiles against reservation data." They also indicate that passengers will be scored green, yellow, and red.[441]

Implementation of the e-Borders program started in 2004 and is expected to be complete by 2018.[442]

German "Trawling"

After September 2001, German police units started collecting data on young men with Islamic backgrounds from universities, registration offices, health insurance companies, and Germany's "Central Foreigners Register" (*Ausländerzentralregiste*) using the practice of "trawling" or "dragnet control" (*Rasterfahndung*). Introduced in the 1970s in the wake of the activities of the terrorist group Rote Armee Fraktion, trawling allows vast amounts of data to be collected about individuals and compared with various criteria.

The profile used in the program after 9/11 was that of the Arab students from the University of Hamburg allegedly linked to the 2001 attacks in the United States—effectively making every male Arab student in Germany a suspected terrorist. As a result of the program, approximately 10,000 students have been placed under surveillance in North-Rhine Westphalia alone.[443]

Data Mining and the Democratic Deficit

As with other mass surveillance initiatives, there has been a democratic deficit in the implementation of data-mining programs.

First, there has been a conspicuous lack of transparency about these programs. It is difficult to get information about what projects are being undertaken and how they will operate. Many, like the Canadian initiative, have been set up quietly, under the radar of the public, with little or no democratic debate.

Governments avoid political accountability for data-mining programs. For example, the implementation of the Secure Flight program was postponed until after the American election in November 2004, and government officials would not give details about what they were keeping or dropping from the CAPPS II program until that time.[444] Finally, governments are less than honest about these projects. When programs are canceled under political pressure, governments simply reintroduce them in new packages using new names.

Flawed Facts, Dirty Information, "Guilt by Google," Ethnic Profiling

The post-9/11, data-mining version of the McCarthy era is, perhaps, a bit like the Hollywood film *Minority Report* in which state officials try to use technology to read people's minds in order to stop criminal acts before they happen. However, the technology that is being used in our current post-9/11 world falls far short of the technology of Hollywood fantasy.

First, the factual base on which the technology rests is unreliable. The "best information available" on which data-mining or risk-scoring technology depend is often inaccurate, lacking context, dated, or incomplete. It might even be *dirty information*—extracted by torture or offered by an informant who is vulnerable or who is willfully misleading authorities.

None of the data-mining programs contain a mechanism by which individuals can correct, contextualize, or object to the information that is being used against them or even know what it is. Indeed, operating on a preemption principle, these systems are uninterested in this kind of precision. They would be bogged down if they were held to the ordinary standards of access, accuracy, and accountability.

Second, the criteria used to sort masses of data will always be overinclusive and mechanical. Data mining is like assessing guilt by Google keyword searches. And since these systems use broad markers for predicting terrorism, ethnic and religious profiling are endemic to them. The manager of the TIA program was right when he said that looking for anything useful with data mining was like looking for particular needles in stacks of needles. However, his analogy would have been more accurate if he had talked about looking for a needle in an ocean full of needles.

LOW-TECH "SOLUTIONS" TO RISK ASSESSMENT

Of course, not all risk assessment in the "war on terror" is being done by computer data mining. As in the McCarthy era, human beings are also making judgments about who might present a "risk" to the state.

In the post-9/11 climate, where law-enforcement and security intelligence agencies are being blamed for failing to stop the attacks on U.S. soil, there are strong bureaucratic incentives for officials to err on the side of caution. After all, who would want to be responsible for failing to receive, gather, share, or flag information regarding someone who later took part in an attack? As with data mining, a preemption principle is at work when human beings are making the risk assessments.

This kind of environment leads to indiscriminate interpretations of information and indiscriminate actions on the part of authorities. And, as with high-tech risk assessment, ethnic and religious profiling are endemic.[445]

Guilt by Association

The cases of Maher Arar and the other Canadians described in chapter 1 are prime examples of how, in the new world of risk assessment, people are being treated as guilty by association, no matter how tenuous their association with someone else suspected of terrorism may be. The presence of one known terrorist supporter, Ahmed Said Khadr, raising funds intermittently in Canada for a distant project about which most people had no direct or inside knowledge, had devastating effects on the relatively small Canadian Muslim community. As mentioned earlier, almost all of the Canadians detained outside Canada and all of the five Muslim immigrants held indefinitely inside Canada on security certificates, had some association with Khadr. They were unfortunate to have shared a car ride with him to Toronto, stayed with his in-laws, to have met him fleetingly in Afghanistan, or volunteered to help the refugees he worked with in Pakistan. Or, in the case of Maher Arar, they knew someone who knew Ahmed Said Khadr. In fact, the Mounties created profiles of Maher Arar and Monia Mazigh's two children for use in a kind of lookout database for suspects.[446] At the time that they were profiled, one child was six years old, the other only five months old!

How safe would any of us be, if we could be targeted on the basis of any association we had made in the many aspects of our lives? In relatively small religious or immigrant communities where most people know each other or have some shared acquaintances, hardly anyone would be safe.

In other countries, the same thing is going on, and guilt by association is in many cases *codified* in legislation, in the definition of "terrorism," and in the drafting of new "participation" and "glorification" offenses. Upholding the release of a Libyan man who had been held without charges on secret evidence for fifteen months under the UK Anti-terrorism, Crime and Security Act, Britain's most senior judge, Lord Chief Justice Woolf, asked government lawyers, "If I was a grocer and I delivered groceries to somebody who was a member of al-Qaida, do I fall within that [the act's definition of a terrorist]?"[447]

Indiscriminate Sharing of Information

UN Security Council Resolution 1373 called on all states to "take steps to prevent the commission of terrorist acts, including the provision of early warning to other states by exchange of information." The Smart Border Agreement and accompanying Action Plan negotiated between Canada and the United States call for the sharing of information and intelligence in a timely way[448] and for joint intelligence teams.[449] The Europol–U.S. agreement gives an unlimited number of U.S. agencies access to Europol information for the purposes of *the prevention*, detection, suppression, investigation, and prosecution of any specific criminal offenses, and any specific analysis.

The Arar case is a good example of how indiscriminately governments are sharing information and what personal and social consequences indiscriminate sharing can lead to. The RCMP did not have reasonable grounds to suspect Maher Arar of anything when they passed his name on to foreign agencies without any caveats and left him to his fate.

The case underlines that while the timely sharing of information between countries is an important part of combating terrorist acts and other crimes, there need to be appropriate criteria about the quality of the information that can be passed on to foreign countries and instructions or conditions about how the information can be used.

Using Information Obtained by Torture and Tipping Off Torturers

Another example of indiscriminate behavior on the part of authorities carrying out "low-tech" risk assessment is their use of torture.

Repressive regimes are not the only ones using torture to make risk assessments. Testimony from the Arar Inquiry has revealed that Canadian agencies may, in some circumstances, share information with foreign agencies they suspect are engaged in torture and that they will receive and use information from foreign agencies obtained through torture if it is corroborated by other sources.[450] This is done even though Canada is a signatory to the UN Convention against Torture.

As the Arar, El Maati, and Almalki stories demonstrate, Canadian authorities may also wait for people to go abroad in order to have them questioned without a lawyer present and intimidated or mistreated by foreign security forces. Two more stories amplify this suspicion. In September 2004, the brother-in-law of Maher Arar, who had just moved back to Tunisia, was questioned by Tunisian secret police. According to Arar's family, the Tunisian questioners had information to which only Canadian authorities would have had access. Canadian authorities had had ample opportunity to interview the brother-in-law during the four years he was living in Canada, but had not done so.[451] Another man, Kassim Mohamed, who divides his time between Toronto and Egypt, was questioned by CSIS in Canada after videotaping Toronto landmarks for his children, who attend school in Egypt. He was then cleared to go to Egypt. When he arrived in Egypt, he was immediately arrested and held for two weeks, handcuffed and blindfolded, in a prison in Cairo.[452]

In the UK, the intelligence service MI5 appears to have tipped off the CIA so that a British citizen of Iraqi origin, Wahab al-Rawi, could be seized by the CIA when he arrived in The Gambia for a business trip on a flight from London and thereby deprived of his rights under British law. Al-Rawi has said that when he asked to see the British consul, the CIA agent interrogating him laughed, saying, "Why do you think you're here? It's your government that tipped us off in the first place."[453]

The English Court of Appeal ruled in August 2004 that the use of evidence obtained under torture was legal in the UK, as long as the UK neither "procured nor connived at" torture.[454] But on December 8, 2005, the British House of Lords ruled that evidence that may have been obtained by torture cannot be used against terror suspects in British courts.[455] "The rejection of torture by the common law has a special iconic importance as the touchstone of a human and civilized legal system," one of the Law Lords wrote.

Shoot-to-Kill Policies

In some countries, police can shoot to kill you if they make a negative low-tech risk assessment about you. While the assessment often starts with some kind of lead, it often ends in a moment's judgment based on woefully inadequate information. In the wake of the September 11 attacks, the UK adopted a shoot-to-kill policy to deal with possible suicide bombers.[456] Jean Charles de Menezes was shot point-blank in the head in a crowded subway car by police making a split second assessment about him.[457] They were wrong. The same kind of assessment was made when 250 police[458] surrounded the home of two brothers in London and shot one of them in the chest without warning as he came down the stairs in his pajamas.[459] The police found nothing in their extensive searches to justify their suspicions. In both cases, the police apologized.

The Madrid Investigation: Sloppy Mistakes

In the low-tech version of risk assessment, many "false positives" are the result of sloppy police work and crude profiling on the part of authorities.

The home of Brandon Mayfield, an American citizen and lawyer in Oregon, was secretly searched and he was thrown in jail for two weeks when the FBI matched his fingerprint to a print found on a plastic bag used by terrorists in the Madrid train bombing of March 2004. The print was of poor quality, and the Spanish authorities who had provided it warned American investigators early in the case that the print did not match those of Mayfield.[460] In addition to this, there was no record of Brandon Mayfield having traveled outside the United States for more than a decade.[461] But the U.S. Justice Department used a "material witness" law to round up Mayfield anyway, bolstering their case by painting him as a Muslim extremist. The affidavit that secured his arrest made much of the fact that he had converted to Islam, was married to an Egyptian-born woman, and had once briefly represented one of the "Portland Seven" in a child custody case.[462]

Spanish authorities eventually matched the fingerprint to Ouhnane Daoud, an Algerian living in Spain, against whom they had other evidence.[463] The FBI, which originally claimed to be absolutely certain the print was Mayfield's, then backtracked and changed its position completely, saying the fingerprint was "of *no* value for identification purposes."[464]

Getting People off the Street: Indefinite, Arbitrary Detentions

In the low-tech version of risk assessment, governments wanting to eliminate risk have indiscriminately swept people off the streets—using detentions without charge and indefinite confinements that violate constitutional guarantees and human rights obligations.

Under international human rights law, arbitrary detentions are justified only in a time of public emergency that threatens the life of the nation and only if the state publicly declares such an emergency. Then, the derogation from rights may only be carried out "to the extent strictly required by the exigencies of the situation," and without discrimination.[465]

INITIAL SWEEPS OF IMMIGRANTS: As described earlier, U.S. authorities detained masses of people immediately after September 11, 2001. It did so without declaring the state of emergency required under international human rights law. The Bush administration had initially sought power to detain noncitizens without charge and without judicial review through the USA PATRIOT Act, but Congress had refused this request. Undeterred, the administration created the power on its own by quietly issuing an administrative order. The order allowed INS to hold noncitizens on immigration charges for forty-eight hours and to extend that time indefinitely "in the event of an emergency or other extraordinary circumstances."[466]

The move was an endrun around democratic processes and around the constitutional protections for accused people in criminal processes. In criminal cases, the U.S. Constitution requires charges to be laid in a timely manner and guarantees detainees the right of habeas corpus.[467] The U.S. Supreme Court has held that the government must charge a detainee and a judge must determine there is probable cause to substantiate the charge within forty-eight hours.[468] By holding people on immigration charges while they were, in fact, being investigated for links to criminal activity (terrorism), the government deliberately sought to deny them these constitutional rights.[469]

Again, not one of the people held on immigration grounds in the initial sweeps, which picked up nearly two thousand people, was charged with any criminal offense relating to the attacks, and not one was confirmed to have links to Al Qaeda.[470]

USE OF MATERIAL WITNESS WARRANTS: The United States has also been "getting people off the street" within its own borders by abusing "material witness" laws that allow police to hold someone for questioning without having probable grounds to hold them as criminal suspects (as in the Brandon Mayfield case). The Justice Department has refused to say how many people have been detained under material witness warrants for counterterrorism cases, despite repeated congressional inquiries. But Human Rights Watch and the American Civil Liberties Union have been able to identify seventy people. Sixty-four of these individuals were of Middle Eastern or South Asian origins, seventeen were U.S. citizens, and except for one person, all were Muslims. Only a few were ever charged with anything related to terrorism. Nearly half of them were never brought before a court or grand jury to testify. The Justice Department used false or flimsy evidence to secure warrants and assert that they were flight risks and had to be incarcerated.[471] Their stories are as harrowing as that told by Brandon Mayfield.

"Five to six cars surrounded my car," Mohdar Abdullah told Human Rights Watch. "The agents pulled out shotguns and told me to get out of the car or they will shoot me. They told me they were about to shoot me . . . I asked what's going on? I've been so helpful. But three guys told me to put my hands on the car, they patted me down and shackled me. I asked what am I arrested for? Am I charged with something? . . . I got no answer. They shoved me against the car and handcuffed me . . . They told me to 'shut the fuck up.'"[472]

Ayub Ali Khan described being transferred to solitary confinement in a six-by-five-foot cell, very much like the one Maher Arar languished in, except that it was cleaner and the lights were kept on twenty-four hours a day. "Guards came every ten to fifteen minutes and banged on the door. . . . I didn't sleep for one or two months. The guards would bang on the door all night. They would say, 'This is the guy—the Taliban guy' or call me 'Khan Taliban.' The guards said so many bad things, they told me: 'You won't ever see your family. You're going to die here. Do you smell the WTC [World Trade Center] smoke? You're gone. How would you like to die? With the electric chair?' . . . [Whenever I was taken out of my cell] they would twist my hands. My feet were shackled and guards would step on [the] chains. I got a deep cut on my feet . . ."[473]

Speaking of the use of material witness warrants since 9/11, a district court judge has declared, "The government's treatment of material witness information is deeply troubling. . . . The public has no idea whether there are forty, four hundred, or possibly more people in detention on material witness warrants."[474]

DESIGNATING PEOPLE AS ENEMY OR UNLAWFUL COMBATANTS: The U.S. government is also holding foreigners and U.S. citizens by designating them as "enemy" or "unlawful" combatants. The term is purportedly drawn from the Geneva Conventions, but in fact does not exist in them or in customary international humanitarian law and has been devised by the Bush administration to *deny* prisoners rights under the Geneva Conventions, under the U.S. Constitution, and under ordinary criminal law. Some "enemy combatants" are being held on U.S. soil, and many more are being held in Guantánamo Bay, a territory in Cuba leased by the United States, or in the numbers of extraterritorial dungeons being run by agencies like the CIA. Since invading Afghanistan in 2001, the United States has held more than eight hundred individuals from more than forty countries in military custody at Guantánamo Bay. As of September 2006 there were approximately 455 still detained there indefinitely. Some were captured during the war in Afghanistan, but others were taken into U.S. custody in places as far flung as Bosnia, The Gambia, and Thailand.[475] At the Bagram detention center in Iraq, there were approximately 560 detainees when the International Red Cross visited them in May 2006.[476]

The U.S. court cases examining the constitutionality of these detentions are still in full flow, but those that have already been decided, and a proposed new congressional amendment purporting to govern all detainee lawsuits, demonstrate well the kind of risk assessment that the executive branch is engaging in.

The first two cases I describe involve U.S. citizens who have been designated enemy combatants by President George W. Bush.

The FBI picked up Jose Padilla at the Chicago's O'Hare airport in May 2002. A Brooklyn-born convert to Islam, Padilla was accused of plotting with Al Qaeda to detonate radioactive, "dirty bombs" in the United States. At first, authorities claimed they were holding him as a material witness for a Manhattan grand jury investigating the September 11 attacks. But days before a hearing that would determine whether the indefinite detention of Padilla as a material witness was legal, the government switched tactics and designated him an enemy combatant in June of 2002.[477] Padilla then spent more than three years detained in a U.S. Navy brig in South Carolina. He petitioned for habeas corpus all the way up to the U.S. Supreme Court. However, the first time around, the Supreme Court dismissed his case on the basis that it had should initially have been filed in South Carolina. In the new claim, filed in that jurisdiction, the Federal District Court ruled in March 2005 that "the president ha[d] no power, neither express nor implied, neither constitutional nor statutory, to hold petitioner as an enemy combatant."[478] But the Court of Appeals nixed the District Court judgment. It took two years for the case to work its way back up to the Supreme Court. But less than a week before the government was to file its argument with the Court, the government changed its tactics again. Attorney General Gonzales announced that Padilla would be *un*designated as an enemy combatant and brought to stand trial in Florida on criminal charges. The Bush administration was clearly trying to avoid another court decision: it argued that the Supreme Court should not hear the case, since the redesignation rendered the matter "moot."

The question that Padilla's lawyers had put to the Supreme Court was an important one: "Does the president have the power to seize American citizens in civilian settings on American soil and subject them to indefinite detention without criminal charge or trial?"[479] A majority of the Supreme Court sided with the Bush administration and refused to hear the case, calling it "hypothetical."

Hamdi v. Rumsfeld[480] was another case involving a U.S. citizen, allegedly captured on the battlefield in Afghanistan. Like Padilla,

Yaser Esam Hamdi was held incommunicado for more than two years on various military brigs without charges or trial. The U.S. Supreme Court found that the president had authority to detain Hamdi pursuant to the same Congressional Authorization of Military Force that the president later relied on in justifying his secret NSA spying program.[481] But Justice Sandra Day O'Connor wrote, "a state of war is not a blank check for the President when it comes to the rights of the Nation's citizens," and the majority held that Hamdi had a right to know the factual basis for his "enemy combatant" classification and to rebut these assertions of fact before a "neutral decision-maker." Nevertheless, within a few months of the Supreme Court decision, the government had still not given Hamdi his day before a neutral decision-maker; instead it gave him a choice between further detention and deportation to Saudi Arabia. Though born in the United States, he was a dual citizen of both countries. Under the "settlement" agreement, Hamdi agreed to relinquish his U.S. citizenship, to be deported to Saudi Arabia, and to abide by numerous conditions that restricted his mobility.[482]

A third case, *Rasul v. Bush*, involved noncitizens of the United States. In *Rasul v. Bush*, the U.S. District Court of Appeals for the District of Columbia ruled that Guantánamo Bay detainees had no right of access to U.S. courts to challenge the basis of their detention, since they were noncitizens held outside the "sovereign territory" of the United States. The ruling was made despite the fact that the 1903 lease signed between the United States and Cuba grants the U.S. government "complete jurisdiction and control" over Guantánamo Bay. The U.S. Navy has described the territory as "a Naval reservation, which for all practical purposes, is American territory. Under the [lease] agreement, the United States has for approximately [one hundred] years exercised the essential elements of sovereignty, without actually owning it."

The Supreme Court reversed the Court of Appeals decision, holding that federal courts did "have jurisdiction to determine the legality of the Executive's potentially indefinite detention of individuals who claim to be wholly innocent of wrongdoing."[483]

Following the Supreme Court rulings in *Hamdi* and *Rasul*, the U.S. authorities instituted a new procedure at Guantánamo Bay. The Combatant Status Review Tribunals (CSRTs), were designed to be a one-time review to determine whether detainees were "enemy combatants." All Guantánamo detainees had received their CSRT hearing by March 2005. Only a handful were determined not to be enemy combatants, and these were kept in detention anyway. Another set of hearings, known as Administrative Review Boards (ARBs) were created by the Bush administration immediately before the Supreme Court heard oral argument in *Rasul.* ARBs are designed to take place annually to assess whether detainees continue to be a threat to the United States. The first round of ARBs was concluded in February 2006.[484] Detainees were not allowed to have lawyers when they went before their CSRTs or to see the evidence against them, and the same conditions apply for the ARBs.[485]

The new procedures did not stop about two hundred detained people from filing habeas corpus petitions in U.S. federal courts pursuant to the *Rasul* and *Hamdi* decisions.[486]

These were thrown into limbo, however, when Congress intervened and passed an amendment to the 2006 National Defense Authorization Bill, known as the Levin-Graham-Kyl amendment, which suspended detainees' right to apply for habeas corpus, replacing it with a one-time appeal to the court that had dismissed the *Rasul* case and another important case I will describe shortly—the U.S. Court of Appeals for the District of Columbia. The one-time review merely covers "whether the formulation and implementation of the practices in place at Guantánamo Bay are constitutional and, in each individual case, whether the military correctly followed procedures." This falls short of a right to habeas corpus, one of the oldest individual rights established in the common law. In effect, Congress has given a green light to torture, since the amendment does not allow detainees to challenge their treatment in court either. This is risk assessment's "fire escape" to the McCain amendment, which banned the use of torture in the 2005 defense appropriations bill. In a case challenging the force-feeding of a Guantánamo detainee on hunger strike, the Justice Department argued in April 2006 that the Levin-Graham-Kyl amendment rendered the McCain amendment unenforceable.[487]

If this inconsistency on the part of Congress seemed strange, in an even stranger development, *Senator John McCain himself* negotiated a bill with the White House in September 2006 that also stripped detainees of their right to habeas corpus and their right to challenge their treatment in U.S. courts. I will return to this later.

The last important enemy combatant case that merits description in the context of low-tech risk assessment is the *Hamdan* case. Salim Ahmed Hamdan is a Yemeni who admits to having been Osama bin Laden's personal driver and bodyguard. He is challenging the special military commissions set up by President Bush to try enemy combatants on criminal charges. These commissions violated all due process standards, and even the U.S. military lawyers who were assigned to represent detainees before the commissions were speaking out publicly against them.[488]

In the *Hamdan* case, the District Court found that these commissions were unlawful and could not continue in their current form since the detainees may be "prisoners of war" and therefore entitled to the higher standard of justice required under the Geneva Conventions.[489] The U.S. Court of Appeals for the District of Columbia reversed the decision and rejected Hamdan's case, as mentioned earlier. But the U.S. Supreme Court struck down the military commissions in a powerful decision released in June 2006, holding that the commissions' derogation from due process rights ran afoul of Common Article 3 of the Geneva Conventions and was not authorized by Congress or military necessity.[490] The Court's skeptical view of the president's claim to unfettered power in wartime could pave the way to successful challenges against the warrantless wiretapping of the NSA program, which the Bush adminstration defends with same claim of wartime power.

BUSH'S MYSTERIOUS NEW PROGRAMS: In January 2006, the U.S. Army awarded the Halliburton subsidiary, Kellogg Brown & Root (KBR), a $385 million contract to construct new detention centers inside the United States, to deal with "an emergency influx of immigrants into the U.S., or to support the rapid development of new programs." In February 2006, the *New York Times* confirmed that KBR would build the detention centers "for the Homeland Security Department for an expected influx of immigrants, to house people in the event of a natural disaster, or for new programs that require additional detention space."[491]

Some journalists have speculated that these centers could be used to detain American citizens if the Bush administration were to declare martial law. Others have said they are more likely to be used for the next roundup of Muslims and possibly dissenters in the case of a new terrorist attack.[492] While these ideas might have sounded like conspiracy theories in the past, in the current regime of preemption and risk assessment they may not be so far-fetched.

INDEFINITE DETENTION, CONTROL ORDERS, AND DETENTION WITHOUT CHARGE IN THE UK: In the UK, the Anti-terrorism, Crime and Security Act 2001 permitted the government to hold foreigners in indefinite detention without charge. Unlike the United States, the UK had made a formal declaration of an emergency threatening the life of the nation. Sixteen foreigners were detained in this way, and as of October 2004, seven had been detained for more than two years. None had been charged with a crime.

Indefinite detention was condemned by two UK parliamentary committees, both of which asked that the practice be "replaced as a matter of urgency," arguing that it was unjust and undermined respect for human rights.[493]

Then, in December 2004, the UK House of Lords ruled seven to one that the detentions of foreigners without charge taking place under the act were discriminatory and violated European human rights standards against arbitrary detention and discrimination.[494] Lord Nicholls of Birkenhead wrote that "[i]ndefinite imprisonment without charge or trial is anathema in any country which observes the rule of law."[495] Lord Hoffman rejected the government's contention that a derogation from the prohibition on arbitrary detention was justified on the basis of a "threat to the life of the nation." "Terrorist violence," he wrote, "serious as it is, does not threaten our institutions of government or our existence as a civil community. . . . The real threat to the life of the nation, in the sense of a people living in accordance with its traditional laws and political values, comes not from terrorism but from laws such as these."[496]

The government, faced with releasing the men, immediately enacted a new piece of legislation, the Prevention of Terrorism Act, which allowed the government to impose "control orders" on *anyone* (foreigner or citizen) suspected of links to terrorist activities, but against whom a case could not be proved in court. Control orders had to be approved by a court, but the standard for obtaining them was low. The orders could restrict "suspects" from using computers and cell phones, from traveling outside a geographic area, and even from leaving their home. In December 2005, four men deprived of their liberty for four years, first through illegal detention under the Anti-terrorism, Crime and Security Act 2001 and then through control orders, revealed that *they had not once been questioned* by police or security officials since being arrested.[497] Their risk assessment, it appears, had been conducted without the need of ever hearing from them.

In a decision rendered in June 2006 at the first court level, the British judiciary ruled against the government's legislation again, holding that the restrictions imposed by control orders were so severe that they amounted to deprivation of liberty without a trial. The court quashed the control orders against the six men in the case before it. One was a British citzen and five were Iraqi nationals. The government is appealing the judgment.[498]

Under the recently enacted Terrorism Act of 2006 police can hold terrorism suspects without charges being laid for up to twenty-eight days. Prime Minister Blair had asked for ninety days. If control orders are ultimately upheld, they could be imposed on suspects when the twenty-eight days are up if the government still finds nothing to charge them with.

INDEFINITE DETENTION AND "PREVENTATIVE ARREST" IN CANADA: In Canada, as of April 2006, five noncitizens were being detained indefinitely without charge under "security certificates" issued by the minister of Public Safety and Emergency Preparedness and the minister of Citizenship and Immigration pursuant to the Immigration and Refugee Protection Act.[499] A constitutional challenge against the certificates was argued in the Supreme Court of Canada in June 2006, and a decision is expected in the fall of 2006.

The Canadian Anti-Terrorism Act provides authorities with additional power to detain people without charges using "preventative arrests."[500] Ordinarily, arrest before the commission of an offense is only permitted on the basis of a "reasonable belief" that a person is "about to commit an offense." Preventative arrests allow police to arrest someone where they merely suspect that "detention is necessary in order to prevent a terrorist activity," and the activity need not be imminent. If a judge decides a police officer has reasonable suspicion, she or he can impose conditions on the person, as in a UK control order, for up to twelve months.

Broad Strokes: The UN List

As the mass detentions carried out by the United States described earlier show, low-tech risk assessment, like high-tech risk assessment, often cuts a broad swath. This can also be seen in the list of names compiled pursuant to UN Security Council Resolution 1373, which calls on states to freeze the assets of terrorists or those supporting them.

Given that the terms "terrorist" and "terrorism" have been defined in vague and overbroad ways in many countries, and that the conception the Security Council and many states have about what constitutes "supporting terrorism" is very broad, it is not surprising, perhaps, that the lists which states have made to satisfy Resolution 1373 have cast an extremely broad net. The story of Liban Hussein illustrates just how broad.

On November 7, 2001, the U.S. government issued a list of sixty-two people and businesses whose assets were to be frozen. In a speech that day, President Bush said there was clear evidence that the people on the list were the "quartermasters of terror."[501] The U.S. list was then adopted by the UN in its list for freezing assets. Shortly thereafter, the Canadian government froze the Canadian assets of Liban Hussein, a Somali-born Canadian businessman who ran a money transfer business in Dorchester, Massachusetts, and whose name was on the U.S. and UN lists.[502]

Canada jailed Hussein briefly, made it a crime for anyone to do business with him, and took steps to have him deported to the United States. Then in June 2002, proceedings against him were abruptly terminated when the Department of Justice admitted that further investigation had revealed no evidence to suggest he had anything to do with terrorism. After devastating the man's business, the Canadian government removed his name from its list for freezing assets and settled out of court with him. Eventually his name was removed from the U.S. and UN lists as well.[503]

Reportedly, there are a number of people on the U.S. list who, like Liban Hussein, run money-transfer businesses, known in Somalia as *hawalas*. *Hawalas* are traditional, informal money-transfer businesses that Somalis use to send money to Somalia, since the normal banking system there collapsed in the early 1990s. Around two-thirds of the money transferred to Somalia is sent through al-Barakaat, one of the largest *hawalas*. In Sweden, authorities froze the accounts of three organizers of al-Barakaat, Swedish citizens of Somali origin, in order to comply with the EU and UN lists. But because the three were so obviously innocent, a public campaign started up and quickly raised 22,000 euros for the men. Lawyers for them met with the European Commission, the European Parliament and the UN Commission on Human Rights and also lodged a case at the European Court.

At no time throughout the affair did the United States present any evidence or specific accusations against the three men. To have their names removed from the lists they were ultimately forced to sign a statement for U.S. authorities saying that they had never been and never would be involved in the support of terrorism and would immediately cease all contacts with al-Barakaat. A joint request from Sweden and the United States to the UN Sanctions Committee then resulted in a decision to remove their names from the various lists. A Swedish parliamentary inquiry concluded that although the government should have reacted much earlier, and at the very least should have asked questions before implementing the UN and EU lists, it had not had many options, owing to its obligations in international law.[504]

Disciplining Dissent

In the low-tech version of risk assessment, governments often give way to an impulse to punish dissent.

The American Civil Liberties Union and newspapers across the

United States have documented numerous instances in which U.S. authorities have made extremely questionable risk assessments, targeting citizens who have exercised free speech to criticize the policies of the Bush administration.[505] This is partly the fault of the definition of "terrorist" in the USA PATRIOT Act, which is so broad and overreaching that it wrongly includes legitimate activities of dissent. But the targeting of dissenters is also happening because a climate exists in times of danger in which there is enormous pressure to conform to what is viewed as "normal" and "patriotic" behavior—and an enormous tendency to engage in a "circling of the ideological wagons" and a collective witch hunt for the "enemy within."

Randolph Bourne, a social critic during another highly polarized time in American history, World War I, reflected that war "automatically sets in motion throughout society those irresistible forces for uniformity, for passionate cooperation with the Government in coercing into obedience the minority groups and individuals which lack the larger herd sense."[506] In such a time it can be dangerous to be "different" or to exercise that quintessential right of American democracy—the right to dissent.

A Senate committee, reporting on the elimination of certain restrictions on the FBI's secret monitoring of U.S. citizens, wrote that the agency had adopted the "belief that dissident speech and associations should be prevented because they were incipient steps towards the possible ultimate commission of an act which might be criminal."[507] In the same vein, a spokesperson for the California Anti-terrorism Information Center, evinced the belief that dissenters from the "war on terror," and the war on Iraq in particular, could well be characterized as terrorists: "If you have a protest group protesting a war where the cause that's being fought against is international terrorism, you might have terrorism at that [protest]. You can almost argue that a protest against that [war] is a terrorist act."[508]

By the look of their domestic database on security threats, it seems that the U.S. military holds the same view. In December 2005,

NBC News broke the story that the Pentagon's Threat and Local Observation Notice (TALON) database contained information on nearly four dozen antiwar meetings and protests.[509] One "incident" recorded in the database was a small meeting of Quakers in Florida to plan protests against military recruiting in schools.[510] Another was a street theater performance organized by a peace activist outside the Houston headquarters of the Halliburton corporation.[511] Another was a large antiwar demonstration at Hollywood and Vine in Los Angeles at which effigies of President Bush were carried.[512] Still another was a planned protest against military recruiting at New York University.[513] A Pentagon document marked "SECRET" showed how closely the military was tracking activists, noting "increased communications between protest groups using the Internet," though no "significant connection between incidents" such as "reoccurring instigators" or "vehicle descriptions."[514]

In the Vietnam era, defense officials also spied on Americans protesting against the war. Congressional hearings in the 1970s led to tight restrictions on the kinds of information that the military could collect about people and activities inside the United States."[515] Regulations, for example, require that any information that is "not validated as threatening must be removed from the TALON system in less than 90 days." Evidence suggests that this regulation has not been followed in the past few years.[516]

Other U.S. agencies have also been watching antiwar protesters based on the assessment that they pose a "risk" to the United States. In spring 2004, for example, the FBI served a subpoena on Drake University regarding an antiwar conference that was held there.[517] In 2003, New York police questioned antiwar protesters about their political activities and associations.[518]

Other kinds of dissenters have been targeted, too. Many of these have had their names show up on the U.S. "no fly" list, which I will describe shortly. University campuses have also been targeted as the following story related by the American Civil Liberties Union illustrates:

> A. J. Brown, [a 19-year-old] freshman at Durham Technical College, almost jumped out of her skin when . . . the U.S. Secret Service . . . knocked on her apartment door. They were responding to an anonymous report about an "anti-American" wall poster. . . . Did she have any information about Afghanistan? No. About the Taliban? No. At their request, she filled out a form providing her full name, race, telephone number and other identifying information.
>
> . . . The poster, opposing the death penalty, showed George W. Bush holding a rope against a backdrop of lynch victims, with the text, "We hang on your every word."[519]

The U.S. "No Fly" List

The names of peace activists, civil libertarians, Quakers, a satirical cartoonist, and others have shown up on the U.S. "no fly" list—the low-tech version of the high-tech CAPPS II/Secure Flight passenger screening program.

Jan Adams and Rebecca Gordon were pulled aside in San Francisco International Airport and told they could not board their flight because their names appeared on the list. The two women, who are peace activists and publish a newspaper called *War Times*, were not told how their names got on the list or how they could have them removed. There appeared to be no reason for their inclusion on the list, other than the fact that they had been exercising their right to disagree with the government. An ACLU lawyer, a retired Presbyterian minister, a man who works for the American Friends Service Committee (a Quaker organization whose purpose is to promote peace and social justice), and an ACLU special projects coordinator[520] have also been among the many passengers pulled aside under the U.S. "no fly" list. In Canada, Shaid Mahmood, a Toronto editorial cartoonist who has been critical of U.S. and Israeli foreign policies, was refused the right to buy a ticket by an Air Canada agent because his name appeared on the U.S. list.[521]

The "no fly" list is run by the Transportation Security Administration, with names fed to it by the FBI and intelligence agencies. Airlines are required to stop passengers whose names appear on the list from flying or to subject those identified as "selectees" to more rigorous security screening.

Dozens of men with the misfortune to be named David Nelson have been questioned by ticket agents, pulled off planes, and interrogated.[522] Massachusetts Senator Ted Kennedy was stopped from getting on a plane from Washington to Boston by a ticket agent who reportedly saw his name on the "no fly" list. Eventually Kennedy was allowed to fly home, but he was stopped again on the return journey to Washington. In order to get his name removed from the list he had to personally enlist the help of Homeland Security Secretary Tom Ridge.[523] Most Americans don't have those kinds of connections.

In all, as of December 2005, about thirty thousand people had been wrongly matched to the U.S. "no fly" list.[524]

The Canadian and UK "No Fly" Lists

In September 2004, Canada admitted it was in the process of establishing its own "no fly" list pursuant to the new Public Safety Act. Constitutional and privacy concerns delayed the implementation of the list for a while, but in August 2005, the introduction of a list was announced as the first phase of the Passenger Protect program. Canadian officials have promised that the list will be a short one, but that may not matter much, since there is some evidence to suggest that Canada is already enforcing the U.S. list. In addition to the Shaid Mahmood story described earlier, and similar stories about Canadians denied boarding on domestic flights connected with flights to the United States, the Canadian press reported in January

2005 that dozens of Canadians had been prevented from boarding U.S.-bound planes by Canadian authorities.[525]

The UK e-Borders initiative also includes a "no fly" list component.[526]

Shutting Down Independent Media

The current risk-assessment climate has led to international cooperation in shutting down independent media outlets. In October 2004, two computer servers were seized by the FBI from the England office of the Texas-based Internet company, Rackspace. The servers were hosting the Web sites of Independent Media Centers.[527] The seizure was reportedly made under a UK-U.S. Mutual Assistance Treaty of 1996 but on the request of Swiss and Italian police.[528]

Open Season on Individuals and Groups Challenging Repressive Regimes

In repressive regimes, the risk-assessment model being applied in the "war on terrorism" has allowed authorities to comfortably declare an open season on dissidents and groups challenging their power. PEN International has reported that in Burma, China, Colombia, Democratic Republic of the Congo, Indonesia, Jordan, Pakistan, Turkey, and other countries, authorities have "[found] that defining their opponents as 'terrorist sympathizers' is a convenient way of stifling opposition movements."[529] In Tunisia, the lawyers of individuals charged with terrorism have themselves been charged with terrorism.[530] In India, individuals protesting the clearing of land for a business development have been prosecuted under antiterrorism legislation. In Eritrea, independent newspapers have been shut down and their journalists jailed after being accused of having terrorist ties. In Uzbekistan, members of the Human Rights Society have been jailed on weak evidence alleging they recruited Islamic militants. In Colombia, President Andres Pastrana has said that rebels in a four-decade civil war would be treated as terrorists "[a]nd in that, the world supports us."[531]

One can imagine how much easier it will be for these regimes to punish dissenters when the greater surveillance capabilities and support from other countries is accessible to them under the new global infrastructure for mass surveillance.

A Plethora of Ballooning Watch Lists

Many people might believe that terrorist watch lists are a reliable product of international intelligence cooperation and consensus. But, in low-tech risk assessment, watch lists proliferate, and they are often as dangerously flawed as the watch lists created by high-tech methods.

In addition to the UN list, and the "no fly" list described above, since 9/11 a plethora of low-tech lists have sprung up.

None of these lists were the product of objective, careful international agreement. Even the UN list is a compilation of national products of variable reliability. In many countries the definition of "terrorism" used to create lists is so vague that, as the former director of the Canadian Security Intelligence Service has said of the Canadian definition, it "could easily include behavior that doesn't remotely resemble terrorism."[532]

In addition, the lists reduce complex historical and political conflicts to a matter of proscription, lumping widely different contexts into one category. Opponents of a repressive regime in a liberation movement or a civil war or an occupation could be labeled "terrorists" under many countries' definitions of terrorism, even though they are not targeting civilian populations. The U.S. Military Commission Instruction No. 2 on "Crimes and Elements for Trials by Military Commission" and its Comments, for example, define the offense of "terrorism" as including "an attack against a military objective that normally would be permitted under the law of armed conflict"![533]

Many regimes have pressured other governments to place the names of their opponents on their lists. In the UK, the debate over the first list of twenty-one proscribed groups was limited to half an hour, with no time to discuss each group situation on a separate basis. Jeremy Corbin, MP, complained about the political influence of other governments on the list, saying that he was "very well aware that the Indian government, the Turkish government, the Sri Lankan government, the Iranian government and undoubtedly many other governments have constantly been pressing the British government to close down political activity in this country by their opponents."[534]

There is little or no due process afforded individuals or groups to allow them to challenge the inclusion of their names on a list. And once the "terrorist" label is associated with them, actions are taken against them without normal legal protections being afforded—protections such as presumption of innocence, the right to know the evidence and allegations against one and to respond, the right to remain silent, and habeas corpus. This is the essence of the preemption model: *it treats as intolerable risks the very legal protections that are fundamental to free and democratic societies.* Like an autoimmune disease, it harms the very democratic organism it is supposed to protect.

In the United States there were, until 2004, nine agencies administering twelve different watch lists. Each of these watch lists was created for a different purpose, using different criteria. The government has enough information to justify suspicions that some of the people on these lists are dangerous. Others are suspected of being dangerous, but the evidence is thin. Others should simply not be on any list: they are there like Maher Arar, because they have been found guilty by association, or because of some misspelling of their name, or on the basis of some mistaken assumption about their background, or owing to crude ethnic and religious profiling, or because they have been critical of the government, or because some state agent decided that he or she would rather be "safe than sorry."[535] In short, the U.S. lists have "been created haphazardly and without the carefully constructed checks and balances that such powerful instrument[s] demand."[536] The FBI stopped Air France and British Airways flights to the United States in late 2003, based on matches with names on terrorist watch lists. The suspects turned out to be a five year-old child with a similar name to a wanted Tunisian, a Welsh insurance salesperson, an elderly Chinese woman, and a prominent Egyptian scientist. "A check was carried out in each case and in each case it turned out to be negative," a spokesman for the French interior minister said. "The FBI worked with family names and some family names sound alike."[537]

The National Counterterrorism Center (NCTC) was created in 2004 to be the primary U.S. terrorism intelligence agency and to help merge lists and streamline the more than twenty-six terrorism-related databases compiled by intelligence and law enforcement. It had a central repository of 325,000 names as of February 2006. Though only a fraction of the names belong to U.S. citizens, that's a lot of terrorists. The NSA, the agency performing President Bush's secret domestic spying, is "a key provider of information for the NCTC database."[538]

The FBI's Terrorist Screening Center receives names from the NCTC and consolidates them with its purely domestic terrorism data to create a unified FBI list. In 2005, the FBI list had 270,000 names on it, an even more disturbing number than the NCTC list, perhaps. The FBI, in turn, passes names on to the Transportation Security Administration for the "no fly" list, the State Department for visa lists, and to the Department of Homeland Security.[539]

A combined master list of immigration and terrorist watch lists from the State Department, Customs Service, Drug Enforcement Administration, and the FBI has a reported 13 million names on it.[540]

To date, there has been a troubling involvement of the private sector with the watch lists. As with the surveillance of electronic communications, private organizations and corporations are being turned into the agents of the state. Under a program called Project Lookout, the FBI circulated a list of hundreds of names to corporations. The list, which was full of inaccuracies and contained the names of many people with whom the FBI simply wanted to talk, was widely shared and quickly took on a life of its own.[541] Health insurance giants looked through millions of customer records. Blue Cross found no terrorists, but six thousand false positives (out of 6 million records) were generated, all of whom were investigated further by the company's employees. Aetna searched through 13 million records. The FBI admitted it had no way to remove innocent people from the list, because its distribution had spun out of its control.[542]

As mentioned earlier earlier, financial companies and businesses involved in helping individuals to buy or sell property must verify each customer's identity and then check whether the person is on a government watch list.[543]

⊙ ⊙

The post-9/11 world of "risk assessment"—whether one is experiencing the high-tech version or the low-tech version—is Kafkaesque.[544] It is a world in which individuals are presumed guilty, detained, and not told the charges against them, denied the right to face their accusers, denied the right to know the evidence against them and the criteria by which they are being judged, and given no legal recourse and no one to advocate for them.

CHAPTER ELEVEN

Integration of Security Functions and Loss of Sovereignty

⊙ ⊙

O world, thy slippery turns!
—William Shakespeare, Coriolanus, IV.iv

When all the initiatives described above are viewed together, what emerges are the "contours of a vast, increasingly integrated multinational registration and surveillance system, with information floating more or less freely between subsystems."[545] As this system emerges, the police, security intelligence, and military operations of many nations are becoming increasingly integrated with U.S. operations. National governments are giving up sovereignty and throwing aside national checks and balances in favor of an integrated security space that is largely being designed and controlled by the United States.

Governments are agreeing to joint policing and intelligence operations with the United States. The RCMP had regular meetings with the FBI and CIA regarding Maher Arar, and they shared all the information they had with these agencies, without caveats. In the mutual assistance teams being set up between Canada and the United States, and between the United States and the EU, this kind of sharing takes place all the time, and the U.S. agencies participating in the teams are likely not accountable to national governments and courts. In the Camolin operation the reported function of the

European agencies (and likely of the Canadian and Australian agencies) involved is reportedly to supply dossiers on suspects for the CIA to act on. Help in the U.S. "war on terrorism" also flows the other way. In Indonesia, the FBI trapped the Papuan separatist fighter Anthonius Wamang and turned him over to Indonesian authorities. Wamang, along with ten other men and a teenager, met with FBI agents in a small hotel in the remote region of Papua after having been assured by intermediaries that they would be flown to the United States and allowed to defend themselves against charges that they had murdered two American teachers in 2002. Instead, they were hustled into a windowless truck and delivered to Indonesian police. "Hurry, hurry," the FBI agents told the Papuans as they left the hotel, "The plane is on the runway."[546]

Governments are sharing suspects. There is currently a global pool of suspects (most of whom are being kept in legal "black holes" around the world) to which multiple security services have access. Canadian services could have interviewed Arar, Almalki, and El Maati in Syria if they had chosen to. Canadian Security Intelligence Service (CSIS) agents were in fact traveling to Guantánamo Bay to interview suspects until Canadian courts put a stop to it.[547] And security agencies in other countries are doing the same kind of thing. The story of Khaled El Masri, a German citizen, paints a disturbing picture of how it happens.

El Masri, an unemployed car salesman from the town of Ulm, was traveling to Macedonia for a New Year's vacation when he was seized by Macedonian police at the border, held incommunicado for weeks without charge, then beaten, stripped, and flown to a U.S. jail in Afghanistan where he was held and tortured for five months before being dumped back in Albania.[548] At the request of the United States, Macedonia held El Masri in a hotel room for twenty-three days so that the CIA could question him, then allowed him to be rendered by the United States to Kabul. "We consider the Americans as our partners," a senior Macedonian official later told the *New York Times*, "[W]e cannot refuse them."[549] El Masri begged his Macedonian captors to call the German embassy. "I'm a German citizen. Please tell them I am here!," he pleaded. "They don't want to talk to you," they replied.[550] According to the *Times*, the German embassy had been contacted within days of El Masri's detention: "Unofficially they knew," said the Macedonian official interviewed.[551]

El Masri had been picked up because his name was on an Interpol "terrorist" list, but it was a case of mistaken identity: he merely shared the name of someone on the list. While in Afghanistan, El Masri says he was interrogated three times by a man who he later identified as a senior German police official. The official denies he visited El Masri in Afghanistan, claiming he was on "on holiday" at the time, though he can't remember where. German police and prosecutors have opened an investigation into whether German officials had any involvement in the case. This was scant consolation for El Masri, however. "I feel deceived and betrayed by my own country" he said in an interview.[552]

In June 2006, these feelings were reinforced when Germany's external intelligence service, the BND, admitted it knew about the U.S. seizure and detention of its fellow citizen sixteen months before the country was officially informed of the abduction.[553]

You may comfort yourself with the thought that if you are mistakenly caught up in the global mass surveillance net, your government will help and protect you. But El Masri's story and others in this book should be convincing that this is a naïve assumption. It is much more likely that your government will be powerless to protect you or that it is "conspiring" with the United States goverment against you. As was painfully illustrated by the Arar case, while part of his national government may have been making genuine efforts to secure his release, that part was either unaware or not in control of what other parts and agencies were doing and these may have been complicit in his continued detention and torture. At the same time, Syria, the government of his country of origin was willing to torture him on behalf of the United States and these agencies. In the case of the Somali Swedes, the Swedish government was powerless to have their names removed from the UN list. It had to beg the United States to take the names off, and its citizens were forced to sign a statement for U.S. authorities swearing that they never had supported terrorism and that they would cease all contact with the *hawala*, al Barakaat.[554] In the case of the British citizens seized in The Gambia, it appears that it was British agencies that tipped off the CIA there. In other cases of kidnapping and rendition it appears that the national agencies of the persons taken were notified in advance by U.S. agencies. Recent evidence suggests that Canada and EU countries have been allowing CIA "rendition" planes, like the one that carried Maher Arar to Jordan, to land and refuel on their territory.

In addition to the increasing integration of police and security intelligence functions that has occurred in tandem with the emergence of a global registration and surveillance infrastructure, there has also been an increasing integration of military functions. In particular, U.S. military presence around the world has increased, compromising national sovereignty and national jurisdiction over the treatment of suspects. The excuse of fighting an indefinitely long "war on terror" has given the neoconservatives in the Bush administration license to do exactly what they said they would do in their seminal documents.

Remember the Project for a New American Century's *Rebuilding America's Defenses* report? It called for an increased U.S. military presence around the world; for U.S. troops to perform global "constabulary" duties: for military bases in the Middle East, Southeast Europe, in Latin America, and in Asia where they did not exist before; and for American leadership in place of the UN's. Those goals are now being achieved in a variety of ways under the banner of the "war on terror," and they have implications for the way in which intelligence is shared and acted upon.

First, the Bush administration is installing "forward operating bases" or "lily pads" in strategic regions like the Middle East, southeast Europe, Central Asia, and Latin America in order to increase the reach of its military forces and secure "enduring access" for "episodic employment."[555] This involves storing military equipment and weapons in strategic areas that can be used by troops when they are needed for regional enforcement of U.S. hegemonic interests. The beauty of "lily pads" is that the host governments can tell their citizens that there are no U.S. bases on their territory.[556]

Second, the United States is reasserting a military presence in places where it had formerly withdrawn. In the Philippines, where years of U.S. military presence were ended as a result of popular protest, the United States managed to reestablish its presence after 9/11, ostensibly to assist in the capture of Philippine-based terrorists, which would ordinarily be a law-enforcement function of the Philippine state. This was done without a treaty or even the usual "status of forces" agreement.[557]

Third, the Bush administration is providing new military advice and training in places like Colombia, Indonesia, Georgia, and Malaysia. U.S. aid is increasingly turning into "technical assistance," bolstering security apparatuses in countries which have strategic value to the United States.

Finally, the administration is increasing covert operations abroad, situating small teams of Special Operations personnel in a growing number of American embassies outside of war zones. As of early 2006, Special Operations personnel had been sent to twenty embassies in Africa, Southeast Asia, and South America.[558] To extend its reach to more countries 12,000 new positions will be added to the Special Operations forces between 2007–11 beefing up the already expanded complement of 51,000 Navy SEALs, Green Berets, Army Rangers, and other commandos.[559]

The mandate of the new teams is to gather intelligence on terrorists (formerly the domain of the CIA) and, in Pentagon jargon, to "find, fix, finish and follow up" on them.[560] This is "shorthand for locating terrorist leaders, tracking them precisely, capturing or killing them, and then using the information gathered to plan another operation."[561] It could also be shorthand for assassinating opponents of the United States government in other countries.

When the first Special Operations personnel were dispatched under the new program starting in 2003, they were called "Operational Control Elements," but the name was later changed to the more tactful moniker, "Military Liaison Elements."[562] In Paraguay, members of one these "Military Liaison Elements" were recalled after killing a thief who attacked them as they stepped out of a taxi. The incident embarrassed senior embassy officials who should have been told the team was operating in the country.[563] Under a classified order made in 2005, however, Special Operations no longer need the approval of the State Department to go into a country.[564]

Whether it was Special Operations forces or the CIA, in two reported instances, U.S. agents have used "actionable" intelligence to try to assassinate people they were after inside the territory of other states. In the first case, in Yemen, all the passengers in a vehicle were killed when they were hit by a missile fired by an unmanned U.S. drone. In the second case in Pakistan, also involving an unmanned drone, as many as seventeen innocent men, women, and children were killed. The Pakistani foreign ministry lodged a strong protest with the United States, and Pakistanis demonstrated in the streets, but U.S. officials said that Pakistan had "signed off on the strike beforehand and even assisted with gathering pre-attack intelligence."[565] Yemeni intelligence was also apparently cooperating with the United States in respect of the strike in their country.[566] How, it must be asked, would people in the United States react if a foreign government sent assassins into their country or bombed a market, a street, or a school in order to target individuals they were after? How would they react if their government assisted in the attack?

There are various forces at work driving countries to submit to the demands of the United States. There is certainly some belief among governments that better sharing and cooperation among states is necessary in order to effectively counter international terrorism, and this may be true. However, many of the agreements and arrangements which governments have made are irresponsible in terms of the sovereign powers they cede, the lack of adequate conditions and controls they contain, and the lack of due process and rule of law they afford citizens.

Some of the willingness of governments to acquiesce to U.S. demands for an integrated security space is rooted in opportunism. U.S. bilateral demands and those channeled through international forums give governments the excuse to do what they otherwise might not be able to do; that is, tighten the grip of their own social control at and within their own borders. This is the eternal tendency of governments and law enforcement, and it is the reason why democracies have entrenched rights and other institutional checks and balances.

In many cases, however, governments are driven by economic interests. The EU, for example, feared the economic consequences of its airline industry's being denied landing rights in the United States when demands for PNR sharing were made; this was part of what led it into negotiations for a formal agreement on PNR sharing.[567] In Canada, where 30 percent of the economy depends on exports to the United States,[568] where a border open to the flow of export traffic is critical, and where powerful business interests have been lobbying for years for what has become known in Canada as "deep" integration with the United States,[569] the government was quick to negotiate the Smart Border Agreement and Action Plan that were, in essence, a blueprint for many of the registration and surveillance initiatives described in this book.

Many other countries that depend on trade with, or aid from, the United States have found themselves in similar situations. Like Canada and the EU, Southeast Asian governments, especially those of the Philippines, Singapore, Thailand, Malaysia and Indonesia, have cooperated closely with the United States in its global campaign against terrorism. The collaboration ranges from interviewing alleged terrorists based on shared intelligence as the Malaysians interviewed Abdullah Almalki, to arresting them and allowing U.S. agents access, to facilitating the extradition of detainees to the United States, to legislating antiterror laws to serve the U.S.-led antiterrorism campaign,[570] to, as mentioned earlier regarding the Philippines, allowing U.S. military forces to lead special operations against terrorist groups in the country.[571]

Arab countries like Syria, Jordan, and Egypt have their own reasons for acting as "the boots of the West," as Ahmad El Maati's Egyptian guard so eloquently described it. Many of them have complicated relationships with the United States because of U.S. relations with Israel, and some are fighting their own battles against fundamentalist Islamic opponents. As a result, they see the "heavy lifting" they are doing for the United States in the war against Islamic terrorists as both an opportunity to help themselves and to improve their relations with an important power in their region.[572]

Whatever states' reasons are for cooperating in the global project for mass surveillance and other aspects of the integrated security space, the net result is increasing hegemony for the United States—just what the neoconservatives in the United States have long desired. Though whether it will be a stable or beneficial hegemony for the United States is another question. More likely, it will turn into a "monkey's paw"[573] story for everyone.

CHAPTER TWELVE

The Corporate-Security Complex

◎ ◎

It is expected that once the public becomes accustomed to using biometrics at borders, their use in commercial applications will follow. . . . The large-scale introduction of biometric passports in Europe provides a unique opportunity. . . . Firstly, the creation of a demand market based on user acceptance. . . . Second, the fostering of a competitive supply market.

—Report of the European Union's Joint Research Centre

"You need to educate yourself," he said with a sneer. "I mean, that's a classic journalist's question, but why are you hassling these guys? They're engineers. They make a product. They don't sell it. What the hell is it to them what anyone does with it?"

"Well, it's quite an issue," I said. "This is the equipment of totalitarianism, and the only things that can keep a population safe are decent law and proper oversight. I want to know what they think when they learn that China, or Syria, or Zimbabwe is getting their hands on it."

He sneered again. "Do you think for a minute that Bush would let legal issues stop him from doing

> *surveillance? He's got to prevent a terrorist attack that everyone knows is coming. He'll do absolutely anything he thinks is going to work. And so would you. So why are you bothering these guys?"*
>
> *"It's a valid question," I inisisted. "This is powerful stuff. In the wrong hands, it could ruin political opponents; it could make the state's power impossible to challenge. The state would know basically everything. People would be getting rounded up for thought crimes."*
>
> *"You're not listening," he said. "The NSA is using this stuff. The DEA, the Secret Service, the CIA. Are you kidding me? They don't answer to you. They do whatever the hell they want with it. Are you really that naïve? Now leave these guys alone; they make a product, that's all. It's nothing to them what happens afterward. You really need to educate yourself."*
>
> —Surveillance equipment salesman speaking with journalist Thomas Greene at the ISS World Conference, May 2006.

In Dwight Eisenhower's farewell address at the end of his presidency in 1961, he warned the American people about the rise of a powerful "military-industrial complex" that threatened the foundations of American democracy: "This conjunction of an immense military establishment and a large arms industry is new in the American experience. . . . The potential for the disastrous rise of misplaced power exists and will persist. We must never let the weight of this combination endanger our liberties or democratic processes. We should take nothing for granted."[574]

Today, the same warning could be made with respect to the new symbiotic relationship that is developing between an immense security/intelligence establishment and an ambitious information technology industry. This new *corporate-security complex* is an aggressive driver of the project for globalized, mass registration and surveillance.

In the official Washington of the 1990s, there was a general scramble, not just on the part of the neoconservatives, but also on the part of the whole military and security apparatus. They needed to find a new rationale that would sustain the level of military spending on which their jobs and, to some extent, the American economy had come to depend after the World War II and during the subsequent Cold War.[575] For this sector, the "war on terror" was heaven sent, offering them a new raison d'être and an opportunity to acquire a long-held "wish list" of investigative and surveillance powers. At the same time, new information technologies, largely being developed by the private sector, offered exciting new possibilities for expanding their surveillance capabilities.

But the private sector offered more than just technology to government agencies. It offered a way around some of the laws and accountability mechanisms that restricted them. For example, contracting with private data-aggregation corporations allows government agencies to access massive databases of personal information they would not under privacy and other laws have been able to maintain themselves. Contracting with private corporations for the development of data-mining projects, similarly allows government agencies to evade privacy protections. To some degree, it also allows them to shield the projects from public scrutiny.

As Roch Tassé of the International Campaign Against Mass Surveillance (ICAMS) has observed, for information-technology corporations, the business generated by the "war on terror" has been a boon after the sector's disastrous economic downfall in the mid- to late 1990s. It offers them a critical opportunity for recovery and expansion that they have been quick to seize—setting in motion a powerful lobby that promotes technological products to governments that have big budgets to spend on the preemption of risk.[576]

Billions of dollars, euros, and other currencies fuel the corporate security complex.

Prior to 9/11, counterterrorism research and development in the United States amounted to only about $500 million per year, with a majority of it being spent by the Department of Defense because of the perception that U.S. troops abroad were most at risk. After 9/11, funding for the Department of Homeland Security alone was $1.5 billion in 2002 and then more than doubled to $3.3 billion in 2003.[577] In 2006 security R&D rose to $4.4 billion.[578] While some of this money is being spent on projects not related to surveillance, the figures give one an idea of the large amounts of money available for security projects. And these figures do not necessarily include money spent on implemented programs.

A security research program announced by the EU in February 2004 is intended to make the EU the rival of the United States in security technology. Dubbed the European Security Research Programme (ESRP), it is explicitly aimed at building a "security culture" in Europe with the help of the security industry and the research community. The program is charged, among other things, with "[demonstrating] the appropriateness and acceptability of tagging, tracking and tracing devices by static and mobile multiple sensors that improve the capability to locate, identify and follow the movement of mobile assets, goods and persons, including smart documentation (e.g. biometrics, automatic chips with positioning) and data analysis techniques (remote control and access)."[579]

The ESRP was developed on the basis of recommendations made by a "Group of Personalities" (GoP) that included representatives from eight multinational companies (including four of the EU's largest arms companies and some of its largest IT companies) and seven "research" institutions (including the Rand Corporation).[580] In 2004, a budget of €65 million was allocated for "preparatory action." In the twenty-four projects funded by the "preparatory action" budget, the big four arms dealers on the GoP did particularly well. Thales is participating in five projects, the EADS group is leading three projects, and Finmeccanica companies are involved in at least three projects.

On the GoP's recommendation, the ESRP is overseen by a European Security Research Advisory Board (ESRAB). Industry occupies fourteen of the fifty ESRAB seats and interior ministries and military and security agencies occupy eighteen.[581] By 2007, the European Commission will be providing the ESRP with more than a billion euros a year.[582]

In Canada, the Liberal government announced a $7.7 billion package (in Canadian dollars) for security spending over a five-year period in its 2001 budget. The package included substantial spending on surveillance and security technology.[583] Much of this money has already been spent, and the Conservatives, elected in early 2006, have allocated another $705 million for transportation (in Canadian dollars), border, and financial system security in their first budget.[584]

The major surveillance projects undertaken by the United States government—such as the Terrorism [Total] Information Awareness System, MATRIX, US-VISIT, CAPPS II, and Secure Flight programs—and the e-Borders project undertaken by the UK government—have provided massive business opportunities and profits for technology corporations.

Prior to being forced by Congress to abandon research on Terrorism [Total] Information Awareness system in the fall of 2003, the Defense Advanced Research Projects Agency oversaw a budget of roughly $2 billion and relied heavily on outside contractors. Between 1997 and 2002, it granted contracts to data-aggregator companies worth $88 million. Among these, thirteen contracts worth more than $23 million went to Booz Allen Hamilton Inc., and twenty-three contracts worth $27 million were granted to Lockheed Martin. Other contractors were Schafer Corporation, SRS Technologies, Adroit Systems, CACI Dynamic Systems, Syntek Technologies, and ASI International.[585]

Although TIA was shelved at the federal level, the MATRIX program has been in the process of implementation at the state level since 2002. As mentioned earlier, the contract for the program was awarded to Seisint Inc., based in Boca Raton, Florida. According to the American Civil Liberties Union, a former company of Seisint's originator, Hank Asher, "administered a contract that stripped thousands of African Americans from the Florida voter rolls before the 2000 elections, erroneously contending that they were felons."[586] In January 2003, Florida Governor Jeb Bush appears to have arranged a meeting at the White House to allow Seisint to demonstrate to Vice President Dick Cheney, FBI Director Robert Mueller, and Homeland Security Director Tom Ridge how the MATRIX could be used for law enforcement and to seek extra funding.[587] Subsequently the Department of Justice gave Seisint $4 million and the Department of Homeland Security contributed $8 million to the project.[588]

In July 2004, Siesint was sold to the LexisNexis Group for a reported $775 million. Hank Asher made $250 million from the sale. LexisNexis predicted that Seisint revenue would grow by more that 40 percent in 2004, helping to boost the revenue of the LexisNexis risk-management division to around $300 million annually.[589]

Companies like LexisNexis, Lockheed Martin, Acxiom, and ChoicePoint have been major winners in supplying governments with their ever-increasing needs for data. ChoicePoint alone claims to have contracts with some thirty-five U.S. government agencies. These include its $8 million contract with the U.S. Justice Department that allows the FBI to tap into the company's vast database of personal information from their squad rooms.

The US-VISIT program has been another goldmine for the corporate sector. In May 2004, the Department of Homeland Security issued a call for bids to develop the program. Accenture, the winner, beat out Computer Sciences and Lockheed Martin.[590] The Accenture team includes AT&T Corp., Datatrac Information Services Inc., Dell

Inc., Deloitte Consulting LLP, Raytheon Co., Sandler and Travis Trade Advisory Services Inc., Sprint Corp., SRA International Inc., and Titan Corp.[591] While the ten-year contract has a $10 billion ceiling and original estimates for US-VISIT were set at $7.2 billion up to 2014, GAO auditors reported in 2003 that the costs would likely rise into the "tens of billions."[592] This seems likely, given that the system is being built by Accenture on top of aging computer databases and software and will need significant upgrades. Accenture is also working with the government as a "partner," with no clear idea of how the system will ultimately work or whether it can be completed over the next ten years. Accenture gets paid for tasks along the way, even if the final system does not work.[593]

Between January 2004 and January 2006, US-VISIT had processed more than 44 million visitors and flagged one thousand people with criminal or immigration violations.[594] Not one reported terrorist. If the program ultimately costs $20 billion, which in light of the GAO auditor report seems conservative, that yields a cost of $20 million per person caught.[595]

Lockheed Martin, a giant of the military-industrial complex, received a five-year, $12.8 million contract to assist the Transportation Security Administration in the development of the CAPPS II program[596] Before the program was canceled, more than $60 million had been spent on the development of computer technology intended to verify individuals' identities against commercial databases.[597]

CAPPS II relied heavily on data and identity-matching algorithms developed by Acxiom. The Little Rock–based company is the world's largest processor of consumer data, collecting and manipulating more than a billion records a day, and is rapidly expanding its reach in Europe and Asia.[598] Since 9/11, Acxiom has been lobbying for federal contracts in homeland security with the help of retired general and presidential candidate Wesley Clark and Bill and Hillary Clinton. Clark has also lobbied on behalf of Lockheed Martin.[599]

As of January 2006, the Secure Flight program, which succeeded CAPPS II, had spent $200 million[600] and had repeatedly received failing grades in government oversight reports.[601] Controversially, of the money spent, a contract worth $475,000 was given to EagleForce Associates of Virginia, to test the use of commercial data in the program.[602]

The main contract for the e-Borders project being implemented in the United Kingdom is expected to cost £4 million and take between five and fifteen years to implement. It will involve the design, development, implementation, support, and operation of the IT systems that will link border control authorities. The government is already in discussions with private-sector suppliers.[603] Already up and running is the first stage of e-Borders called Project Semaphore. It involves the processing of API and PNR data and was awarded to IBM as a three-year contract in November 2004.[604]

The biometric registration of populations through passports, visas, and ID cards offers the prospect of huge profits for corporations globally. Once a fairly muted industry owing to the privacy concerns of clientele and potential clientele, overnight biometrics became an acceptable security solution and its corporate developers vocal proponents of the technology.[605] Corporations that specialize in biometrics—such as Byometric Systems (Germany), Bioscrypt (Canada), and BioDentity (Canada)—are aggressively looking for a piece of the antiterrorism action. At a public conference organized by the Liberal government to "debate" the introduction of national ID cards in Canada in 2003, the biometric industry was one of the biggest participants. On its Web site, BioDentity quotes a Frost & Sullivan claim that "[c]utting-edge security systems could have prevented the catastrophe—the worst terrorist attack in U.S. history."[606]

The contract awarded by the Swedish government to Setec, a Finnish company, to supply biometric passports and ID cards over the next five years is worth €100 million.[607] Another lucrative contract with the Danish government will see Setec provide 3 million Danes with biometric passports.[608]

In Canada, ACME-Future Security Controls, an Ottawa-based company, was chosen by the Canadian Air Transport Security Authority to develop a secure identity card, using biometric technologies, for individuals accessing restricted areas of airports.[609]

In Asia, the Indian smart card industry is growing at a rate of 45 percent annually and will be worth $6 billion by 2010. Companies like Sony, Infineon, and Hitachi are "licking their lips."[610]

IT corporations, such as Oki, have recently moved into the biometrics sector as well, anticipating big profits. Oki now specializes in iris scans and is working for the German government on a pilot project in the Frankfurt airport.[611]

Companies are looking aggressively for business across borders. Unisys, a company based in the U.S. which won the contract for the U.S. "Registered Traveler Program" in 2004,[612] has developed ID cards for Panama and Malaysia and has been lobbying to get a contract for the impending U.K. ID card.[613] Unisys has also been awarded a contract to test the operational impact of biometric technology for Citizenship and Immigration Canada.[614] SITA Information Networking Computing, an IT company registered in the Netherlands, is now implementing "intelligent border services" in Bahrain, Australia and New Zealand, including a tracking system that analyzes the travel patterns of high risk passengers.[615] Siemens, a company based in Germany, is now providing passports to the U.K. government, national ID cards with chips and biometrics to Macau, ID cards to Bosnia-Herzegovina and Italy, and visas to Norway.[616] In 2002, the France-based Thales Group sought and won the contract for the Chinese ID card.[617] In September 2004, the Canadian government facilitated the mission of a Canadian trade delegation to China to promote the sale of surveillance and security technology to the Chinese government, including closed circuit television devices, night-vision products, face recognition technology and computer systems for monitoring the Internet.[618]

In the fray of all the activity described above, corporations are constantly "pushing the envelope" of social control by technological means—egging on governments to embrace bigger, newer, more expensive and more intrusive systems of social control.

It is not implausible, in the new world order, that corporations will sell governments on the idea that their populations should have their brains scanned with neuro electric sensors whenever they enter an airport, in order to asses whether they are having agitated thoughts.[619] Or that their populations should be biometrically registered by DNA. Or that they should be required to have micro chips implanted under their skin, so that the state might better identify, locate and screen them.

In 2006 it was reported that an Ohio company had become the first-known business to have implanted RFID transmitters into the arms of two of its employees. VeriChip, the company that made the chips, says that its products combine "access control with the location and protection of individuals." George Monbiot, a journalist who writes frequently for *Le Monde* and the *Guardian*, has made some chilling observations about how this kind of technology could easily become normalized in our societies:

> The transmitters are tiny (about the size of a grain of rice), cheap ($150 and falling), safe and stable. Without being maintained or replaced, they can identify someone for many years. They are injected, with a local anesthetic, into the upper arm. They require no power source, as they become active only when scanned. There are no technical barriers to their wider deployment. . . . A tag like [those injected into the two employees] has a maximum range of a few meters. But another implantable device emits a signal that allows someone to be found or tracked by satellite. . . .

> At first the tags will be more widely used for workers with special security clearance. No one will be forced to wear one: no one will object. Then hospitals—and a few in the United States are already doing this—will start scanning their unconscious or incoherent patients to see whether or not they have a tag. Insurance companies might start to demand that vulnerable people are chipped.
>
> The armed forces will discover that they are more useful than dog tags and more useful for identifying injured soldiers or for tracking troops who are lost or have been captured by the enemy. Then sweatshops in developing countries will begin to catch on. . . . After that, it surely won't be long before asylum seekers are confronted with a similar choice: You don't have to accept the implant, but if you refuse, you can't stay in the country.
>
> . . . As it is with all such intrusions on our privacy, it won't be easy to put your finger on exactly what's wrong with this technology. It won't really amount to a new form of control, as all the people who accept implants will already be subject to monitoring or tracking of one kind or another. It will always be voluntary, at least to the extent that anything the state or our employers want us to do is voluntary. But there is something utterly revolting about it. It is another means by which the barriers between ourselves and the state, ourselves and the corporation, ourselves and the machine are broken down. In that tiny capsule we find the paradox of 21st century capitalism: A political system that celebrates choice, autonomy and individualism above all other virtues demands that choice, autonomy and individualism are perpetually suppressed.[620]

Eisenhower's warning that we should take nothing for granted, it would appear, has never been more relevant.

CHAPTER THIRTEEN

The End of Democracy?

◉ ◉

ROPER: So now you'd give the Devil the benefit of the law!
MORE: Yes. What would you do? Cut a great road through the law to get after the devil?
ROPER: I'd cut down every law in England to do that!
MORE: Oh? And when the last law was down, and the Devil turned round on you—where would you hide, Roper, the laws all being cut flat? This country's planted thick with laws from coast to coast—man's laws, not God's—and if you cut them down—and you're just the man to do it—d'you really think you could stand upright in the winds that would blow then? Yes, I'd give the Devil benefit of the law, for my own safety's sake.
—Robert Bolt, A Man for All Seasons

The fate of every democracy, of every government based on the sovereignty of the people, depends on the choices it makes between these opposite principles, absolute power on the one hand, and on the other the restraints of legality and the authority of tradition.
—John Acton, historian

> *The accumulation of all powers, legislative, executive, and judiciary, in the same hands, whether of one, a few, or many, and whether hereditary, self-appointed, or elective, may justly be pronounced the very definition of tyranny.*
> —James Madison

The purported aim of the people behind the Project for the New American Century—the neoconservative architects of the "war on terrorism," the war in Afghanistan, the war in Iraq, and the possible war in Iran—was to spread democracy around the world. The achievement of this, for some neoconservatives, would mean "the end of history,"[621] the end of dialectical ideological struggles, since the whole world would finally have agreed that the most desirable form of government *was* democracy.

The terrible truth is that the achievement of the neoconservatives' aims is more likely to result in the *end of democracy*, since they have been subverting it both at home and abroad. The subversion of democracy abroad is not surprising since it follows a long pattern of American foreign policy in regions deemed strategic. The subversion of democracy inside the United States is not surprising either, perhaps, when one considers that the goal of the neoconservatives is unrivaled American hegemony and that where there is empire abroad there is often tyranny and propaganda at home.[622] Those in power who are pursuing an imperial project need to maintain tight control at home in order to extract the political, material, and human resources they need for their project and, at the same time, to avoid being overwhelmed by dissent and popular unrest.

The neoconservatives claim they are spreading democracy, but democracy is more than periodic free elections and majority rule. Democracy is a whole set of institutions; institutions that are premised on the rule of law and the idea that the state's power is only legitimate when based on the sovereign will of the people.

There can be no proxy governments where there is real democracy. In a democracy, *no one* is above the law. In a democracy, the state is answerable to the people, *all* of the people, whether they be part of a minority or a majority; and (especially in liberal democracies) the state is answerable to the individual. There are strong checks, therefore, on the state's ability to wield powerful tools of social control in a democracy. There are limits on the state's power to intrude into the private sphere of the individual. There is a right against self-incrimination and a right to be treated as innocent until proven guilty. There is no duty on the part of individuals or private enterprises to assist police in investigations. There are checks on how personal information is accessed, used, and disseminated. And in a democracy, the division of power between coequal branches of government—judicial, legislative, and executive—allow each to act as a check on the other, so that the rights and freedoms of the people may be preserved.

In a surveillance society, all of these maxims are turned on their head: government need not represent the people; the ruling class is above the law; the people and the individual are answerable to the state; their rights and protections are subordinated to the state's interest; and the executive branch of government usurps the constitutional power of the other branches of government. Democracies are essentially rights-based societies. Police states are utilitarian, and usually narrowly utilitarian as they tend to favor the ruling class.

The global project for mass registration and surveillance that the neoconservative government in the United States is pushing, and that governments and corporations are building around the world in the name of protecting freedom and democracy, will have specific, long-term, and insidious effects on freedom and democracy.

As they pursue globalized, mass surveillance, misguided governments are breaking down all kinds of democratic institutions by doing the following:

- Suspending judicial oversight over law-enforcement agents and public officials
- Placing unprecedented power in the hands of the executive arm of government
- Making end runs around the oversight and debate normally provided by the legislative arm of government
- Inviting unelected, unaccountable supranational bodies to set policy for them
- Abandoning well-established privacy protections for citizens
- Ignoring constitutional guarantees
- Rolling back criminal law and due process protections (such as the presumption of innocence, habeas corpus, attorney-client privilege, public trials, the right to know the evidence against one and to respond, reasonable grounds for search and seizure, and the right to remain silent) that balance the rights of individuals against the power of the state
- Turning the private sector into the agent of the state
- Systematically violating basic human rights
- Flouting the rule of law itself

The effects of the global project for mass registration and surveillance on democracy will be long term because in the North, South, East and West, governments in democratic countries have been able to make these changes by declaring a state of crisis. But the "war on terror"—the "long war" as the Bush administration is cleverly trying to rebrand it[623]—is a war without end. The state of crisis, they tell us, is permanent, not temporary. As a result, democratic societies are gradually becoming surveillance societies—or worse, increasingly authoritarian police states.

At the same time, the prospects for freedom in undemocratic countries are fading and are unlikely to be rekindled in the foreseeable future. Emboldened by the abandonment of democratic values in Western countries, those in power in these countries are abandoning democratic reforms and tightening their mechanisms of control. In Russia, for example, President Vladimir Putin announced, in September 2004, plans for a sweeping political overhaul in the name of fighting terrorism, strengthening the president's already extensive control over the legislative branch and regional governments.[624]

The effects of globalized, mass registration and surveillance will be insidious because by the time we are aware of what they have done to our democratic societies, it may be too late to reverse them.

In the eighteenth century, English philosopher Jeremy Bentham proposed an architectural design for what he considered the perfect prison. It enabled one unseen warden to watch all of the prisoners in an institution. Bentham called his design the "Panopticon." His idea was that if prisoners never knew when they were actually being watched—only that they might be watched at any time—they would begin to modify their behavior. Fearing they could be seen, and fearing punishment for transgressions observed, they would begin to internalize the rules of the institution so that actual punishment would eventually be rendered superfluous.[625]

As we begin to realize that every transaction in our personal lives is accessible to state agents, if not in real-time, then later, and that our innocent actions and beliefs can be easily misconstrued by risk assessors in our own and other countries—we will begin to internalize the social control that is being exerted on us, watching what we say, what we criticize, whom we associate with, and what we profess to believe in. French philosopher Michel Foucault wrote, “In appearance [panopticism] is merely the solution to a technical problem, but, through it, a whole new type of society emerges [transported] from the penal institution to the entire social body.”[626]

CHAPTER FOURTEEN

A Loss of Moral Compass—Abduction, Torture, Assassination, and Murder

◎ ◎

First they came for the Socialists, and I didn't speak up,
because I wasn't a Socialist.
Then they came for the Trade Unionists, and I didn't speak up,
because I wasn't a Trade Unionist.
Then they came for the Jews, and I didn't speak up,
because I wasn't a Jew.
Then they came for me, and there was no one left
to speak up for me.
—version of poem written by Martin Niemöller

One commentator, reflecting on the implications of biometric registration and mass surveillance, has written: "There has been an attempt in the last few years to convince us to accept as the humane and normal dimensions of our existence, practices of control that had always been properly considered inhumane and exceptional."[627]

To this observation, it could be added that once societies begin to accept inhumane and exceptional practices of social control, they begin to lose their moral compass.

It is now clearly documented that the United States and other countries participating in the global surveillance project are engaging in inhumane treatment, torture, abduction, assassination, and murder. So that the worst that individuals have to fear from the global surveillance system is something far darker than "mere" loss of privacy, civil liberties, freedom of movement, or even democratic patrimony.

THE GLOBAL GULAG

Detention Centers Used by the United States

When Alexander Solzhenitsyn wrote *The Gulag Archipelago* in the last half of the twentieth century, he described a physical chain of island prisons clustered in Soviet Russia's northern seas and Siberia. But the description was metaphorical as well as physical: the archipelago was a cluster of prisons around which swirled the sea of normal society.[628] Before and during Solzhenitsyn's time, people were often sent to the gulag secretly, without due process, and many disappeared, never to be seen again.[629]

Like the Soviet system that Solzhenitsyn described, the United States has been operating an archipelago of prison camps and detention centers around the world that remains largely unseen by the world. Some of are being run directly by the United States—including Camp Delta at Guantánamo Bay in Cuba; Bagram Air Base and other military bases in Afghanistan; Camp Justice on British Diego Garcia; a floating detention center on board a U.S. naval vessel in the Indian Ocean; Camp Cropper at Baghdad International Airport and other detention centers in Iraq; the U.S. airbase in Qatar; a jail with an undisclosed location referred to by the CIA as "Hotel California";[630] another known as "Bright Light,"[631] and other CIA centers disclosed and undisclosed in Guantánamo Bay,[632] Afghanistan, Pakistan, Thailand, Jordan, Qatar, and elsewhere.[633] In November 2005, the *Washington Post* broke the story that the United States had also set up covert detention centers in "several democracies in Eastern Europe," including one in "a Soviet-era compound" where the CIA has "been hiding and interrogating some of its most important al Qaeda captives."[634] According to the *Post*, "The existence and locations of the facilities—referred to as 'black sites' in classified White House, CIA, Justice Department and Congressional documents—are known to only a handful of officials in the United States and, usually, only to the leader and a few top intelligence officers each host country."[635]

Other detention centers are run by allies of the United States in its "war on terror," in close cooperation with, and sometimes the financial assistance of U.S. agencies like the CIA.[636] These centers are located in Jordan, Syria, Egypt, Morocco, Saudi Arabia, Uzbekistan, and Pakistan—countries with documented records of using torture in interrogation and indefinite detention.[637] Among the worst are the Far' Falastin interrogation center in Damascus, Syria, where Maher Arar was held, and the Scorpion jail and Lazoghly Square secret police headquarters in Cairo.[638] Former CIA agent Bob Baer, who worked covertly for the United States across the Middle East until the mid-1990s has said, "If you want a serious interrogation, you send a prisoner to Jordan. If you want them to be tortured, you send them to Syria. If you want someone to disappear—never to see them again—you send them to Egypt."[639]

Although difficult to verify, Pentagon figures and estimates of intelligence experts put the number of people being held by the United States, directly or at its request, at more than 9,000 as of May of 2004[640] and there may be even more at the time of writing, in September 2006.

THE PRACTICE OF RENDITION

Many detainees held by the Unites States have been captured on the battlefield in Afghanistan and Iraq and have been shipped off to detention centers beyond these theaters of war,[641] in contravention of Article 49 of the Fourth Geneva Convention, which provides that "[i]ndividual or mass forcible transfers, as well as deportations of protected persons from occupied territory to the territory of the Occupying Power or that of any other country . . . are prohibited, regardless of their motive." However, the Bush administration has also moved detainees to and between detention centers using an existing American practice of abduction known as "extraordinary rendition."

The practice was developed as "rendition to justice" in the late 1980s, reportedly to allow U.S. agents to apprehend wanted persons in so-called "failed states" like Lebanon,[642] where lawful extradition procedures were either ineffectual or nonexistent. Before September 2001, the CIA was authorized by presidential directives to carry out renditions, but the rules were restrictive, requiring review and approval by interagency groups led by the White House. The purpose of the procedure at that time was to bring prisoners to the United States or to other countries to face criminal charges.[643]

According to current and former government officials, days after September 11, 2001, President Bush signed a directive that gave the CIA expansive authority to use rendition *without* case-by-case approval from the White House, the State Department, or the Justice Department.[644] Since then, the program has "expanded beyond recognition—becoming, according to one former CIA official, 'an abomination.'"[645] Rendition is now being used—not to bring a small number of individuals charged with criminal offenses to face trial in the United States—but to transfer a large group of individuals who will likely never have criminal charges brought against them to detention centers outside of the United States, and solely for the purpose of detention, interrogation, and torture.[646] As another CIA official has said of the current practice, "It's not rendering to justice. It's kidnapping."[647]

This new form of rendition has become one of the principal strategies of the United States in the "war on terror."[648]

Under the new form of rendition, the United States picks up

individuals around the world with the help of its allies, and transfers them to extraterritorial detention centers on jets operated by the U.S. Special Collection Service. The service runs a fleet of luxury planes and military transports that has moved thousands of prisoners around the world since September 11, 2001—much as the CIA's secret fleet—"Air America"—moved prisoners in the 1960s and 1970s.[649] Maher Arar was transported to Jordan (on his way to Syria), in this way.

DISAPPEARANCE

The operations of the Special Collection Service air fleet, and of the detention centers to which it delivers detainees, are shrouded in secrecy.[650] With few exceptions, when detainees arrive at their destinations either as rendered suspects or as prisoners captured in a theater of war, they disappear.

The Geneva Conventions require the prompt registration of detainees captured in theaters of war so that their treatment can be monitored.[651] Under the Rome Statute of the International Criminal Court, "enforced disappearance" is a "crime against humanity" and is defined as "the arrest, detention or abduction of persons by, or with the authorization, support or acquiescence of, a State or a political organization, followed by a refusal to acknowledge that deprivation of freedom or to give information on the fate or whereabouts of those persons, with the intention of removing them from the protection of the law for a prolonged period of time."[652] While the United States is not a signatory to the Rome Statute, the statute's definition arguably codifies existing international law regarding disappearances.

Although the United States has released the names of a few of the high-level Al Qaeda suspects it holds,[653] and other detainees' names have become public through families' and activists' efforts as in the case of Maher Arar, the United States does not release any details about the people it renders to foreign prisons[654] or about most of the people it holds in CIA-run detention centers.[655] The latter have been called "ghost detainees" by Human Rights Watch, since the Bush administration has consistently refused to reveal their fate or locations.[656] Recent additions to their ranks came from the Iraq theater of war when a number of detainees were kept off the registers shown to the Red Cross there with the approval of U.S. Secretary of Defense Donald Rumsfeld.[657]

The Bush administration also refused to release the names of detainees held at Guantánamo Bay to lawyers and the public right up until February 2006 when it decided it wouldn't appeal a federal judge's order to provide names that had been blacked out in documents released under a Freedom of Information Act claim filed by the Associated Press.[658] Most of these detainees were transferred from the Afghan theater of war, but many have been rendered there from other countries.[659]

In 2002, at a joint hearing of the House and Senate Intelligence Committees, Cofer Black, then head of the CIA Counterterrorist Center, spoke of the United States' new forms of "operational flexibility" in dealing with suspected terrorists: "This is a highly classified area. All I want to say is that there was 'before 9/11,' and 'after' 9/11. After 9/11 the gloves come off."[660]

THE ASSERTION OF A LEGAL BLACK HOLE AND AUTHORITY TO TORTURE

The Bush administration has asserted that neither the U.S. Constitution[661] nor the Geneva Conventions[662] nor international human rights law[663] apply to "enemy" or "unlawful combatants" in the "war on terror." In other words, according to the United States, these detainees exist in a legal "black hole." They are in a no-man's-land where the United States, and by implication its allies, are free to act outside the law or to pick and choose what parts of the law they will apply—as in the Military Orders and Instructions[664] for the detainees in Guantánamo Bay.

While there is some basis in United States jurisprudence to suggest that the U.S. Constitution does not apply to aliens outside the U.S.,[665] the Bush administration's assertions in respect to the Geneva Conventions and human rights obligations are false. Under the Geneva Conventions there is no such category as "enemy" or "unlawful" combatant. In armed conflict like the war in Afghanistan or the war in Iraq, all persons are covered under the Geneva Conventions either as "civilians" or "combatants."[666] In respect of human rights law, under the International Covenant on Civil and Political Rights (to which the United States is a signatory) states arguably bear obligations wherever they have jurisdiction.[667] Under the Convention Against Torture and Other Cruel, Inhuman, or Degrading Treatment or Punishment (to which the United States is a signatory) states are responsible for taking effective legislative, administrative, judicial, or other measures to prevent acts of torture in any territory under their jurisdiction.[668] Finally, it is clear that, under the customary international law of human rights the detainees have due process rights and protections against torture, arbitrary and prolonged detention, and extrajudicial killing.[669]

The Bush administration has repeatedly denied that it has a policy of torture or that it condones the torture of detainees. As President Bush himself told the media in June 2004, after the photographs of the abuse of prisoners at the Abu Ghraib prison in Iraq were released, "Let me make very clear the position of my government and our country. We do not condone torture. I have never ordered torture. I will never order torture. The values of this country are such that torture is not a part of our soul and our being."

Evidence proving the contrary beyond any possible doubt, countinues to mount daily, however.

Newsweek magazine has reported that after September 11, 2001,

President Bush signed a secret order authorizing the CIA to set up detention centers outside the United States and "to question those held in them with unprecedented harshness."[670]

According to *Newsweek*, agreements were then negotiated with foreign governments with respect to these sites, giving U.S. personnel and private contractors immunity for their actions there.[671]

Newspapers have also reported on a series of internal legal memoranda, collectively referred to as "the torture memos." These memoranda, some of which were leaked and some of which were made public by groups such as the New York University School of Law's Center on Law and Security, advise the Bush administration, in essence, on how to engage in practices of inhumane treatment and torture and how to justify or redefine the conduct. According to the *New Yorker*, most of the memoranda "were generated by a small hawkish group of politically appointed lawyers in the Justice Department's Office of Legal Counsel and in the office of Alberto Gonzales."[672] At the time the memoranda were written, Gonzales was White House legal counsel. Subsequently, he has been appointed by President Bush to be the attorney general of the United States.

A series of memoranda written in January 2002 by the Justice Department provided legal arguments to support Bush adminstration officials' assertions that detainees captured in the Afghan theater of war did not have to be treated in accordance with the Geneva Conventions, creating the new category not found in the Geneva Conventions—"illegal enemy combatant."[673]

An August 2002 memorandum signed by Attorney General Jay S. Bybee, defined torture as the intent to inflict suffering "equivalent in intensity to the pain accompanying serious physical injury, such as organ failure, impairment of bodily function, or even death." According to newspaper reports, the memorandum "also claimed that torture only occurs when the intent is to cause pain. If pain is used to gain information or a confession, that is not torture."[674] These definitions of torture, of course, do not accord with international law.[675] But a senior administration official is reported to have said that the memorandum's conclusions align closely with the prevailing White House view of interrogation practices.[676]

Another memorandum advised interrogators on how to shield themselves from liability under the Convention Against Torture and the federal Torture Act of 2000, by contending that prisoners were in the custody of another government and that U.S. officials were only receiving information from the other country's interrogations.[677]

A memorandum prepared by a Defense Department legal task force drew on earlier memos to declare that the president could override international treaty prohibitions and federal anti-torture law under his authority as commander in chief to approve any technique necessary to protect the nation's security. This, of course is the same theory that the Bush administration used to justify the secret NSA program; to insist that the president can control what information is revealed to Congress under the legislation renewing provisions in the PATRIOT Act; and to insist that he was not bound by the McCain amendment forbidding torture, which I will discuss more fully in a moment. The memorandum also stated that executive and military officials could be immune from domestic and international prohibitions against torture for a variety of reasons, including a belief by interrogators that they were acting on orders from superiors "except where the conduct went so far as to be patently unlawful."[678] This advice contradicts the Convention Against Torture, which states that "[n]o exceptional circumstances whatsoever . . . may be invoked as a justification of torture," and, in particular, that "[a]n order from a superior officer or a public authority may not be invoked as a justification of torture."[679]

According to the *New York Times*, "a secret memo issued by Administration lawyers authorized the CIA to use novel interrogation methods—including 'water-boarding,' in which a suspect is bound and immersed in water until he nearly drowns."[680]

In June 2004, U.S. Secretary of Defense Donald Rumsfeld admitted that, acting upon a request by George Tenet, then-director of the CIA, Rumsfeld had ordered an Iraqi national held in Camp Cropper, a high security detention center in Iraq, to be kept off the prison's rolls and not presented to the International Committee of the Red Cross. The prisoner, referred to as "Triple X," was reportedly a senior member of Ansar al-Islam, an organization apparently responsible for several attacks in Iraq and linked to Al-Qaeda. Rumsfeld also admitted that there have been other cases in which detainees have been held secretly.

Earlier, a U.S. Army investigation into the abuses of detainees at Abu Ghraib prison in Iraq sharply criticized this practice of keeping "ghost detainees." According to the report of Maj. Gen. Antonio Taguba:

The various detention facilities operated by the 800th MP Brigade have routinely held persons brought to them by Other Government Agencies (OGAs) [i.e. the CIA] without accounting for them, knowing their identities, or even the reason for their detention. The Joint Interrogation and Debriefing Center (JIDC) at Abu Ghraib called these detainees "ghost detainees." On at least one occasion, the 320th MP Battalion at Abu Ghraib held a handful of "ghost detainees" (6-8) for OGAs that they moved around within the facility to hide them from a visiting International Committee of the Red Cross (ICRC) survey team. *This maneuver was deceptive, contrary to Army Doctrine, and in violation of international law.*

Source: The United States' "Disappeared": The CIA's Long-Term "Ghost Detainees," Human Rights Watch Briefing Paper, October 2004: http://www.hrw.org/backgrounder/usa/us1004/.

A memorandum from Secretary of Defense Donald Rumsfeld to General James T. Hill of April 2003 outlined permitted interrogation techniques for detainees in U.S. custody, including stress and duress methods.[681]

Finally, an FBI e-mail released in December 2004 under a Freedom of Information Act request repeatedly referred to an executive order that permitted military interrogators in Iraq to place detainees in painful stress positions, to use hoods, to intimidate detainees with military dogs, and to use other coercive methods.[682]

After the Abu Ghraib scandal in Iraq, the August 2002 memorandum signed by Jay Bybee was formally rescinded by the Justice Department and replaced by a legal opinion that stated torture should be more broadly defined.[683] However, the Bush administration fought vigorously against legislative efforts to restrict the CIA. In early 2005, "Republican leaders, at the White House's urging, [blocked] two attempts in the Senate to ban the CIA from using cruel and inhumane interrogation methods. An attempt in the House to outlaw extraordinary rendition, led by Representative Markey, also failed."[684]

The administration also supported provisions[685] in the Republican House version of the 9-11 Recommendations Implementation Act (H.R. 10) that suspended U.S. obligations under the Convention Against Torture and authorized U.S. authorities, without judicial review, to send foreigners on "national security" grounds to any country that would accept them, even if they were likely to be tortured or abused there.[686] The provisions were retroactive, applying to anyone then in detention and anyone already deported or rendered to a country where they faced torture.[687] Where no country would accept an individual they provided for indefinite detention in the United States.[688] On the floor of the House, Representative Edward Markey decried, "It's outrageous that these provisions have been snuck into the 9-11 bill behind closed doors when the 9-11 Commission specifically called for the United States to 'offer an example of moral leadership in the world, committed to treat people humanely, abide by the law. . . .' Nothing could be further from the 9/11 Commission's intent."[689] In a push back against the White House, the provisions were defeated in the

House-Senate conference in December 2004, which settled the final version of the bill.[690]

MORE EVIDENCE OF AN INTENT TO TORTURE—THE McCAIN AMENDMENT

In October 2005, Republican Senator John McCain introduced an amendment to the defense appropriations bill that prohibited U.S. personnel from subjecting prisoners anywhere in the world to cruel, inhuman and degrading treatment. While the Senate approved the amendment ninety to nine, President Bush threatened to veto any legislation containing its language. The overwhelming support for the amendment in Congress, however, made it virtually veto-proof.[691] Vice President Dick Cheney fought hard to have the CIA exempted from the ban,[692] and at one point, the White House asked Congress to insert a presidential waiver to the restrictions contained in the amendment and was refused.[693] After a protracted stand-off, though, the president finally agreed to sign the bill with the amendment as introduced, in late December 2005.[694]

In signing the bill into law, however, the president inserted the following signing statement describing how the executive branch would interpret the amendment: "The executive branch shall construe Title X in Division A of the Act, relating to detainees [the McCain amendment regarding cruel, inhuman and degrading treatment], in a manner consistent with the constitutional authority of the President to supervise the unitary executive branch and as Commander in Chief and consistent with the constitutional limitations on the judicial power, which will assist in achieving the shared objective of the Congress and the President, evidenced in Title X, of protecting the American people from further terrorist attacks."[695]

Here again is the doctrine by which the administration justified its secret NSA domestic spying program, its right to ignore reporting provisions in the PATRIOT Act renewal legislation, and its right to ignore its international treaty obligations and federal laws prohibiting torture. Here again is the rationale of preemption, justifying just about anything when applied to foreign policy, security intelligence, law enforcement, and the exercise of government power.

After hearing of the signing statement while away on vacation, Senator McCain vowed to monitor the administration's compliance with the law closely and to see that Congress enforced it.[696] In the meantime, however, the Levin-Graham-Kyl amendment was passed in the 2006 defense appropriations bill. It made certain that no detainees could challenge their treatment in U.S. courts, severely undermining the McCain amendment.

And then in September 2006 McCain, himself, along with Senators John Warner and Lindsey Graham, made things even worse. In another abject example of Congress's incapacity to rein in the Bush administration, they brokered a deal with the administration on military commissions. In return for getting the administration to agree to have military commissions abide by the rules of courts martial in regard to secret evidence (which days after, the administration was already starting to wiggle out of), these three senators agreed to make evidence obtained by torture admissible; to give the president power to interpret the Geneva Conventions and U.S. law implementing them; to give U.S. officials amnesty for any war crimes committed in the last nine years; and to give the president power to declare almost anyone, anywhere in the world, an enemy combatant, and to detain them indefinitely. Moreover, nailing down the earlier Levin-Graham-Kyl amendment, the senators agreed to prohibit detainees from bringing habeas corpus challenges to their indefinite detention in U.S. courts.[697] This was significant, since, like the earlier Levin-Graham-Kyl amendment, the agreement flew in the face of the U.S. Supreme Court's decision in *Rasul v. Bush*, which affirmed detainees' rights to habeas corpus before American courts. Most detainees currently held by the U.S. are facing indefinite detention, since the Bush administration plans to bring only a score of detainees to trial before its military commissions.

The bill passed in the House of Representatives and the Senate in September 2006. In its final form, it looked a lot like the original White House draft. It included a narrow definition of torture "that was a virtual reprise of the deeply cynical memos" on torture that the administration's lawyers had produced.[698] On October 18, 2006 the President signed it into law.[699] So that in the end, the administration got almost everything it wanted from Congress.

TORTURE COMMITTED BY U.S. PERSONNEL

Diliwar[700] was a twenty-two-year-old Afghani whose family had bought him a used Toyota sedan to drive in order to make a living as a taxi driver. Days after he set out to begin his new career in his "prized possession," his mother asked him to gather his three sisters from their nearby villages in order to celebrate the Muslim holiday of Id al-Fitr. Diliwar needed money for gas, however, and so he drove to the town of Khost to pick up some fares there. He found three men headed back his way, and on the journey they passed a base where American troops were stationed, called Camp Salerno. It had been hit with a rocket attack that morning. Afghani militiamen stopped the taxi at a checkpoint and found a broken walkie-talkie belonging to one of the passengers and an electric stabilizer used to regulate current from a generator. Diliwar and his passengers were detained and turned over to the American troops.

The passengers were eventually flown to Guantánamo Bay and detained there for more than a year until they were sent back to Afghanistan with letters stating they posed "no threat" to the United States. Diliwar was not so lucky.

When Diliwar was hit by American soldiers, he would cry out, "Allah! Allah! Allah!" "Everybody heard him cry out and thought it was funny," Specialist Corey E. Jones told investigators. "It became a kind of running joke, and people kept showing up to give this detainee a common peroneal strike just to hear him scream out 'Allah.' It went on over a twenty-four-hour period, and I would think it was over one-hundred strikes."

After a while, Diliwar's screaming began to annoy the soldiers. He was kept chained up by his wrists to the top of his cell for most of four days between interrogations in which he was kicked mercilessly, shoved, shouted at, and humiliated by a female soldier.

At his final interrogation, an interpreter who was present noticed that Diliwar's legs were bouncing uncontrollably and that his hands were numb. Diliwar begged the soldiers for water. One of them punched a hole in the bottom of a bottle of water and offered it to Diliwar. As he "fumbled weakly" to unscrew the cap of the bottle, the water poured out over his orange overalls. Then the soldier snatched the bottle back and began squirting the remaining water hard, into Diliwar's face.

They tried to force Diliwar to his knees, but his mashed up legs could no longer bend. "Leave him up" the leader ordered as Diliwar was finally dragged back to his cell. Hanging alone, shackled from the ceiling, Diliwar died soon after.

One of the coroners later said that the tissue of Diliwar's legs "had basically been pulpified. I've seen similar injuries in an individual run over by a bus."

A sergeant, speaking voluntarily to interrogators almost two years later, added the final chilling detail about Diliwar's ordeal: most of the interrogators had believed he was innocent.

Evidence of torture committed by U.S. personnel is extensive. In U.S. detention centers, prisoners have been doused with cold water and subjected to freezing temperatures,[701] beaten,[702] denied medical treatment,[703] subjected to severe sleep deprivation,[704] bound in awkward, painful positions for hours,[705] blindfolded and thrown against walls,[706] forced off bridges,[707] subjected to loud continuous music and noises,[708] shot,[709] asphyxiatied,[710] "water-boarded,"[711] had their seven- and nine-year-old sons picked up to induce them to talk,[712] been covered with their own urine,[713] been strangled,[714] had lighted cigarettes put in their ears,[715] been chained in the fetal position for twenty-four hours or more,[716] humiliated by female personnel,[717] bitten by dogs,[718] banged headfirst repeatedly into doors,[719] forced to sodomize themselves,[720] held naked for long periods,[721] and thrown on top of each other and jumped on.[722] As of the end of February 2006, nearly one hundred prisoners had died in U.S. custody in Iraq and Afghanistan alone, with at least thirty-four of these suspected or confirmed as homicides.[723]

A review of this record, alongside the memoranda, executive orders, legislative developments, and presidential signing statements described earlier, show that Diliwar's story and the revelations at the Abu Ghraib prison in Iraq, which shocked the conscience of the American people in 2004, were by no means isolated phenomena. On the contrary, they were part of a wider system of abuse fostered, if not sanctioned, by the top levels of the U.S. government.

The Plan to Build Permanent Prisons outside the United States

Michael Scheuer, a counterterrorism expert with the CIA until 2004, helped establish the practice of rendition. In an interview he pointed to the folly of the whole project: "Are we going to hold these people forever? Once a detainee's rights have been violated you absolutely can't reinstate him into the court system. You can't kill him either. All we've done is create a nightmare."[724]

"A senior U.S. official told the *New York Times* in January 2005 that three quarters of the 550 prisoners then at Guantánamo Bay no longer had any intelligence of value. But they would not be released out of concern that they posed a continuing threat to the U.S."[725]

In January 2005, the *Washington Post* and other newspapers broke the story that the U.S. government was thinking of building jails in foreign countries, "mainly ones with grim human rights records, to which it [could] secretly transfer detainees (unconvicted by any court) for the rest of their lives . . . beyond the scrutiny of the International Committee of the Red Cross, or any other independent observers or lawyers."[726]

One proposal is for the United States to build new prisons in Afghanistan, Saudi Arabia, and Yemen. Those countries would run the prisons, but U.S. officials would have access to "monitor human rights compliance."[727] As of March 2005, the United States had already transferred sixty-five detainees from Guantánamo Bay to other countries, including Pakistan, Morocco, France, Russia, and Saudi Arabia so that they can be either prosecuted (an unlikely prospect) or detained indefinitely. The Defense Department has also asked Congress for funds to build a new prison at Guantánamo Bay, since, officials say, any remnant population of detainees that could not be transferred to other countries would likely be held there indefinitely since charges will never be brought against them.[728]

MURDER AND ASSASSINATION BY U.S. PERSONNEL

In Chapter 11, I discussed the expansion by the United States of covert military special operations around the world. These teams are charged with locating, capturing, and/or killing terrorist suspects and using the intelligence gained in one operation to plan another.

The White House has also charged the CIA to conduct covert operations in the "war on terror." On September 17, 2001, Bush signed a "presidential finding" authorizing the action and giving the agency permission to "kill, capture and detain members of al Qaeda anywhere in the world."[729]

The day after the attacks of September 11, 2001, the CIA's Counterterrorism Center (CTC) had a list of "High Value Targets" in Al Qaeda, to which names were added as the 9/11 investigation unfolded. According to the *Washington Post*, "The CTC chief of operations argued for creating hit teams of case officers and CIA paramilitaries that would covertly infiltrate countries in the Middle East, Africa and even Europe to assassinate people on the list, one by one. . . . But many CIA officers believed that the al Qaeda leaders would be worth keeping alive to interrogate about their networks and other plots. Some officers worried that the CIA was not very adept at assassination."[730]

Assassination was ruled out by the CIA and its masters as a main strategy in the "war on terror" in favor of the secret, indefinite detention of terrorist suspects. But the stories of assassination operations in Yemen and Pakistan show that it has still been reserved as an option.

And so has the murder of innocent civilians who get in the way.

THE PARTICIPATION OF OTHER WESTERN DEMOCRACIES

Western democracies, my own country Canada included, love to paint a picture of themselves defending democracy and human rights in the rest of the world. Yet the new paradigm of a global pool of detainees held and transferred between centers around the world and accessible to the security agencies of the United States and its allies in the "war on terror," is not the policy of the United States alone. It is a policy that is being embraced, acquiesced to, or made use of by many of its Western democratic allies.

The UK allows the CIA to operate one of its extraterritorial detention centers on the British island of Diego Garcia. The Swedes have allowed U.S., UK, and German agencies to question suspects held in Sweden[731] and have cooperated in the rendition of two asylum applicants from Sweden to Egypt by U.S. agents. Evidence shows that these individuals were tortured there. One was subsequently released, and one was sentenced to twenty-five years' imprisonment by a military court that did not meet international standards for fair trial.[732] In Canada, there are the stories of Maher Arar, Abdullah Almalki, Ahamd El Maati, Muayyed Nurredin, and Kassim Mohamed. In Britain there is the story of Wahab al-Rawi.

While in a few cases, Western governments or agencies have protested the kidnapping of their nationals by United States agents, the protests have either been disingenuous or have not affected relations with the U.S. to any great extent. The case of Maher Arar prompted Prime Minister Jean Chretién's successor, Paul Martin, to seek an assurance from President Bush that Canada would be notified the next time the United States wanted to render a Canadian to a foreign dungeon. While spun by the government as "talking tough" with the Americans to defend Canadian sovereignty, the deal was, in fact, hypocritical and rather pathetic—next time, if we're not involved ourselves, they'll tell us when the CIA plane takes off. In early 2006, Canada was accused by human rights groups of "running interference" for the United States by working hard to dilute key provisions of a new United Nations treaty on forced disappearances.[733]

In Germany, the government has been investigating the El Masri case, but there have been no ramifications yet in terms of Germany's support for the U.S.-led war on terrorism.

In Italy, where CIA agents dressed as Italian police abducted Muslim cleric Hassan Mustafa Nasr on the streets in Milan, spraying him with chemicals, bundling him into a van, and flying him from Venice to a U.S. base in Germany and thence to Egypt, prosecutors have issued arrest warrants for twenty-two CIA agents.[734] At the time of his disappearance, Italian authorities had been investigating Nasr, and they were not at all pleased to find him whisked out of the country. Nasr was reportedly tortured in Egypt and then briefly released. Since then, he has disappeared again.[735] While Italian police and prosecutors may not have known that Nasr was about to be whisked away by the CIA, security experts say that is likely that the Italian government knew of the rendition and had an understanding with the U.S. government.[736] The STRATFOR corporation says that this "is often part of the agreement between the United States and foreign governments for permission to carry out renditions in their territory. In exchange, the host country can be expected to deny knowledge of the rendition and feign outrage when it comes to light, thereby minimizing the political fallout."[737] This would explain why, despite the prosecutions brought by independent prosecutors, there has been no cooling of Italian-U.S. relations over the affair—at least on the Italian side.[738]

Concerned parliaments in Sweden, Canada, Italy, France, and the Netherlands have forced governments to establish inquiries into the rendition of their citizens or residents. But whether these inquiries will be able to penetrate the secrecy their governments want to maintain will be interesting to see. In Canada, Justice Dennis O'Connor, the respected and experienced judge who conducted the "public" inquiry into the role of Canadian officials in Maher Arar's rendition, has been prevented from disclosing summaries of evidence in the case, as well as portions of his report, released in September 2006. In a departure from the usual practice used when showing redacted information, the government used asterisks rather than blacked out words in the O'Connor report.

In late 2005, news started breaking in Canada and a number of European countries about stopovers of CIA rendition flights. The *Guardian* reported that CIA aircraft had flown into and out of British airports at least 210 times since September 11, 2001.[739] The *Toronto Star* reported in January 2006 that at least 55 CIA "ghost flights" had passed through Canada.[740] Spanish police began investigating reports of CIA rendition flights out of the Palma de Mallorca airport.[741] James Risen, National security reporter for the *New York Times*, has said that the flights are operating with the complicity of the host governments. In the case of Canada, he said, the

Canadian Security Intelligence Service and the prime minister "would have approved the use of Canadian airspace, but kept other government agencies in the dark."[742]

In December 2005, just before leaving on her state visit to the EU, U.S. Secretary of State Condoleezza Rice told reporters that "the United States does not use the air space or airport of any country for the purpose of transporting a detainee when we believe he or she will be tortured. With respect to detainees, the United States government complies with its laws, its Constitution and its treaty obligations. . . . The United States has fully respected the sovereignty of other countries that have cooperated in these matters."[743]

Whether one believes Western governments are cooperating with the United States in its rendition program or not, it is clear that many of them, including the governments of Austria, Canada, Germany, Sweden, Turkey, and the UK, have themselves sought to deport terrorist suspects to countries where torture is a widespread or a systemic problem, including Egypt, the Philippines, Russia, Sri Lanka, Syria, and Uzbekistan.[744]

NEW LICENSE FOR BRUTAL REGIMES

At the same time, regimes whose human rights abuses have, in the past, elicited sharp criticism from Western governments are now being tolerated, supported, and even bolstered by those governments.

Since it launched its military campaign in Chechnya, Russia's leaders have characterized the armed conflict there as counterterrorism, glossing over the political aspects of it. But world leaders were critical of the gross human rights abuses of the Russian operation, which have included the indiscriminate bombing of civilian populations, village massacres, disappearances, mass arbitrary detentions, and torture. Weeks after the 9/11 attacks, however, democratic leaders like German Chancellor Gerhard Schroeder and Italy's

Prime Minister Silvio Berlusconi were saying that they would have to judge Russian operations in Chechnya differently.[745]

In Egypt, governments have ruled under an emergency law continuously since 1981 and have routinely used their authority under the law to "arrest people at will and detain them without trial for prolonged periods, refer civilians to military or exceptional state security courts, and prohibit strikes, demonstrations, and public meetings." On the extension of the law in February 2003, a U.S. State Department spokesperson stated that the United States "under[stood] and appreciate[d] the Egyptian government's commitment to combat terrorism and maintain stability."[746]

In Georgia, where operations against Chechen rebels in the Pankisi Gorge have been brutal, involving extrajudicial execution, disappearances, arbitrary detention, and discrimination on the basis of racial and ethnic identity, the United States has established a $64 million "Train and Equip" program "to strengthen Georgia's counter-terrorism capability." At least six U.S. military personnel were present in Georgia as of October 2002 to provide training.[747] *Time* magazine has reported that Georgian operatives have "disappeared" and killed suspects based on "real-time intelligence" provided by the United States Georgian officials have also admitted to the secret and extralegal rendition of individuals into United States custody.[748]

In Indonesia, the United States has renewed its links with the Indonesian military, which had been cut after the violence orchestrated by that military in East Timor in 1999. After September 11, 2001, the U.S. military training program was reinstated and a new $50 million program announced to assist Indonesian security forces in their counterterrorism efforts. In December 2002, a Kuwaiti citizen married to an Indonesian woman was arrested "and handed over to the U.S. authorities as part of an intelligence operation involving Indonesia's intelligence service and the CIA."[749]

In Malaysia, nearly one hundred men have been held for alleged links to terrorist groups under the country's draconian Internal

Security Act (ISA)—some for more than three years.[750] Prior to 9/11, the U.S. government had been extremely critical of the Malaysian government's detentions of opponents under the ISA, and relations between the two countries were strained.[751] Since then, U.S. officials have praised the detentions[752] and President Bush has referred to the country as a "beacon of stability."[753] The United States has helped Malaysia to set up the Southeast Asia Regional Center for Counterterrorism and provided training there for Malaysian government officials.[754] "The Malaysian government regularly shares intelligence information with the U.S. government, and has offered the U.S. access to detainees in Malaysia. When the U.S. interrogated thirteen Malaysian students detained without trial in Karachi, Pakistan, in September 2003, the Malaysian government remained silent rather than protest the detentions."[755] When the thirteen returned to Malaysia, the government detained them.[756] Detainees who have refused to cooperate with security officials in Malaysia have been told that they could be transferred to U.S. custody in Guantánamo Bay, Cuba.[757]

Former British ambassador to Uzbekistan, Craig Murray, has claimed that U.S. agents sent detainees from Afghanistan to that country to be interrogated using torture. Murray was removed from his post after sending a memo to the British foreign minister in which he reported that the CIA station chief in Tashkent had "readily acknowledged torture was deployed [in Uzbekistan] in obtaining intelligence [from U.S. suspects]."[758] In Uzbekistan, Murray has stated, the "partial boiling of a hand or an arm is quite common [in interrogation]."[759] "I have seen postmortem photos of a corpse. These show that the person was boiled to death."[760]

In Latin America, the United States has intensified its support of the Colombian military in order to help it win a four-decade-old war against the leftist Revolutionary Armed Forces of Colombia (FARC) and the National Liberation Army (ELN).[761] The head of the U.S.

Southern Command told a congressional panel in March 2004 that Washington "must take comprehensive measures in our region to combat terrorism" including, he said, strengthening Latin American militaries. He also suggested that Latin American countries should be encouraged to break down legal barriers between civilian policing, intelligence functions, and military functions.[762] Latin American militaries, in the past, have been responsible for some of the worst human rights abuses in the region.

Brutal or repressive regimes have been quick to point to the current practices of the United States to justify their own practices. The Liberian government claimed that an editor of one of Liberia's independent newspapers whom it had arrested could be held incommunicado and tried before a military court since he was an "illegal combatant" involved an Islamic fundamentalist war.[763] Egypt's President Mubarak has said, "There is no doubt that the events of September 11 created a new concept of democracy that differs from the concept that Western states defended before these events, especially with regard to freedom of the individual." The U.S. decision to authorize the use of military tribunals in its "war on terror," he said, "proves that we were right from the beginning in using all means, including military tribunals."

CHAPTER FIFTEEN

Illusions of Security

◎ ◎

Those who would give up essential liberty to purchase a little temporary safety deserve neither liberty nor safety.
—attributed to Benjamin Franklin

The global surveillance initiatives that governments have embarked upon do not make us more secure. They only create illusions of security. Illusions that do little to catch or stop terrorists and that ensnare the innocent, divert resources away from better initiatives, obscure our public policy debates, and betray our real personal and collective security.

LESS THAN A LITTLE TEMPORARY SAFETY

Sifting through an ocean of flawed information with a net of bias and faulty logic, the initiatives described in this book yield a tidal wave of false leads and useless information. The information used will never be fully accurate, contextualized, and complete; the biometrics will never be foolproof; and the predictive judgments made about individuals, whether by human or artificial intelligence, will never be reliable. But even if they were, they would provide less than a little temporary safety from terrorist attacks.

There is a widely held public opinion that governments should have known about and prevented the 9/11 plot. In fact, the traditional systems of intelligence and law enforcement that were in place at the time *did* yield information about the likelihood of an attack on U.S. soil by Muslim extremists using airplanes, and some of the key players in the 9/11 attacks were under investigation by the CIA and FBI before the events.[764] The Joint Inquiry into the circumstances surrounding the 9/11 attacks conducted by the U.S. Senate and House intelligence committees reported that while the intelligence community did not have information on the "time, place and specific nature" of the 9/11 attacks, it had "amassed a great deal of valuable intelligence" that warned of the attacks.[765] The community's failure, according to the Joint Inquiry, was its inability "to discern the bigger picture . . . to capitalize on both the individual and collective significance of available information. . . . No one will ever know what might have happened had more connections been drawn between these disparate pieces of information. . . . The important point is that the Intelligence Community, for a variety of reasons, did not bring together and fully appreciate a range of information that could have greatly enhanced its chances of uncovering and preventing Usama bin Ladin's plan to attack these United States on September 11, 2001."[766]

If U.S. agencies could not "see the forest for the trees" when they had specific information about a specific kind of threat and specific individuals, would it have helped them to sift through information on the lives of hundreds of millions of people?

If there was failure in communication or analysis on the part of U.S. security agencies, there was also political failure on the part of the White House. While the Bush administration refuses to reveal what it was briefed about and when, prior to the attacks, sources indicate that it was briefed,[767] and the record shows that it took no steps to heighten security in appropriate areas.

Under Attorney General John Ashcroft, the FBI's counterterrorism program faced pressures for funding cuts. Despite the numerous intelligence warnings about the importance of the Al Qaeda threat, the CIA unit focusing on bin Laden could not get the funding it needed. Lieutenant General Michael V. Hayden, director of the National Security Agency (NSA) and chief of Central Security Service from March 1999 to May 2005, said that he knew in 2001 that the NSA needed to improve its coverage of Al Qaeda but that he was unable to obtain the resources for that effort.[768]

Neither bureaucratic failure nor the failure of political leadership would have been improved in any way by mass surveillance of the whole population. The 9/11 experience itself shows that authorities had enough trouble appreciating the significance of the specific, relevant information they did have. They did not need the ocean of general, irrelevant information they are now collecting, and very possibly they would have drowned in it altogether.

Since the president's secret NSA program started trawling through the international calls and e-mails made and received by Americans, the FBI has been complaining that the flood of telephone numbers, e-mail addresses, and names it is receiving from the NSA has been swamping investigators, requiring hundreds of them to track down thousands of tips each month. Officials, including those who knew about the secret program, said that the torrent of tips led them to few suspects they did not already know about inside the country and "diverted agents from counterterrorism work they viewed as more productive. . . . We'd chase a number, find it's a school teacher with no indication they've ever been involved in international terrorism—case closed," said one former FBI official, who was aware of the program and the data it generated for the bureau. "After you get a thousand numbers and not one is turning up anything, you get some frustration."[769]

On the other side of the fence, private-sector banks have been complaining that their onerous new obligations to report to government are undermining efforts to deter terrorist financing. In a January 2005 letter to the Treasury Department, banking officials said that because of the heavy penalties for failing to report and the lack of clarity about what is to be reported, "many banks, now in a defensive mode, are sending the government far more reports than ever before on 'suspicious activities' by their customers—and potentially clogging the system with irrelevant data—for fear of being penalized if they fail to file the reports as required."[770] "'Law enforcement is shooting the messenger', said Herbert A. Bierne, a senior enforcement official with the Federal Reserve System's board of governors. 'You shoot the messenger, you stop getting the messages.'"[771]

At the same time that the new global, mass surveillance initiatives threaten to overwhelm authorities in a sea of information, the dragnet they create is easily circumvented by determined terrorists who are either not known to authorities or who use identity theft or false identities to evade them. Sophisticated terrorist groups often look for "clean skins" who have no criminal records or known terrorist associations to commit their attacks. And, as long as technology and procedures exist to create identity documents, means to evade them will also exist. Several of the big database companies on which the mass surveillance project relies have had major security breaches within the last few years. Hackers breaching the security of the Seisint division of LexisNexis stole from the MATRIX the personal information, including social security numbers and driver's license details, of 310,000 individuals.[772] Thieves posing as legitimate businesses accessed the personal records of 35,000 individuals stored in the databases of ChoicePoint, a company that, as mentioned earlier, maintains background information on virtually every U.S. citizen and sells it to the private sector and thirty-five government agencies including the FBI.[773] Hackers also broke into the Arkansas file server of Acxiom, the world's largest collector and processor of personal data, twice in 2004, copying the records of millions of individuals. Acxiom cooperated closely with the FBI in the wake of the 9/11 attacks, has participated in research with the Pentagon and other U.S. agencies regarding the sharing, linkage, and consolidation of data, and as mentioned earlier, received the main contract for the CAPPS II program.[774]

Finally, the more states rely on one biometric identity document as the gold standard for identifying individuals, the easier it will be for terrorists and others to breach security once they obtain the document. Speaking about a proposed "trusted traveler" ID card system, security expert Bruce Schneier has suggested that identity documents, and particularly voluntary documents, arbitrarily create two categories of people, "trusted people with a card" and "less trusted people without a card," as well as a third category: "bad guys with a card."[775]

THE DIVERSION OF RESOURCES

In terms of countering terrorism, the global surveillance dragnet diverts crucial resources and efforts away from the kind of investments that *would* make people safer. There are many things that we can responsibly do to decrease the risk and consequences of terrorist attacks, including protecting critical infrastructure, controlling nuclear and biochemical materials, screening baggage and containers for electronic devices and radioactivity, locking cockpits and putting air marshals on planes, and improving our first-response systems. In terms of ferreting out terrorists, however, what is required is good information about specific threats, not crude racial profiling and useless information on the nearly 100 percent of the population that poses no threat whatsoever.

Good information about specific threats is usually obtained through human not technological intelligence, by agents capable of infiltrating the circles where these threats exist. As security experts admitted in the aftermath of 9/11, these were the kind of critical resources that were lacking in U.S. security agencies at that time. There was a dearth of agents who possessed the background and languages relevant to the threat and a dearth of agents on the ground collecting human intelligence. Even translators were lacking. The Al Qaeda messages that were reportedly intercepted by the

NSA on September 10, 2001 ("Tomorrow is zero hour," "The match is about to begin"), were not translated until days later. Three years after the attacks, more than 120,000 hours of recorded telephone calls had yet to be translated by the FBI.[776]

Moreover, the global surveillance dragnet alienates the very communities from whom intelligence agencies currently need assistance, making it difficult to get crucial tips from them and difficult to recruit the law-enforcement and intelligence officers needed from their ranks. The racial profiling that is endemic to the dragnet approach harasses and targets these communities wholesale. Ronald Noble, the black American who runs the 181-nation Interpol agency, says he himself has been singled out when traveling because of his looks: "I perspire and I'm the head on an international law enforcement agency. . . . You have a lot of abuses that are never, ever checked."[777]

Surveillance does nothing to address what many say are the root causes of terrorism—dispossession, poverty, lack of opportunity, and political repression. Despite claims that it is spreading democracy around the world, the U.S. foreign policy gives more support than ever to repressive regimes. And U.S. foreign aid is declining while military expenditures are rocketing. In 2000, the United States spent $281 billion on the military. Under Bush's 2007 budget request submitted in February 2006, Pentagon spending will rise to almost $440 billion, not including the $120 billion that the administration is asking for as a supplement to fund military operations in Iraq and Afghanistan through September 2006. Compare that to the proposed budget for aid, which will remain at $24 billion, equal to what the Bush administration spends in Iraq every five months. And consider that the president is calling for a 20 percent reduction in development aid and similar cuts in disaster assistance and child survival and health programs. Meanwhile, some $6.2 billion are earmarked for the security apparatuses of states that are considered key strategic allies in the "war on terror." There is no new support for democracy promotion and other institutional initiatives meant to strengthen states and make them more responsive to their citizens.[778]

Despite Western governments' enormous spending on counterterrorism initiatives, nonstate terrorism is a statistically *insignificant* threat to people's security in most countries around the world. Annual State Department reports mandated by Congress provide relatively reliable annual figures on the total number of terrorist attacks and the total numbers of deaths and injuries caused by them for the years 1995 to 2003. Summarized below,[779] they show that the "mean" number of deaths each year has been in the hundreds. The average number, including the 9/11 attack figures, is 774.

YEAR	ACTS	KILLED	WOUNDED
2004	NA	NA	NA
2003	208	625	3646
2002	199	725	2013
2001	346	3547	1080
2000	423	405	791
1999	392	233	706
1998	273	741	5952
1997	304	221	693
1996	296	311	2652
1995	440	165	6291

The reports were discontinued in their numerical form in 2004 amid controversy that the numbers for that year had been inflated.[780] Numerical reporting was then taken over by the U.S. National Counterterrorism Center (NCTC), which reported 11,111 attacks and 14,600 deaths (the highest recorded) for the year 2005. These numbers are probably grossly inflated, since they include insurgent attacks in Iraq and attacks by insurgent groups like the Revolutionary Armed Forces of Colombia (FARC) in Columbia and the Lord's Resistance

Army in Uganda. Also, a majority of the reported deaths occurred in Iraq alone (thanks, many would say, to U.S. policies there).[781]

While no death caused by terrorism is acceptable, the figures, even when inflated, are small compared to the approximately 1.2 million deaths and 48 million injuries caused by car accidents each year,[782] They are *miniscule* compared to the number of deaths and human misery caused globally by *starvation*, *war*, *disease*, *lack of health care*, *environmental catastrophes*, and *ordinary crime*.

THE BETRAYAL OF OUR REAL SECURITY

The "hook" politicians use to peddle their counterterrorism measures is that "guaranteeing security is the paramount responsibility of governments." With this simple idea, they have succeeded for too long in obscuring public policy debate.

When I think back to those days of the 9/11 carnage and the anthrax scare we lived through as a family in New York, I feel how seductively simple that equation is: "Give up some of your civil liberties, temporarily, to save your lives." Very soon, however, first as a lawyer, then as a citizen, I began to realize that there was something greater at stake than even our temporary safety. I watched as my profession perverted important legal principles and the rule of law itself for political masters, and I sensed as a citizen that the way of life my forefathers and mothers had fought for hung in a balance.

Democratic institutions and rights are the bulwark of real personal and collective security, as we the people should know only too well from the long and bitter struggles that have been required to attain them in most countries. They keep us secure in our homes, secure in our persons, secure in our freedoms and our polity. They protect us from oppression, tyranny and unnecessary wars. They constitute, as Benjamin Franklin might say, our *essential* liberty. Without them, I have come to understand in an almost visceral way, we can be neither safe nor free.

Globalized, mass surveillance and the preemptive model of security that promotes it threaten our essential liberty. They create a world in which we can, at any time, be blacklisted; dragged out of a line, our office, or our homes; presumed guilty; detained; tortured; not told the charges against us; denied the right to face our accusers; denied the right to know the evidence against us and the criteria by which we are being judged; and given no legal recourse and no one to advocate for us. Today, it is Muslims and immigrants among us who are most in danger, but tomorrow, new groups could easily be targeted.

Mass surveillance and the preemptive model of security also threaten our lives by exacerbating global insecurity. The West's unjust targeting and stereotyping of Muslims, combined with its rhetoric about a "clash of civilizations" and collusion with repressive regimes—and the brutal, lawless treatment meted out to civilian populations and detainees—engender hatred against Western countries and their partners, fomenting only more insurgent opposition and terrorism. The new doctrine of preemptive war advocated by the neoconservative forces in the United States, moreover, threatens to unleash an era of unimaginable violence and disorder.

Today we do, indeed, stand at a crossroads. A crossroads between instinct and understanding. A crossroads between what we can responsibly do to protect ourselves from terrorist violence and what we cannot afford to do. Now, more than ever, we as citizens must determine which path our governments take.

Our future depends on it.

Notes

◉ ◉

Note: Dates in square brackets after on-line addresses refer to the most recent dates the Web sites or on-line documents were accessed.

Prologue

1. Kerry Pither, *The Deportation and Imprisonment of Maher Arar: Chronology of Events, December 20, 2001 to September 23, 2003*, April 29, 2003 entry. http://www.maherarar.ca .cms.images.uploads/mahersstory.pdf. [Kerry Pither]
2. Jeff Sallot, "PM vows help for Canadian held in Syria: Questions still linger about RCMP connection," *Globe & Mail*, June 25, 2003, cited in Kerry Pither, *supra* note 1. [Jeff Sallot, "PM vows help for Canadian held in Syria: questions still linger about RCMP connection"]
3. Robert Fife, "Al-qaeda targeted U.S. Embassy: Syrian tip led to arrest of accused terrorists planning Ottawa attack," *National Post*, July 25, 2003, cited in Kerry Pither, *supra* note 1.
4. Robert Fife, "RCMP didn't turn in Arar U.S. says: Embassy statement conflicts with claims by Powell, Cellucci," *National Post*, August 1, 2003, cited in Kerry Pither, *supra* note 1.
5. Ibid.
6. Public Statement by Syrian Ambassador to Canada Ahmad Arnous, dated October 16, 2003, cited in Kerry Pither, *supra* note 1.
7. Letter from Monia Mazigh to U.S. Ambassador Paul Cellucci, dated April 28, 2003, cited in Kerry Pither, *supra* note 1.
8. Letter from U.S. Ambassador Paul Cellucci to Monia Mazigh, dated May 27, 2003, cited in Kerry Pither, *supra* note 1.
9. Gwynne Dyer, *Future Tense: The Coming World Order* (Toronto: McClelland & Stewart, 2004), p. 152.
10. Ibid.
11. Ibid., p. 151.
12. Ibid.
13. See Noam Chomsky, *Power and Terror: Post 9/11 Talks and Interviews*, ed. John Junkerman and Takei Masakazu (New York: Seven Stories Press, 2003).

Chapter One

14. Transcript of June 29, 2005 testimony of Sergeant Mike Cabana before the Commission of Inquiry into the Actions of Canadian Officials in Relation to Maher Arar, p. 7880.

15. Kerry Pither, *Abdullah Almalki Chronology,* October 11, 2001, entry. http://www.mun.ca/serg/almalkichronology.pdf. [Kerry Pither, *Almalki Chronology*]
16. Ibid.
17. Ibid.
18. Ibid., citing documents released by the Arar Commission of Inquiry.
19. Cabana testimony, *supra* note 14, p. 7785.
20. Cabana testimony, *supra* note 14, p. 7782.
21. Cabana testimony, *supra* note 14, p. 7787.
22. Cabana testimony, *supra* note 14, pp. 7785–86.
23. Cabana testimony, *supra* note 14, pp. 7911 and 7915. One meeting, of May 31, 2002, was held in the United States.
24. Cabana testimony, *supra* note 14, p. 7907.
25. Michael den Tandt, "9/11 crisis led to RCMP to share its secrets," *Globe & Mail*, June 30, 2005. See also Cabana testimony, *supra* note 14, p. 7907.
26. Cabana testimony, *supra* note 14, p. 7888.
27. Commission of Inquiry into the Actions of Canadian Officials in Relation to Maher Arar, *Report of the Events Relating to Maher Arar: Analysis and Recommendations* (Ottawa: Her Majesty the Queen in Right of Canada, 2006) pp. 24–25 (released September 18, 2006). [Arar Commission Report]
28. Cabana testimony, *supra* note 14, p. 7880.
29. Arar Commission Report, *supra* note 27, p. 28.
30. Ibid., p. 28.
31. Cabana testimony, *supra* note 14, p. 7958.
32. Cabana testimony, *supra* note 14, p. 7995. See also, CBC news story, "U.S. offered to return Arar to Canada, inquiry hears," June 1, 2005.
33. Cabana testimony, *supra* note 14, p. 7985.
34. Cabana, testimony, *supra* note 14, pp. 7962–86.
35. Commission of Inquiry into the Actions of Canadian Officials in relation to Maher Arar, Summary of Information Received at *In Camera* Hearings, December 20, 2004, para. 19. [Arar Inquiry Summary of Information]
36. Statement given by Maher Arar to the Canadian people on November 4, 2003. http://www.maherarar.ca/cms/images/uploads/Maher_statement_nov4.pdf. [Arar Statement]
37. Commission of Inquiry into the Actions of Canadian Officials in relation to Maher Arar, Report of Professor Stephen J. Toope, Fact Finder, October 14, 2005, p. 13. [Toope Report]
38. Arar Statement, *supra* note 36.
39. Cabana testimony, *supra* note 14, p. 7949 and 7962.
40. Arar Statement, *supra* note 36.
41. In respect of the October 17, 2002, questions, see Garvie Report, pp. 28–29. But compare with Arar Commission Report, p. 200. In respect of the January 15, 2003, set of questions, see Arar Commission Report, pp. 206-214.
42. Cabana testimony, *supra* note 14, p. 8032.
43. Toope Report, *supra* note 37, p. 13.
44. James Travers, "How CSIS botched Arar file," *Toronto Star*, June 9, 2005.
45. Arar Inquiry Summary of Information, *supra* note 35, para. 33.
46. Ibid.
47. Neco Cockburn, "MP blasts RCMP, CSIS for Arar's treatment," *Ottawa Citizen*, June 1, 2005.

48. Robert Fife, "CIA foiled Al- Qaeda plot to attack Ottawa," *CanWest News Service*, July 25, 2003, cited in Kerry Pither, *supra* note 1.
49. Seymour Hersh, "The Syrian Bet," *The New Yorker,* July 28, 2003, issue. [Seymour Hersh, "The Syrian Bet"]
50. "No Al-Qaida plot in Canada: RCMP," *Canadian Press*, July 25, 2003, cited in Kerry Pither, *supra* note 1.
51. Jeff Sallot and Colin Freeze, "It was hyped as a TERRORIST map. It was cited by Egyptian Torturers. It is a VISITOR'S GUIDE to Ottawa," *Globe & Mail*, September 6, 2005. [Jeff Sallot and Colin Freeze, "It was hyped as a TERRORIST map"]
52. Heather Sokoloff, "Criticized for slowness: Graham to thank Britain for speeding prisoners' release," *National Post*, August 9, 2003, cited in Kerry Pither, *supra* note 1.
53. Cabana testimony, *supra* note 14, pp. 7872, 8029–30; Michelle Shephard, "Envoy says he doubted Arar's story," *Toronto Star*, June 15, 2005. [Michelle Shephard, "Envoy says he doubted Arar's story"]
54. Kerry Pither, *supra* note 1, August 18, 2003, entry.
55. Irwin Cotler, "Six steps to freedom: What Canada must do to secure justice for Maher Arar," *Globe & Mail*, September 2, 2003, cited in Kerry Pither, *supra* note 1.
56. Letter from Prime Minister Jean Chretién to Dr. Monia Mazigh, dated September 4, 2003, cited in Kerry Pither, *supra* note 1.
57. Editorial, "When Canadians are jailed abroad," *Globe & Mail*, September 4, 2003.
58. Kerry Pither, *supra* note 1, September 3, 2003, entry.
59. Ibid., September 10, 2003, entry.
60. Ibid., September 11, 2003, entry.
61. Kerry Pither, *Maher Arar: Chronology of Events, September 26, 2002 to October 5, 2003*, July 2003 entry. http://www.maherar.ca/cms/images/mahersstory.pdf. [Kerry Pither, *Maher Arar: Chronology of Events*]
62. Michelle Shephard, "Envoy says he doubted Arar's story," *supra* note 53.
63. Arar Commission Report, supra note 27, pp. 208–209.
64. Kerry Pither, *supra* note 61, August 14, 2003, entry. See also, Arar Commission Report, *supra* note 27, pp. 387–392. Due to the refusal of the government to disclose critical parts of its testimony to Maher Arar, he was unable to testify before the Commission without prejudice, and as of September 2006 had not done so. Where there is conflict between the chronology prepared by Kerry Pither and Maher Arar and the testimony of Canadian consul, whose credibility was put into doubt by revelations in the Commission report, I have chosen the chronology version of the facts.
65. Kerry Pither, *supra* note 1, August 14, 2003, entry.
66. Arar Statement, *supra* note 36.
67. Ibid.
68. Ibid.
69. Toope Report, *supra* note 37, p. 19.
70. Author's interview with Kerry Pither.
71. Except where otherwise indicated, all of the information and quotations regarding Ahmad El Maati comes from the chronology prepared on his behalf by Kerry Pither and submitted to the Arar Commission of Inquiry, except when other sources are indicated. [Kerry Pither, *Ahmad Abou el Maati: Chronology*]
72. Jeff Sallot and Colin Freeze, "It was hyped as a TERRORIST map," *supra* note 51.

73. *Los Angeles Times*, "U.S. strikes back: The investigation," October 12, 2001.
74. Jeff Sallot and Colin Freeze, "It was hyped as a TERRORIST map," *supra* note 51.
75. Kerry Pither, presentation to the Annual General Meeting of the International Civil Liberties Monitoring Group, March 10, 2006.
76. Kerry Pither, *Ahmad Abou el Maati: Chronology*, August 15, 2002, entry, citing documents released by Arar Commission of Inquiry.
77. Kerry Pither, *Almalki Chronology, supra* note 15. All of the information regarding Abdullah Almalki is taken from this chronology prepared by Kerry Pither on behalf of him and his lawyer Paul Copeland and submitted to the Arar Commission of Inquiry, except where other sources are cited. [Kerry Pither, *Abdullah Almalki: Chronology*]
78. Kerry Pither, *Abdullah Almalki: A brief biography*.
79. Colin Freeze, "The Khadr Effect," *Globe & Mail*, October 3, 2005.
80. Ibid.
81. Ibid.
82. Ibid.
83. Ibid.
84. Kerry Pither, *Abdullah Amalki: A brief biography*, *supra* note 78.
85. Kerry Pither, *Almalki Chronology, supra* note 15.
86. Toope Report, *supra* note 37, p. 6.
87. All of the information about Al Boushi comes the article, "Canadian 'recovering' after Syrian incarceration: Businessman reunites with son in Toronto, won't comment on 3 1/2 years spent in prison," *Globe & Mail*, January 10, 2006.
88. Toope Report, *supra* note 37, p. 20.
89. Ibid, pp. 20–21.
90. Steven Frank, "Seeking the Truth," *Time* (Canadian edition), December 27, 2004–January 3, 2005, p. 71.
91. Tim Harper, "U.S. ruling dismisses Arar lawsuit," *Toronto Star*, February 17, 2006.
92. Toope Report, *supra* note 37, pp. 19–21.
93. Ibid., p. 20.
94. Ibid., p. 22.
95. Ibid., pp. 22–23.
96. Brian Murphy, of the Canadian development nongovernmental agency (NGO), Inter Pares.

Chapter Two

97. Leslie Cauley, "NSA has massive database of Americans' phone calls," *USA Today*, May 11, 2006. [Leslie Cauley]
98. U.S. Attorney General Alberto Gonzales, quoted in Dan Egan, "Gonzales Defends Surveillance," *Washington Post*, February 7, 2006.
99. Eric Lichtblau and James Risen, "Domestic Surveillance: The program; Spy agency mined vast data trove, officials report," *New York Times*, December 24, 2005. See also, Barton Gellman, Dafna Linzer and Carol D. Leonnig, "Surveillance Net Yields Few Suspects," *Washington Post*, February 5, 2006. [Gellman, Linzer and Leonnig]
100. Gellman, Linzer and Leonnig, *supra* note 99.

101. Lowell Bergman, Eric Lichtblau, Scott Shane, and Don van Natta Jr., "Spy Agency Data After Sept.11 Led F.B.I. to Dead Ends," *New York Times*, January 17, 2006. [Bergman, Lichtblau, Shane, van Natta Jr.]
102. Ibid.
103. James Risen and Eric Lichtblau, "Bush Lets U.S. Spy on Callers Without Courts," *New York Times*, December 16, 2005.
104. Ibid.
105. Gellman, Linzer and Leonnig, *supra* note 99.
106. Bergman, Lichtblau, Shane, van Natta Jr., *supra* note 101.
107. Editorial "Bush's High Crimes," *Nation,* January 9, 2006, p. 3.
108. David E. Sanger, "In Speech, Bush Says He Ordered Domestic Spying," *New York Times*, December 18, 2005. [David Sanger]
109. Editorial, "Bush's High Crimes," *Nation*, *supra* note 107, p. 3.
110. See Elizabeth Holtzman (Former Member, House Judiciary Committee, Nixon Impeachment Proceedings), "The Impeachment of George W. Bush," *Nation*, January 30, 2006. [Elizabeth Holtzman]
111. Lewis H. Lapham, "The Case for Impeachment: Why We Can No Longer Afford George W. Bush," *Harper's Magazine*, March 2006. [Lewis Lapham]
112. Pub. L. No. 95-511, 92 Stat. 1783.
113. Elizabeth Holtzman, *supra* note 110, p. 13.
114. Charles Babington, "Activists on Right, GOP Lawmakers Divided on Spying," *Washington Post*, February 7, 2006.
115. Sheryl Gay Stolberg, "Republican Speaks Up, Leading Others to Challenge Wiretaps," *New York Times*, February 11, 2006. [Sheryl Gay Stolberg]
116. David E. Sanger, *supra* note 108.
117. Ibid.
118. Patricia Williams, "Foggy Bottom," *Nation,* February 6, 2006, p.9.
119. Sheryl Gay Stolberg, *supra* note 115.
120. Carol D. Leonnig, "Secret Court's Judges Were Warned About NSA Spy Program," *Washington Post*, February 9, 2006.
121. Ibid.
122. Elizabeth Holtzman, *supra* note 110, p. 9.
123. Eric Lichtblau and Scott Shane, "Basis for Spying in U.S. Is Doubted," *New York Times*, January 7, 2006.
124. See Wikipedia, "Unitary Executive Theory": http://en.wikipedia.org/wiki/Unitary_Executive_theory.
125. Dan Egge, "Warrantless Wiretaps Possible in the U.S," *Washington Post*, April 7, 2006.
126. Lesley Cauley, *supra* note 97.
127. Ibid.
128. Ibid.
129. Seymour Hersh, "Listening In," *New Yorker*, May 29, 2006 (posted May 22, 2006). [Seymour Hersh, "Listening In"]
130. Ibid.
131. Ibid.
132. Ibid.
133. Ibid.

134. Ibid.

Chapter Three

135. Between 1996 and 1999, the number of deaths in the world caused by terrorist acts committed by nonstate actors was only 11,000. The number of deaths caused by car accidents in the United States alone during that period was 160,000. Jonathon Barker, *The No Nonsense Guide to Terrorism* (Oxford: New Internationalist, 2003), p. 39. Figures since 9/11 do not change the equation.
136. Gwynne Dyer, *supra* note 9, p. 119.
137. Gwynne Dyer, *supra* note 9, pp. 119–120. See also, Francis Fukuyama's influential article "The End of History?" about the dialectical victory of American-style liberal democracy over all alternative forms of government, first published in the summer 1989 issue of the *National Interests*. See further Samuel P. Huntington, "The Clash of Civilizations," first published in *Foreign Affairs*, 72, 3 (1993).
138. Gwynne Dyer, *supra* note 9, pp. 122–123.
139. Gwynne Dyer, *supra* note 9, p. 124.
140. The signatories were Elliott Abrams, Gary Bauer, William J. Bennett, Jeb Bush, Dick Cheney, Elliot A. Cohen, Midge Decter Forbes, Paula Dobriansky, Steve Forbes, Aaron Friedberg, Francis Fukuyama, Frank Gaffney, Fred C. Ikle, Donald Kagan, Zalmay Khalilzad, I. Lewis Libby, Norman Podhoretz, Dan Quayle, Peter W. Rodman, Stephen P. Rosen, Henry S. Rowan, Donald Rumsfeld, Vin Weber, George Weigel, and Paul Wolfowitz.
141. Gwynne Dyer, *supra* note 9, p. 120.
142. Gwynne Dyer, *supra* note 9, p. 125.
143. Joshua Micah Marshall, "Practice to Deceive: Chaos in the Middle East is not the Bush hawk's nightmare scenario—it's their plan," *Washington Monthly*, April 2003; Gwynne Dyer, *supra* note 9, p. 125.
144. Joshuah Micah Marshall, *supra* note 143.
145. Bruce Murphy, "Neoconservative clout seen in U.S. Iraq policy," *Milwaukee Journal Sentinel*, April 5, 2003.
146. Ibid. Bruce Murphy quoting Heritage Foundation fellow John C. Hulsman.
147. Lewis H. Lapham, *supra* note 111, p.29.
148. Bruce Murphy, *supra* note 145.
149. PBS *Frontline*, "Chronology: The Evolution of the Bush Doctrine," quoting *The National Security Strategy of the United States of America*, September 2002 (http://www.whitehouse.gov/nsc/nss.html). http://www.pbs.org/wgbh/pages/frontline/shows/iraq/etc/cron.html.
150. Ibid.
151. Ibid.
152. Bruce Murphy, *supra* note 145.
153. BBC News, "Blair terror speech in full." http://www.bbc.co.uk.
154. Oliver Burkeman and Julian Borger, "War critics astonished as US hawk admits invasion was illegal," *Guardian*, November 20, 2003.
155. U.N. CHARTER, arts. 24 and 39; see also, Rome Statute of the International Criminal Court, U.N. Doc. A/CONF.183/9 (1998), art. 5(1)d.

156. This formulation, communicated by the Americans to the British in the nineteenth century Caroline case, is often cited as authoritative. 2 MOORE, DIGEST OF INTERNATIONAL LAW 412 (1906), quoting U.S. Secretary of State Daniel Webster's remarks in a diplomatic note to the British in the Caroline case. Respected international legal scholar Oscar Schachter believed the Caroline formulation did not, in fact, accurately reflect state practice; however, he thought "it is safe to say it reflects a widespread desire to restrict the right of self defense when no attack has actually occurred." Schachter thought it was a better formulation to say that customary international law recognized "there may well be situations in which the imminence of an attack is so clear and the danger so great that defensive action is essential for self preservation." Oscar Schachter, *International Law: The Right of States to Use Armed Force,* 82 MICH. L. REV. (1984), pp. 1634–35.
157. In the Nicaraguan case before the International Court of Justice, the United States tried to argue that it had the right to define the circumstances in which self-defense was necessary (and lost). In Kosovo, along with other NATO countries, it tried a new legal justification called humanitarian intervention.
158. Joshua Micah Marshall, *supra* note 143.
159. Bruce Murphy, *supra* note 145.
160. Jay Bookman, "The president's real goal in Iraq," *Atlanta Journal-Constitution*, September 29, 2002.
161. Speech by Stephen J. Hadley at the Institute of Peace, March 17, 2006.

Chapter Four

162. For an excellent analysis of the USA PATRIOT Act, see Nancy Chang's free report posted to the Center for Constitutional Rights Web site here: http://www.ccr-ny.org/v2/reports/docs/USA_PATRIOT_ACT.pdf, or her groundbreaking book, *Silencing Political Dissent, How Post-September 11 Anti-terrorism Measures Threaten Our Civil Liberties* (Seven Stories Press/Open Media Series, 2002). http://www.sevenstories.com/Book/?GCOI=58322100208840.
163. Reg Whitaker, *The End of Privacy* (New York: The New Press, 1999), p. 25. [Reg Whitaker]
164. Ibid.
165. Ibid. p. 45.
166. Ibid.
167. Estanislao Oziewicz, "Shroud lifting on global gulag set up to fight 'war on terror'," *Globe & Mail,* May 13, 2004. [Estanislao Oziewicz]

Chapter Five

168. Thomas Mathiesen, *On Globalistion of Control: Towards an Integrated Surveillance System in E.U.rope* (London: Instant Print West, November 1999), p. 3. Available from Statewatch here: http://www.statewatch.org, or e-mail office@statewatch.org). [Thomas Mathiesen]
169. Peter Reydt, "How IBM helped the Nazis," book review of Edwin Black, *IBM and the Holocaust*, World Socialist Web sites, June 27, 2001. http://www.wsws.org/articles/2001/jun2001/ibm-j27.html.
170. Ibid.

171. "Once the Belgians had decided to limit administrative posts and higher education to the Tutsi, they were faced with the challenge of deciding exactly who was Tutsi. Physical characteristics identified some, but not for all. Because group affiliation was supposedly inherited, genealogy provided the best guide to a person's status, but tracing genealogies was time-consuming and could also be inaccurate, given that individuals could change category as their fortunes rose or fell. The Belgians decided that the most efficient procedure was simply to register everyone, noting their group affiliation in writing, once and for all. All Rwandans born subsequently would also be registered as Tutsi, Hutu, or Twa at the time of their birth. The system was put into effect in the 1930s. Human Rights Watch, *Leave None to Tell the Story: Genocide in Rwanda*, April 1, 2004. http://www.hrw.org/reports/1999/rwanda/Geno1-3-09.htm.
172. Deepa Fernandes, "Targeted: Homeland Security and the Business of Immigration," manuscript (New York: Seven Stories, fall 2006), p. 99.
173. Ibid., p. 102.
174. Rachel Meeropol, "The Post 9-11 Terrorism Investigation and Immigration Detention" in ed. Rachel Meeropol, *America's Disappeared* (New York: Seven Stories Press, 2005) [Rachel Meeropol]
175. Ibid. The Inspector General's Report states 762 people were arrested in the initial sweeps, but the number may well be based on an incomplete record. Office of the Inspector General, United States Department of Justice, *The September 11 Detainees: A Review of the Treatment of Aliens Held on Immigration Charges in Connection with the Investigation of the September 11 Attacks*, June 2003. http://www.usdoj.gov/oig/special/0306/index.htm. [Office of the Inspector General, *Report on Detainees*]
176. Ibid.
177. Nina Bernstein, "U.S. is Settling Detainee's Suit in 9/11 Sweep," *New York Times*, February 28, 2006. [Nina Bernstein]
178. Tim Harper, "U.S. 'mistreated' immigrants in 9/11 roundup," *Toronto Star*, June 3, 2003.
179. Rachel Meerpol, *supra* note 174, p. 153–154, citing the Supplementary Inspector General Report, pp. 10, 11, 17, 21, 26.
180. Nina Bernstein, *supra* note 177.
181. Tim Harper, "U.S. 'mistreated' immigrants in 9/11 roundup," *supra* note 178.
182. See 67 Fed. Reg. 52584 (Aug. 12, 2002) codified at 8CFR 264.1 (f); and 67 Fed. Reg. 67766(Nov. 6, 2002) requiring citizens and nationals of Iran, Iraq, Libya, Sudan and Syria to appear for Special Registration; 67 Fed. Reg. 70525 (Nov. 22, 2002) requiring citizens and nationals of Afghanistan, Algeria, Bahrain, Eritrea, Lebanon, Morocco, North Korea, Oman, Qatar Somalia, Tunisia, United Arab Emirates, and Yemen to appear for special registration; and 67 Fed. Reg. 77642 (Dec. 18, 2002) requiring citizens and nationals of Pakistan and Saudi Arabia to appear for special registration. See also, National Security Entry-Exit Registration (NSEERS) Summary Chart, February 25, 2003. http://64.233.167.104/search?q=cache:-34s3QXmzLMJ:www.oiss.wayne.edu/Forms/PDF/NSEERS_SUMMARY_CHART.pdf+NSEERS&hl=en.
183. Asian American Legal Defense and Education Fund (AALDEF), *Special Registration: Discrimination and Xenophobia as Government Policy*, 2004, p. 1. http://www.aaldef.org/images/01-04_registration.pdf.

184. All of the quotes and information for this story come from Paula Simons, "Canadian citizenship proves worthless at the U.S. border: Security concerns shouldn't override human rights," *Edmonton Journal*, November 6, 2002.
185. All of the information and quotes for this story come from CBC News, "Canadian passport 'meant nothing' to U.S. immigration officials," CBC.ca, January 13, 2003.
186. Editorial, "Registration of residents from terrorism states is INS fiasco," *Guardian Weekly*, January 16-22, 2003.
187. Ibid.
188. Immigration Policy Center, "Targets of Suspicion: The Impact of Post-9/11 Policies on Muslims, Arabs and South Asians in the United States," *Immigration Policy in Focus*, 3, 2 (May 2004) p. 7. http://www.ailf.org/ipc/ipf051704.pdf. See also, Flynn McRoberts, "Muslim exodus from U.S. unravels tight knit enclaves," *Chicago Tribune*, November 18, 2003.
189. Andrea Elliot, "In Brooklyn, 9-11 Damage Continues," *New York Times*, June 7, 2003.
190. Flynn McRoberts, *supra* note 188.
191. Ibid.
192. Ibid.
193. See the Consular Services at the U.S. Mission in Canada Web site. http://www.amcits.com/nseers.asp?print-version.
194. Lynn Waddell, *Special Report: Immigration Law elusive refuge: detention rates increase in name of homeland security, but advocates on both sides worry about tactics*, FIAC, January 27, 2005.
195. The US-VISIT program requirements apply to all visitors except (as of October 2006) Mexican citizens holding "border crossing cards" or "laser visas" and most Canadian citizens. See U.S. Department of Homeland Security, *US-VISIT Fact Sheet: U.S.-Canada Land Borders*, and *US-VISIT Fact Sheet: U.S.-Mexico Land Borders.* http://www.dhs.gov/dhspublic/interapp/editorial/editorial_0435.xml.
196. Associated Press, "U.S. eye scan plan under scrutiny: U.S. demanding biometric technology in passports; world may not be ready," *Okanagan,* August 24, 2003.
197. See Statewatch, "Biometrics—the E.U. takes another step down the road to 1984," *Statewatch News online,* September 2003. http://www.statewatch.org/news/2003/sep/19E.U.biometric.htm; E.U.ractive, News, February 7, 2005. http://www.euractiv.com/Article?tcmuri=tcm:29-133939-16&type=News.
198. Alloire Gilbert, "States to test ID chips on foreign visitors," CNet News.com, January 26, 2005. http://news.com.com/States+to+test+ID+chips+on+foreign+visitors/2100-1039_3-5552120.html. See also, Office of the Inspector General, Enhanced Security Controls *Needed for US VISIT's System Using RFID Technology* (redacted), June 2006.
199. Bruce Schneier, "RFID Passport Security Revisted," Schneier on Security, August 9, 2005. http://www.schneier.com/blog/archives/2005/08/rfid_passport_s_1.html.
200. Wilson P. Dizard III, "Special Report: DHS's double duty," *Government Computer News*, December 13, 2005.
201. See the Department of Homeland Security's Web page about US-VISIT here: http://www.dhs.gov/dhspublic/interapp/press_release/press_release_0710.xml.
202. Ryan Singel, "CAPPS II stands alone, feds say," *Wired News*, January 13, 2004. http://www.wired.com/news/privacy/0,1848,61891,00.html?tw=wn_story_related. [Ryan Singel]

203. Eric Lichtblau and John Markoff, "U.S. Nearing Deal on Way to Track Foreign Visitors," *New York Times*, May 24, 2004. [Lichtblau and Markoff]

204. The *Federal Register* notice states that "[i]t is . . . anticipated that CAPPS II will be linked with the U.S. Visitor and Immigrant Status Indicator Technology (US-VISIT) program at such time as both programs become fully operational, in order that processes at both border and airport points of entry and exit are consistent." See also, Questions Submitted for the Record by Senator Ron Wyden, Oversight Hearing for Transportation Security, September 9, 2003. http://www.eff.org/Privacy/cappsii/20030909_wyden_questions.php. "U.S. officials said they are considering merging the two programs." Sara Kehaulani Goo, "U.S. to Push Airlines for Passenger Records: Travel Database to Rate Security Risk Factors," *Washington Post*, January 12, 2004; and Interim Final Rule and Notice, 69 Federal Register 467 (January 5, 2004). http://a257.g.akamaitech.net/7/257/2422/05jan20040800/edocket.access.gpo.gov/2004/pdf/03-32331.pdf. The rule "requires the integration of all databases that process or contain information on aliens." Compare, Ryan Singel, *supra* note 202.

205. Lynda Hurst, "Bio-Security Still a Fantasy; Airport Screening Won't Work: Experts; No information to identify terrorists," *Toronto Star*, January 24, 2004. See also, American Civil Liberties Union, "ACLU Criticizes Plans to Go Forward with CAPPS II, Calls Dragnet Profiling Approach Fake Security on the Cheap," Media Release, January 12, 2004. http://www.aclu.org/SafeandFree/SafeandFree.cfm?ID=14699&c=206. The term "black box" is also used to refer to Internet monitoring devices on Internet service provider networks to monitor user traffic. Little is publicly known about the workings of these, except that they are like the "'packet sniffers' typically employed by computer network operators for security and maintenance purposes. Packet sniffers are specialized software programs running in a computer that is hooked into the network at a location where it can monitor traffic flowing in and out of systems. Sniffers can monitor the entire data stream, searching for key words, phrases, or strings such as net addresses or e-mail accounts. They can then record or retransmit for further review anything that fits their search criteria. Black boxes are apparently connected directly to government agencies by high-speed links in some countries. Privacy International, *Privacy and Human Rights 2003, Executive Summary*. http://www.privacyinternational.org/survey/phr2003/threats.htm.

206. *Uniting and Strengthening America by Providing Appropriate Tools Required to Intercept and Obstruct Terrorism* (USA PATRIOT Act) *of 2001*, Pub. L. No. 107-56, sec. 215 (Washington: GPO, 2001). http://thomas.loc.gov.

207. Owing to public concerns expressed about privacy, the Lockheed Martin group was eventually only awarded a contract to assist in the census by providing advanced systems and processing technologies. *Statistics Canada*, "Role of private contractors in the census," n.d. http://www12.statcan.ca/english/census06/info/outsource/outsourcing.cfm.

208. See British Columbia Ministry of Health Services, "Government Moves to Improve MSP and Pharmacare Services," news release, November 4, 2004; and "Backgrounder: Maximus BC/Alternative Service Delivery," both available on-line here: http://www.healthservices.gov.bc.ca/msp/.

209. B.C. Hydro, "B.C. Hydro and Accenture Agreement Designed to Save $250 Million in Costs," news release, February 28, 2003. http://www.bchydro.com/news/2003/feb/release4622.html.

210. Carol D. Leonnig, "Secret Court's Judges Were Warned About NSA Spy Program," *supra* note 120.

211. See Patrick Healy, "Colleges giving probers data on foreign students' finances," *Boston Globe*, October 3, 2001; and American Association of Collegiate Registrars and Admissions Officers, "Preliminary Results of the AACRAO Survey on Campus Consequences of the September 11 Attacks," October 4, 2001. http://www.aacrao.org/transcript/index.cfm, both cited in Jay Stanley, *The Surveillance-Industrial Complex: How the American Government Is Conscripting Businesses and Individuals in the Construction of a Surveillance Society*, written by Jay Stanley (New York: ACLU, 2004), p. 14. http://www.aclu.org/SafeandFree/SafeandFree.cfm?ID=16226&c=207. [Jay Stanley, *The Surveillance Industrial Complex*]
212. Stephanie Stoughton, "Poll: Firms Relaxed Privacy Rules," *Boston Globe*, October 8, 2001, cited in Jay Stanley, *The Surveillance Industrial Complex*, *supra* note 211.
213. Eunice Moscoso, "Demand for data by feds on rise," Cox Washington Bureau, August 17, 2003. http://www.federalobserver.com/print.php?aid=6378, cited in Jay Stanley, *The Surveillance Industrial Complex*, *supra* note 211.
214. See the Web site of InfraGard: Guarding the Nation's Infrastructure. http://www.infragard.net. As of November 22, 2004, the number of InfraGard members was given as 14,536.
215. Chris Seper, "Combating Cybercrime: FBI's InfraGard Program Promotes Security Awareness," *Cleveland Plain Dealer*, November 4, 2002. http://www.infragard.net, cited in Jay Stanley, *The Surveillance Industrial Complex*, *supra* note 211.
216. Ryan Singel, "JetBlue Shared Passenger Data," *Wired News*, September 18, 2003; Ryan Singel and Noah Schachtman, "Army Admits to Using JetBlue Data," *Wired News*, September 23, 2003. http://www.wired.com/news/privacy, both cited in Jay Stanley, *The Surveillance Industrial Complex*, *supra* note 211.
217. Electronic Privacy Information Center, "Northwest Airlines gave NASA Personal Info on Millions of Passengers; Disclosure Violated Privacy Policy," press release, January 18, 2004. http://www.epic.org/privacy/airtravel/nasa/pr1.18.04.html. See also, Sara Kehaulani Goo, "Northwest Gave U.S. Data on Passengers," *Washington Post*, January 18, 2004, both cited in Jay Stanley, *The Surveillance Industrial Complex*, *supra* note 211.
218. Sara Kehaulani Goo, "American Airlines Revealed Passenger Data," *Washington Post*, April 10, 2004, cited in Jay Stanley, *The Surveillance Industrial Complex*, *supra* note 211.
219. John Schwartz and Micheline Maynard, "FBI Got Records on Air Travelers," *New York Times*, May 1, 2004, cited in Jay Stanley, *The Surveillance Industrial Complex*, *supra* note 211.
220. DoubleClick, "Abacus B2C Alliance." http://www.doubleclick.com/us/products/direct_marketing/abacus_b2C_alliance/.
221. Jim Krane (Associated Press), "Information bank reaches into Latin America: U.S. buys access to personal data," *Daily News* (Los Angeles), April 20, 2003.
222. Ibid. According to ACLU researchers, no country in Latin America has protections in place against the export of data.
223. Ibid.
224. In the novel *Brave New World*, a totalitarian government controls society through the use of science and technology. Aldous Huxley, *Brave New World*, 1932, 1946 (New York: Harper Collins,1998).

Chapter Six

225. "Smart cards make inroads into Asia," *Asian Times*, October 2004. [Smart cards make inroads in Asia]
226. House of Commons Canada, Interim Report of the Standing Committee on Citizenship and Immigration, *A National Identity Card for Canada?* October 2003, pp. 16–23. http://www.parl.gc.ca/InfocomDoc/Documents/37/2/parlbus/commbus/house/reports/cimmrp06-e.htm. [*A National Identity Card for Canada?*] See also, Julian Ashbourn, background paper for the Institute, DG JRC- Sevilla, European Commission, January 2005, p. 27.
227. Initially, the United States exempted twenty-eight visa waiver countries from the requirements of the US-VISIT program, provided they implemented biometric passports by an October 2004 deadline. However, when it became clear that countries were not going to be able to meet the deadline, the US-VISIT program was extended to all countries including Canada. Once visa-waiver countries implement machine-readable biometric passports, fingerscanning of their nationals under the U.S. VISIT program may stop, but it may also continue if the passports adopted do not incorporate a fingerprint biometric. See http://news.bbc.co.uk/2/hi/americas/3595221.htm; Tim Harper, "U.S. to Screen Canadians," *Toronto Star*, January 6, 2004.
228. See Statewatch, "E.U. Summit: Agreement on "harmonised" biometric identification linked to E.U. databases," *Statewatch News online*, June 2003. http://www.statewatch.org/news/2003/jun/22bio.htm.
229. At the outset of its deliberations, ICAO promised to design standards that upheld national data protection laws and cultural practices in the domestic and transborder use of information, but it did none of this. See Open Letter to ICAO, March 30, 2004. www.privacy-international.org/ issues/terrorism/rpt/icaoletter.pdf.
230. Bruno Waterfield, "EU passport to European fingerprint database," theparliament.com, February 18, 2004. http://www.eupolitix.com/EN/News/200402/1c70db13-14e7-4a32-af69-1b26c445e804.htm.
231. International Civil Aviation Organization, "Biometric Technology in Machine Readable Travel Documents—The ICAO Blueprint," FAL-12-WP/4, 5/11/03, Presented to the Twelfth Meeting of the Facilitation Division of the International Civil Aviation Organization, March 22-April 2, 2004, Cairo, Egypt. http://www.icao.int/icao/en/atb/fal/fal12/documentation/fal12wp004_en.pdf.
232. Tom Young, "Biometric passports get cracked," Vnunet.com, August 7, 2006. http://www.vnunet.com/computing/news/2161836/kacers-crack-biometric.
233. John Oates, "US gets RFID passports," *Register*, August 15, 2006.
234. "RFID Passports: Not Dead Yet: State Department Adds Protections But Still Clings to RFID Fantasy," RFIDkills.com.
235. Bruce Schneier, "RFID Passports," October 14, 2004, weblog. http://www.schneier.com/blog/archives/2004/10/rfid_passports.html.
236. See *A National Identity Card for Canada?*, *supra* note 226.
237. With the release of the Commons Committee report in early October, Citizenship Minister Denis Coderre was immediately put on the defensive. See, for example, Tyler Hamilton, "Security-as-Theatre, Intrusive, Ineffective Smoke and Mirrors Security Fails," *Toronto Star*, September 1, 2003. [*Tyler Hamilton*] At a public forum on national ID cards

organized by Coderre's Ministry and held on October 7 and 8, 2003, civil society groups and privacy commissioners criticized Coderre's proposal to introduce a national ID card, and also the heavy participation of industry in the forum.

238. The Canadian Press, "Ottawa to introduce biometric passports," *Toronto Star*, July 18, 2004.
239. Ibid.
240. *National ID Cards and REAL ID Act*, Electronic Privacy Information Center. http://www.epic.org/privacy/id_cards/.
241. Ibid.
242. The U.S. Congress set October 26, 2004 as the deadline by which both U.S. and foreign passports were to be upgraded to include biometric identification, but the U.S. along with other countries was unable to meet the deadline. See, "Iris-recognition will become common at border crossings into the United States by the end of the year," *National Post*, August 28, 2004, p. FP7; Tyler Hamilton, *supra* note 46.
243. Bruce Schneier, "REAL ID" Schneier on Security, May 9, 2005. http://www.schneier.com/blog/archives/2005/05/real_id.html.
244. Ibid.
245. Brian Bergstein, "National ID, State Nightmare," *Guardian*, January 12, 2006.
246. Hibel v. Sixth Judicial District Court, 124 S. Ct. 2451 (2004).
247. Kamal Ahmed, "Ministers to dump 'useless' identity card," *Observer*, October 12, 2003.
248. At the G8 meeting, the U.K. Home Secretary said that biometric data would be included in U.K passports from 2006. Kristina Merkner and Elise Kissling, "Germany to shape E.U. passport rules," *Frankfurter Allgemeine Zeitung (F.A.Z.)*, June 27, 2003.
249. Phillip Johnston, "ID cards 'could fall foul of human rights law'," *Daily Telegraph*, February 3, 2005.
250. Tanya Branigan, "Lords could sink ID Bill, admits Clarke," *Guardian*, February 11, 2005. http://www.guardian.co.uk/idcards/story/0,15642,1410578,00.html.
251. Alan Cowell, "A Bit of Good News," *New York Times*, February 14, 2006.
252. BBC, "Deal Paves the Way for ID Cards, March 30, 2006. http://news.bbc.co.uk/1/hi/uk_politics/4856074.stm.
253. George Monbiot, "The Perpetual Surveillance Society," *Alternet*, February 23, 2006. http://www.alternet.org/rights/32645.
254. Tim Harper, "U.S. opts for security card," *Toronto Star*, January 18, 2006.
255. Beth Gorham, "Wilson fears 'invisible barrier'," *Toronto Star*, April 6, 2006.
256. Ibid.
257. BBC News, "Concern over biometric passports," March 30, 2004. http://newsvote.bbc.co.uk/mpapps/pagetools/print/news.bbc.co.uk/1/hi/technology/3582461.stm.
258. Government of the United States, "Face Recognition for Identity Confirmation—Inspection of Travel Documents," FAL/12-WP/63, 10/3/04, Presented to the Twelfth Meeting of the Facilitation Division of the International Civil Aviation Organization, March 22-April 2, 2004, Cairo, Egypt. http://www.icao.int/icao/en/atb/fal/fal12/documentation/fal12wp063_en.pdf.
259. Lynda Hurst, *supra* note 205.
260. David Colker and Joseph Menn, "ChoicePoint CEO had Denied any Earlier Breach of Database," *Los Angeles Times*, March 3, 2005. http://www.newsday.com/business/la-fi-choicepoint3mar03,0,6289300.story?coll=ny-business-headlines.

261. Lynda Hurst, *supra* note 205.
262. See, for example, Government of Canada, "The Canadian Advance Passenger Information Program," FAL/12-WP/38,11/12/03, Presented to the Twelfth Meeting of the Facilitation Division of the International Civil Aviation Organization, March 22-April 2, 2004, Cairo, Egypt, point 1.3. http://www.icao.int/icao/en/atb/fal/fal12/documentation/fal12wp038_en.pdf [Canadian Submission on PNR to ICAO)]; Tonda MacCharles, "Air travelers face screening; Canadian program aims at terrorist 'risk scoring' system; Information would be shared with U.S., documents show," *Toronto Star*, January 17, 2004. [Tonda McCharles]
263. Observation made by Brian Murphy, Interpares.

Chapter Seven

264. Privacy International, *First Report on Towards an International Infrastructure for Surveillance of Movement: Transferring Privacy: the Transfer of Passenger Records and the Abdication of Privacy Protection*, February 2004, p. 2. [*Transferring Privacy*]
265. See, for example, "Directive 95/46/EC of the European Parliament and of the Council of 24 October 1995 on the protection of individuals with regard to the processing of personal data and on the free movement of such data," *Official Journal L 281,* 23/11/1995, pp. 0031-0050. http://europa.eu.int/comm/internal_market/privacy/law_en.htm; and the Canadian *Personal Information Protection and Electronic Documents Act,* 2000. http://www.privcom.gc.ca/legislation/02_06_01_e.asp. Habeas corpus laws in Latin America contain similar principles.
266. *The Smart Border Declaration*, December 12, 2001. http://www.dfait-maeci.gc.ca/can-am/menu-en.asp?act=v&mid=1&cat=10&did=1669. [*The Smart Border Declaration*]; *Action Plan for Creating a Secure and Smart Border*, http://www.dfait-maeci.gc.ca/can-am/menu-en.asp?act=v&mid=1&cat=10&did=1670. [*Smart Border Action Plan*]
267. *An Act to Amend the Aeronautics Act*, 2001, c. 38, s. 1. http://laws.justice.gc.ca/en/2001/38/text.html.
268. *Transferring Privacy*, *supra* note 264, p. i.
269. "E.U.-US PNR: Council to ignore parliament and go ahead with 'deal,' *Statewatch News online*, April 2004. http://www.statewatch.org/news/2004/apr/13ep-vote-pnr-court.htm. [Council to ignore parliament]
270. "All the national authorities competent for data protection in Europe have declared these transfers incompatible with European privacy laws." Letter from Graham Watson MEP, Enrique Baron Crispo MEP, and Johanna Boogerd-Quaak MEP, rapporteur, to fellow Members of the European Parliament, dated April 2004 [MEP letter]. See also *Transferring Privacy*, *supra* note 264, p. 2.
271. *Transferring Privacy*, *supra* note 264, p. 5.
272. MEP letter, *supra* note 270.
273. Ibid.
274. In the current agreement, the retention period is 3.5 years. *Transferring Privacy*, *supra* note 264, p. 11.
275. *Transferring Privacy*, *supra* note 264, p. 10.
276. Council to ignore parliament, *supra* note 269.
277. Ian Black, "E.U. hands over data on air travelers," *Guardian*, May 18, 2004. [Ian Black]

278. Nicola Clark and Matthew L. Wald, "Hurdle for U.S. in Getting Data on Passengers," *New York Times*, May 31, 2006.
279. Observation made by Ben Hayes, Statewatch.
280. See *Transferring Privacy, supra* note 264, pp. 5–9; and Privacy International, "Report on Transfers of Air Passenger Data to the U.S. Department of Homeland Security," media release, February 2, 2004.
281. See Statewatch, *Observatory on E.U. PNR Scheme*. http://www.statewatch.org./eu-pnrobservatory.htm.
282. "In September 2003, the Commission decided to accelerate work on developing an international arrangement for PNR data transfers within ICAO. The Commission services have prepared a working paper to this effect that will be submitted by the Community and its Member States to ICAO shortly." Commission of the European Communities, COMMUNICATION FROM THE COMMISSION TO THE COUNCIL AND THE PARLIAMENT: *Transfer of Air Passenger Name Record (PNR) Data: A Global E.U. Approach*, Brussels: European Union, 2003, COM(2003) 826 final, December 16. European Community and its Member States, "An International Framework for the Transfer of Passenger Name Record (PNR) Data," FAL/12-WP/75, 15/3/04, Presented to the Twelfth Meeting of the Facilitation Division of the International Civil Aviation Organization, March 22-April 2, 2004, Cairo, Egypt. http://www.icao.int/icao/en/atb/fal/fal12/documentation/fal12wp075_en.pdf [E.U. submission to ICAO]
283. Ibid., point 1.1. Regarding the existence of the UK program see, Statewatch, "UK: e-Border plan to tackle 'threats'," *Statewatch Bulletin*, vol. 15 (3/4).
284. Canadian Submission on PNR to ICAO, *supra* note 262, point 1.3. See also, Beth Gorham, "Domestic Passengers to be screened: Ottawa looking at kinds of information that can be collected," *Vancouver Sun*, January 31, 2004, reporting plans to expand the Canada Customs and Revenue Agency database on air passengers on incoming international flights to passengers arriving by bus, boat and train.
285. Under the Canadian *Public Safety Act*.
286. Spokesperson Suzanne Luber said the new program replacing the Computer Assisted Passenger Prescreening Systems (CAPPS II) will cover all passengers traveling to and from the United States and within the country. Tim Harper, "U.S. ditches travel surveillance plan," *Toronto Star*, July 16, 2004.
287. Statewatch, "UK: e-Border plan to tackle 'threats'," *supra* note 283.
288. John Lettice, "Got a ticket? Get a record. E.U.-US data handover deal leaks," *Register*, February 3, 2004. http://www.theregister.co.uk/2004/02/03/got_a_ticket_get/.
289. Barry Newman, "How tools of war on terror ensnare wanted citizens," *Wall Street Journal*, November 1, 2005.
290. Ibid.
291. Ibid.
292. Kent v. Dulles, 357 U.S. 116 (1958).

Chapter Eight

293. Three examples of such legislation are the USA PATRIOT Act, the Colombian Anti-Terrorism Act, and the Canadian Anti-Terrorism Act.

294. Matt Richtel, "Live Tracking of Mobile Phones Prompts Court Fights on Privacy," *New York Times*, December 10, 2005. [Matt Richtel]
295. Ibid.
296. Ibid.
297. Breaking News, "New Case Reveals Routine Abuse of Government Surveillance Powers," Electronic Frontier Foundation, September 2005. http://www.eff.org/news/archives/2005_09.php#004002.
298. Matt Richtel, *supra* note 294.
299. Ibid. The judges were sitting in cases in New York, Texas, and Maryland.
300. Barton Gellman, "The FBI's Secret Scrutiny," *Washington Post*, November 6, 2005.
301. Eric Lichtblau, "F.B.I. Using Patriot Act, Demands Library's Records," *New York Times*, August 26, 2005.
302. Ibid.
303. Charles Doyle, *Administrative Subpoenas and National Security Letters in Criminal and Intelligence Investigation: A Sketch*, CRS Report for Congress, April 15, 2005.
304. Barton Gellman, "The FBI's Secret Scrutiny," *supra* note 300.
305. Ibid.
306. Ibid.
307. Ibid.
308. Ibid.
309. Ibid.
310. Ibid.
311. Ibid.
312. Ibid.
313. Ibid.
314. Doe v. Ashcroft, 334 F. Supp. 2d 471 (S.D.N.Y. 2004).
315. Barton Gellman, "The FBI's Secret Scrutiny," *supra* note 300.
316. Nation in Brief, "U.S. Drops Push to Enforce Gag Order Under Patriot Act," *Washington Post*, April 13, 2006.
317. "U.S. Libraries, Challenging FBI, Shape Debate on Patriot Act," June 20, 2005, Bloomberg.com. http://www.bloomberg.com/apps/news?pid=10000103&sid=aaukulguf7_k&refer=us.
318. Electronic Privacy Information Center, *The USA PATRIOT Act*. http://www.epic.org/privacy/terrorism/usapatriot/.
319. Elizabeth Holtzman, *supra* note 110.
320. 18 U.S.C. s. 3121 et seq.
321. Electronic Privacy Information Center, *The USA PATRIOT Act*, *supra* note 318.
322. Electronic Privacy Information Center, *Carnivore*. http://www.epic.org/privacy/carnivore.
323. Charlie Savage, "Bush shuns Patriot act requirement: In addendum to law, he says oversight rules are not binding," *Boston Globe*, March 24, 2006.
324. Ibid.
325. Statewatch, "Data retention and police access in the U.K.—a warning for Europe," *Statewatch News online*, November 3, 2003. http://www.statewatch.org/news/2005/nov/01uk-eu-police-access-to-data.htm.
326. Stuart Miller, "Blunkett security laws may be illegal," *Guardian*, July 31, 2002.

327. Section 273.65.
328. Barton Gellman, "The FBI's Secret Scrutiny," *supra* note 300. The storage directive, announced in late 2003 reversed long-standing FBI policy that required agents to destroy files on innocent citizens, companies, and residents when investigations were closed. The dissemination directive was made through Executive Order 13388.
329. Ibid.
330. Ibid.
331. Ibid.
332. Ibid. All of the information and quotes about the Las Vegas operation comes from this article.
333. The U.S. Department of Homeland Security maintains a five-color public threat advisory; green, blue, yellow, orange, and red. Level green is the lowest level of threat, red the highest. The current level is displayed on DHS's homepage here: http://www.dhs.gov/dhspublic/.
334. This was among more than forty demands. See Statewatch, "Text of U.S. Letter from Bush with Demands for E.U. for Cooperation," *Statewatch News online*. http://www.statewatch.org/news/2001/nov/06uslet.htm.
335. Statewatch, "Data retention and police access in the UK—a warning for Europe," *supra* note 325.
336. EDRI/Digital Civil Rights in Europe, "Data Retention Directive adopted by JHA Council," March 1, 2006. http://www.edri.org/issues/privacy/dataretention.
337. Directive of the European Parliament and of the Council on the retention of data generated or processed in connection with the provision of publicly available electronic communications services or of public communications networks and amending Directive 2002/58/EC, 2005/0812 (COD) Brussels, February 3, 2006, Article 1.
338. Ibid.
339. Article 12.
340. Article 8.
341. Council of the European Union, *Report of the EU-US informal High Level meeting on Freedom, Security and Justice on 2-3 March 2006*, Brussels, March 27, 2006.
342. Declan McCullagh, "Congress may make ISPs snoop on you," *ZDNet News*, May 16, 2006. http://news.zdnet.com/2100-9588_22-6072601.html.
343. Ibid.
344. Declan McCullagh, "Gonzales pressures ISPs on data retention," *ZDNet News*, May 26, 2006. http://news.zdnet.com/2100-1009_22-6077654.html.
345. Ibid.
346. Declan McCullagh, "Congress may make ISPs snoop on you," *supra* note 342.
347. Anne Broache, "Data retention bill expected next week," *ZDNet News*, September 21, 2006. http://news.zdnet.com/2102-9588_22-6118283.html.
348. Jay Stanley, *The Surveillance Industrial Complex, supra*, note 211.
349. Final Rule, 47 CFR Part 64.
350. Breaking News, "FCC Mandate Forces 'Backdoors' in Broadband ISPs and VoIP," Electronic Frontier Foundation, September 28, 2005. http://www.eff.org/news.archives.2005_09.php#004002.
351. Ibid.

352. Kevin Poulsen, "War of Words Rages over Internet Taps," *Security Focus*, April 14, 2004. http://www.securityfocus.com/news/8454. [Kevin Poulsen]
353. United States, *The National Strategy to Secure Cyberspace*, February 2003. http://www.whitehouse.gov/pcipb/.
354. Treaty Office, *Convention on Cybercrime, list of signatories and ratifications*, Council of Europe. http://conventions.coe.int/Treaty/Commun/ChercheSig.asp?NT=185&CM=12&DF=4/5/2006&CL=ENG.
355. Council of Europe, *Convention on Cybercrime* (Budapest: 2001), arts. 20 and 21. See also art.1 definitions of "computer system" and "service provider." http://conventions.coe.int/Treaty/en/Treaties/Html/185.htm. [*Convention on Cybercrime*]
356. Ibid., arts. 16, 20 and 21.
357. Ibid., arts. 16 and 17.
358. Ibid., arts. 25(4) and (5), and 27.
359. See Kevin Poulsen, *supra* note 352 for a description of what is happening in the United States. In Canada, the federal government released consultation documents on "lawful access" in 2002 and 2005 that suggested that service providers would have to build surveillance capacity into their systems. Department of Justice, Industry Canada and Solicitor General Canada, "Lawful Access—Consultation Document," August 25, 2002. http://www.canada.justice.gc.ca/en/cons/la_al/consultation_index.html.
360. See "Memorandum of Understanding concerning the lawful interception of telecommunications," ENFOPOL 112, 10037/95, Limite, Brussels, 25.11.95.
361. *Convention on Cybercrime*, *supra* note 355.
362. See Privacy International, "Privacy and Human Rights 2003, Executive Summary," pp. 18 and 19. http://www.privacyinternational.org/survey/ phr2003/threats.htm.
363. Originating from a G-8 ministerial subgroup.
364. Seymour Hersh, "Listening In," *supra* note 129.
365. David Akin, "Arrests key win for NSA hackers," *Globe & Mail*, April 6, 2004.
366. ECHELON is a secret program but information about it has been exposed in a 1996 book by Nicky Hager, called *Secret Power: New Zealand's role in the International Spy Network* (Nelson, New Zealand: Craig Potton Publishing, 1996). See also European Parliament, *Report on the existence of a global system for the interception of private and commercial communications (ECHELON interception system) 2001/2098(INI)*, Final A5-0264/2001 PAR 1, July 11, 2001. http://www.europarl.eu.int/tempcom/echelon/pdf/rapport_echelon_en.pdf.
367. United Nations Security Council, *Resolution 1373 (2001)*, S/RES/1373 (2001). http://www.un.org/Docs/sc/committees/1373/resolutions.html.
368. The U.S. Money Laundering Strategy of 2003 deals extensively with terrorist financing. See http://www.treas.gov/offices/enforcement/publications/ml2003.pdf. One of the "Six Key Objectives" of the strategy is "establishing and promoting international standards to be adopted by countries" and "ensuring that countries throughout the world consistently implement these international standards." See further, the work of the Financial Action Task Force (FATF), the Egmont Group of Financial Intelligence Units, the G-20 and the International Financial Institutions, all of which provided a framework for combating money laundering before 9/11. This framework has been expanded to address terrorist financing and envisages sanctions for noncooperating states.
369. See http://europa.eu.int/comm/external_relations/un/docs/eu1373.pdf.

370. Eric Lichtblau, "Feds could access world banking data to sniff out terrorist financing," *New York Times,* April 10, 2005.
371. Ibid.
372. Unless otherwise noted, dollar figures in this document are in U.S. dollars.
373. Jay Stanley, *The Surveillance-Industrial Complex, supra* note 211, p. 18.
374. See further, 2002 FATF guidelines entitled "International Best Practices for Combating the Abuse of Non-Profit Organizations." http://www1.oecd.org/fatf/pdf/SR8-NPO_en.pdf. See also, Statewatch "Charities and NGOs targeted in "war on terror," *Statewatch News online*, January 2005. http://www.statewatch.org/news/2005/jan/08charities.htm.
375. European Union, General Secretariat of the Council of the European Union, *European Union Fact Sheet: Extradition and Mutual Legal Assistance* (Brussels: European Union, June 25, 2003). http://europa.eu.int/comm/external_relations/us/sum06_03/extra.pdf.
376. Eric Lichtblau and James Risen, "Bank Data Is Sifted by U.S. in Secret to Block Terror," *New York Times*, June 23, 2006.
377. Ibid.
378. Ibid.
379. David Martin, "With a Whisper, Not a Bang," *San Antonio Current*, December 12, 2003.

Chapter Nine

380. The Schengen Information System contains records on people wanted by the police or judicial authorities, people to be refused entry at external borders (mainly rejected asylum applicants and people subject to deportation orders), people to be placed under surveillance, and records on stolen vehicles, documents, works of art, and other objects. As of 2004, there were already some 15 million records in the SIS and 125,000 access points.
381. *Smart Border Action Plan, supra* note 266. See also, *Securing an Open Society: Canada's National Security Policy*, April 2004.
382. Statewatch, "EU: JHA Council authorizes signing of EU-USA agreements on extradition and mutual legal assistance," *Statewatch News online*. http://www.statewatch.org/news/2003/jun/01useu.htm.
383. Statewatch, "E.U.: Council capitulates and releases draft E.U.-US agreements," *Statewatch News online*. http://www.statewatch.org/news/2003/may/06useu.htm. On January 3, 2005 *The Guardian* newspaper reported that two organizations in the U.K. set up to help the Palestinian people had their bank accounts abruptly closed without explanation. Both groups claimed their targeting was political. The Palestine Solidarity Campaign, a long-established group, had its account closed by the Alliance & Leicester Bank in July 2004. Zoe Mars, the treasurer for the PSC, said that at the end of 2003 the group sent £750 to a medical charity in Palestine. Five months later it received a letter from its bank saying the transaction had been interrupted by the U.S. treasury, which wanted more information on the transfer. The money eventually went through, but the incident raises important questions about the surveillance of financial transactions by the U.S. government. See Faisal al Yafai, "Palestinian Aid Groups' Accounts Closed," *Guardian*, January 3, 2005. http://www.guardian.co.uk/print/0%2C3858%2C5094894-103690%2C00.html; and Faisal al Yafai, "U-turn over Palestinian help group," *Guardian*, January 10, 2005. http://www.guardian.co.uk/print/0%2C3858%2C5099255-103690%2C00.html.

384. Statewatch, "EU: JHA Council authorizes the signing of EU-USA agreements on extradition and mutual legal assistance," *supra* note 382.
385. "What is 'Camolin'?" *Statewatch Webdiary*, filed January 16, 2006. http://statewatch.org/news/2006/jan/05eu-camolin.htm.
386. Supplemental Agreement between the United States of America and the European Police Office on the Exchange of Personal Data and Related Information. See U.S. Department of State Web site.
387. Ibid., art. 6.
388. Ibid., art. 5.
389. The Hague Programme Strengthening Freedom, Justice and Security in the European Union, adopted at the EU Summit, November 4–5, 2004, art. 2.1. http://www.statewatch.org/news/2004/nov/hague-programme-final.pdf.
390. Statewatch, "Some remarks on Schengen III," *Statewatch News online*, July 2005. http://www.statewatch.org/news/2005/jul/17schengen-III.htm.
391. Statewatch, "EU policy 'putsch': Data protection handed to the DG for "law, order and security," *Statewatch News online*, July 2005. http://www.statewatch.org/news/2005/jul/06eu-data-prot.htm.
392. EU doc no: 7416/05.
393. Kelly Field, "FBI Gets Access to Student Databases," *Chronicle of Higher Education*, September 21, 2004.
394. Barton Gellman, "The FBI's Secret Scrutiny," *supra* note 300.
395. Seisint Inc., "Matrix Michigan Briefing," May 8, 2003, slide entitled "Seisint's Core Capabilities" (document obtained through open records request filed by ACLU), cited in ACLU, *The Surveillance-Industrial Complex*, *supra* note 211, p. 24.
396. See Associated Press, "Early database project yielded 120,000 suspects; Scoring system cited for Matrix project spurs privacy worries," May 21, 2004. http://www.cnn.com/2004/LAW/05/20/terror.database.ap/.
397. Madeleine Baran, "Welcome to the MATRIX: Inside the Government's Secret, Corporate-Run, Megadatabase," *New Standard*, July 9, 2004. http://newstandardnews.net/content/?action=show_item&itemid=662. [Madeleine Baran]
398. Michelle Shephard, "Ex-CIA director backs sharing of data," *Toronto Star*, March 15, 2005.
399. Joe Paraskevas, "Security trumps privacy," *Canwest News Service*, November 5, 2004.
400. Jim Bronskill, "Canada's justice supercomputer plan hits snag," *Globe & Mail*, April 19, 2004.
401. Privacy International, *Terrorism Profile—Colombia*, September 19, 2004. http://www.privacyinternational.org/article.shtml?cmd%5B347%5D=x-347-68924.

Chapter Ten

402. Mark Clayton, "US Plans Massive Data Sweep," *Christian Science Monitor*, February 9, 2006.
403. Reg Whitaker, *supra* note 163, p. 25.
404. Ibid. Quotes are given in reverse order.
405. Ibid., p. 26, citing Owen Lattimore, *Ordeal by Slander* (Boston: Little, Brown, 1950).
406. Ibid., p. 26.

407. Michael Sniffen, "Controversial Terror Research Lives On," *Washington Post*, February 23, 2004. http://www.washingtonpost.com/wp-dyn/articles/A63582-2004Feb23.html. [Michael Sniffen]
408. Ibid.
409. Ibid.
410. Ibid.
411. Jay Stanley, *The Surveillance-Industrial Complex, supra* note 211, p. 24. See also Shannon R. Anderson, "Total Information Awareness and Beyond: The Dangers of Using Data Mining Technology to Prevent Terrorism," Bill of Rights Defense Committee, July 2004. http://www.bordc.org/; and Associated Press, "Congress hides parts of U.S. spying project in other government agencies,"*Daily News* (Kamloops), September 26, 2003.
412. Michael Sniffen, *supra* note 407.
413. United States General Accounting Office, *Data Mining: Federal Efforts Cover a Wide Range of Uses*, GAO-04-548, May 2004. http://www.gao.gov/new.items/d04548.pdf, cited in Jay Stanley, *The Surveillance-Industrial Complex, supra* note 211, p. 24. The CIA and NSA did not participate in the GOA survey.
414. Jay Stanley, *The Surveillance-Industrial Complex, supra* note 211, p. 24.
415. Mark Clayton, *supra* note 402. All of the information and quotes about ADVISE come from this article.
416. Jim DeFede, "Mining the MATRIX," *Mother Jones*, September/October, 2004. [Jim DeFede]
417. Brian Bergstein, "U.S. database contractor gave authorities names of 120,000 'likely terrorists,'" *CP wire*, May 20, 2004.
418. Ibid.
419. American Civil Liberties Union, *MATRIX: Myths and Reality*, ACLU, February 10, 2004. http://www.aclu.org/privacy/spying/14999res20040210.html. [ACLU, *MATRIX: Myths and Reality*]
420. Privacy International, "MATRIX data mining system unplugged," May 5, 2005. http://www.privacyinternational.org/article.shtml?cmd%5B347%5D=x-347-205261.
421. Madeleine Baran, *supra* note 397.
422. Electronic Privacy Information Center, "Passenger Profiling: Overview," 2004. http://www.epic.org/privacy/airtravel/profiling.html.
423. Letter from Joseph Lieberman and Susan Collins of the U.S. Senate to The Honorable Asa Hutchinson, Under Secretary for Border and Transportation Security, U.S. Department of Homeland Security, dated April 14, 2004. The text of this letter is included in a press release of the Senate Committee on Governmental Affairs. http://govt-aff.senate.gov/index.cfm?FuseAction=PressReleases.Detail&Affiliation=C& PressRelease_id=709&Month=4&Year=2004.
424. Sara Kehaulani Goo, "U.S. to Push Airlines for Passenger Records," *Washington Post*, January 12, 2004.
425. Tim Harper, "U.S. 'mistreated' immigrants in 9/11 roundup," *supra* note 178.
426. United States General Accounting Office, *Computer Assisted Passenger Prescreening System Faces Significant Implementation Challenges*, GAO-04-385, February 2004. http://www.gao.gov/cgi-bin/getrpt?GAO-04-385.
427. Mimi Hall and Barbara DeLollis, "Plan to collect flier data canceled," *USA Today*, July 14, 2004.

428. Sara Kehaulani Goo and Robert O'Harrow Jr., "New Airline Screening System Postponed; Controversy Over Privacy Leads to CAPPS II Paring, Delay Until After the Election," *Washington Post,* July 16, 2004 [Goo and O'Harrow]
429. Tim Harper, "U.S. 'mistreated' immigrants in 9/11 roundup," *supra* note 178.
430. See Matthew L. Wald, "U. S. Wants Air Traveler Files for Security Test," *New York Times,* September 22, 2004; and U.S. Department of Homeland Security, Transportation Security Administration, "TSA To Test New Passenger Pre-Screening System," press release, August 26, 2004. http://www.tsa.gov/public/display?theme=44&content=09000519800c6c77.
431. Leslie Miller, "U.S. to test if passenger lists can ID 'sleeper cells,'" *Boston Globe,* July 24, 2005; United States, Government Accountability Office, Memorandum to Congressional Committees re Aviation Security: Transportation Security Administration Did Not Fully Disclose Uses of Personal Information during Secure Flight Program Testing in Initial Privacy Notices, but has Recently Taken Steps to More Fully Inform the Public, July 22, 2005; Matthew L. Wald, "U.S. Wants All Air Traveler Files for Security Test," *supra* note 430.
432. Leslie Miller, *supra* note 431; Patty Donmoyer, "DOJ Assails Secure Flight," *Business Travel News,* September 19, 2005.
433. Bruce Schneier, "Secure Flight," Schneier on Security weblog, July 24, 2005. http://www.schneier,com/blog/archives/2005/07/secure_flight.htm.
434. Associated Press, "TSA's Secure Flight Program Suspended," February 9, 2006.
435. Smart Border Action Plan Status Report, December 17, 2004, Canadian Department of Foreign Affairs. http://www.dfait-maeci.gc.ca/.
436. Author's meeting with Department of Public Safety officials, February 17, 2005.
437. Tonda McCharles, *supra* note 262.
438. Ibid. Under the *Passenger Information (Customs) Regulations* [SOR/2003-219] of the *Customs Act,* Canada is collecting passenger information for incoming flights, and storing this information for analysis for six years. *The Public Safety Ac, 2002,* c. 15, allows the collection of passenger information for outgoing and domestic flights, as well as for incoming flights. The Canadian Risk Assessment Center has access to the former and the latter. Beth Gorman, *supra* note 284.
439. Tonda McCharles, *supra* note 262.
440. Canada, Department of Transportation, *News Release: Government of Canada Moving Forward on Air Passenger Assessment* (Ottawa: Government of Canada, August 5, 2005).
441. Statewatch, "UK: e-Borders plan to tackle 'threats,'" *supra* note 283.
442. *Ibid.*
443. Statewatch, "GERMANY: Police "trawling" for suspect foreigners," *Statewatch Bulletin,* 12, no. 1 (Jan-Feb 2002), p 6.
444. Goo and O'Harrow, *supra* note 428.
445. In 2002 the EU drew up recommendations to the Council of the European Union on the use of "terrorist profiling" . . . "putting together a set of physical, psychological or behavioural variables, which have been identified as typical of persons involved in terrorist activities and which may have some predictive value in that respect." See EU Council doc.: 11858/3/02 REV 3, 18.12.02. http://register.consilium.eu.int/pdf/en/02/st11/11858-r3en2.pdf. The UK and Germany are among a number of countries participating in an expert group on "terrorist profiling" with Europol. See EU Council doc.: 7846/04, 30.3.04. http://register.consilium.eu.int/pdf/en/04/st07/st07846.en04.pdf. The EU is also apparently running a secret program on "radicalism and recruitment," targeting Muslim communi-

ties' places of education and worship. The EU Network of Independent Experts in Fundamental Rights has serious concerns about the development of terrorist profiles. It argued that profiling by police or immigration authorities of potential terrorists on the basis of characteristics such as psycho-sociological features, nationality, or birthplace "presents a major risk of discrimination." It further argued that in order for profiling to be acceptable, a statistical link would have to be proven between the defined characteristics and the risk of terrorism, a link which at present has yet to be demonstrated. See EU Network of Independent Experts in Fundamental Rights thematic report 2003. http://www.statewatch.org/news/ 2003/apr/CFR-CDF.ThemComment1.pdf.

446. Arar Commission Report, *supra* note 27, p. 98.
447. Audrey Gillan, "Keep detainee in jail, appeal told," *Guardian*, March 18, 2004. http://www.guardian.co.uk/terrorism/story/0,12780,1171876,00.html.
448. *Smart Border Declaration, supra* note 266.
449. *Smart Border Action Plan, supra* note 266, art. 25.
450. Testimony of Ward Elcock before the Commission of Inquiry into the Actions of Canadian Officials in Relation to Maher Arar, Public Hearing, June 21, 2004, pp. 161, 251. http://www.ararcommission.ca/eng/11e.htm.
451. CTV.ca News Staff, "Maher Arar suspects he's still being spied on," CTV.ca, September 9, 2004. http://www.ctv.ca/servlet/ArticleNews/story/CTVNews/1094738251010_90147450?s_name=& no_ads=.
452. CBC News Online staff, "Man interrogated by CSIS, RCMP suing to clear his name," *CBC News Online*, October 3, 2004. http://www.cbc.ca/story/canada/national/2004/09/20/ mohamed040920.html.
453. Stephen Grey, "America's Gulag," *New Statesman*, 17, No. 807, May 17, 2004. [Stephen Grey]
454. Human Rights Watch, "United Kingdom: Highest court to rule on indefinite detention," Press Release, October 1, 2004. http://www.hrea.org/lists/hr-headlines/markup/maillist.php.
455. Staff and agencies, "Torture evidence inadmissible in U.K. courts, Lords rules," *Guardian*, December 8, 2005.
456. Jason Bennetto, "Shoot to kill tactic adopted after studying methods of suicide bombers," *Independent*, October 25, 2005.
457. BBC News, "Police shot Brazilian eight times," July 25, 2005. http://news.bbc.co.uk/1/hi/ uk/4713753.stm
458. BBC News, "Man shot in anti-terrorism raid," June 2, 2006. http://news.bbc.co.uk/1/hi/uk/ 5040022.stm.
459. Peter Walker and David Fickling, "Police apologize to East London raid family," *Guardian*, June 13, 2006.
460. Eric Lichtblau, "U.S. Opens 2 Inquiries into Arrest of Muslim Lawyer in Oregon," *Newsweek* (U.S. Edition), June 7, 2004.
461. Andre Murr, "The Wrong Man; Brandon Mayfield speaks out on a badly botched arrest," *New York Times*, June 4, 2004. [Andre Murr]
462. Ibid.
463. Al Goodman, "Spain hunts 'detonator bag' man," CNN.com., May 28, 2004. http://edition.cnn.com/2004/WORLD/europe/05/28/spain.warrant/.
464. Ibid.

465. *International Covenant on Civil and Political Rights*, 999 U.N.T.S. 171, art. 4. The ICCPR entered into force in the United States on September 8, 1992.
466. 8 CFR 287, INS No. 2171-01, September 20, 2001. See also Human Rights Watch, *United States, Presumption of Guilt: Human Rights Abuses of Post-September 11 Detainees*, 14, no. 4 (G), August 2002. http://www.hrw.org/reports/2002/us911/USA0802.pdf.
467. U.S. CONST., Amends. V and XIV. See also, ICCPR, art. 9.
468. County of Riverside v. McLaughlin, 500 U.S. 44 (1991).
469. Human Rights Watch Report, *Presumption of Guilt: Human Rights Abuses of Post-September 11 Detainees*, August 2002. http://www.hrw.org/reports/2002/us911/USA0802-05.htm. [HRW, *Presumption of Guilt*]
470. Tim Harper, U.S. 'mistreated' immigrants in 9/11 roundup," *supra* note 178.
471. Human Rights Watch, "Scores of Muslim Men Jailed Without Charge," June 27, 2005. See also Human Rights Watch, *Witness to Abuse: Human Rights Abuses under the Material Witness Law since September 11*, June 2005, vol. 27, no. 2 (G).
472. Ibid.
473. Ibid.
474. Center for National Security Studies v. U.S. Department of Justice, 2002 U.S. District Court, LEXIS 14168 at *28.(D.D.C., August 2, 2002)
475. Human Rights First, "US Law & Security: Guantánamo Bay," April 2006. http://www.humanrightsfirst.org/us_law/etn/det_fac/Guantánamo.htm. [Human Rights First, "US Law & Security: Guantánamo Bay"]
476. International Committee of the Red Cross, *US detention related to the events of 11 September 2001 and its aftermath—the role of the ICRC*, September 5, 2006. http://www.icrc.org/Web/Eng/siteengo.nsf/html/usa-detention-update-121205?OpenDocument.
477. Adam Liptak, "Still Searching for a Strategy Four Years After Sept. 11 Attacks," *New York Times*, November 23, 2005. [Adam Liptak]
478. Mark Sherman, "U.S. told to charge or free suspect: Bush-appointed judge says government can't keep holding terror suspect after 2 years," Associated Press, March 1, 2005. See also, Neil A. Lewis, "Judge Says Terror Suspect Can't be held as an Enemy Combatant," *New York Times*, March 1, 2005.
479. Adam Liptak, *supra* note 477.
480. Hamdi v. Rumsfeld, 542 U.S. 507 (2004).
481. Authorization for Use of Military Force, 115 Stat. 224.
482. Settlement between the United States of America and Yaser Esam Hamdi, dated September 15, 2004. www.FindLaw.com.
483. Rasul v. Bush, 542 U.S. 466 (2004), 321 F. 3d 1134, reversed and remanded.
484. Human Rights First, "US Law & Security: Guantánamo Bay," *supra* note 475.
485. Emily Bazelon, "The Get-Out-of-Torture-Free Card: Why is Congress banning torture but allowing the use of torture testimony?" *Slate*, December 15, 2005.
486. Lindsey Graham, "Rules for Our War," *Washington Post*, December 6, 2005.
487. David Cole, "Patriot Act Post-Mortem," *Nation*, April 3, 2006, p. 5.
488. Colin Freeze, "Khadr trial process 'offensive' says U.S. defence lawyer," *Globe & Mail*, April 21, 2006.
489. Carol D. Leonnig and John Mintz, "Judge Says Detainees' Trials are Unlawful," *Washington Post*, November 9, 2004.

490. Charles Lane, "High Court Rejects Detainee Tribunals," *Washington Post*, June 30, 2006.
491. "Bush's Mysterious New Programs," Consortiumnews.com, February 22, 2006. http://www.consortiumnews.com/2006/022106a.html.
492. Ibid.
493. Human Rights Watch, "UK: Freedom in the Balance—Britain's Highest Court to Rule on Indefinite Detention," press release, London, October 1, 2004. http://hrw.org/english/docs/2004/10/01/uk9421.htm.
494. A(FC) and others (FC) v. Secretary of State for the Home Department; X(FC)) and another (FC) v. Secretary of State for the Home Department, [2004] UKHL 56, per Lord Hoffman.
495. Ibid., para. 74.
496. Ibid., paras. 96 and 97.
497. Nigel Morris, "Enemies of the State?" *Independent*, December 15, 2005.
498. Simon Freeman, "Judge brands control orders 'unlawful'," *Times*, June 26, 2006.
499. CBC News Online staff, "Security certificates constitutional: court," *CBC.ca News*, December 10, 2004. http://www.cbc.ca/story/canada/national/2004/12/10/security-certificate-041210.html.
500. Anti-Terrorism Act, 2001, c.41, s. 83.3(4).
501. Jake Rupert, "Government pays off victim of smear," *Ottawa Citizen*, October 2, 2003.
502. Ibid.
503. Ibid.
504. See Statewatch, "No charges against Swedish Young Left donation to PLFP," *Statewatch News online*, October, 2004. http://www.statewatch.org/news/2002/oct/11sweden.html. [Swedish Young Left]
505. American Civil Liberties Union, *Freedom Under Fire: Dissent in Post-9/11 America* (New York: ACLU, May 2003). http://www.aclu.org/SafeandFree/SafeandFree.cfm?ID=12581&c=206. [ACLU, *Freedom Under Fire*].
506. Randolph Bourne, "War is the Health of the State," from the first draft of an essay, "The State," which was unfinished at the time of Bourne's death in 1918. http://www.bigeye.com/warstate.htm.
507. Fran Shor, "The Crisis of Public Dissent," Counterpunch.org, September 9, 2004. http://www.counterpunch.org/shor09092004.html.
508. Ian Hoffman, Sean Holstege and Josh Richman, "State monitored war protestors," *Oakland Tribune*, June 1, 2003. http://www.oaklandtribune.com/Stories/0,1413,82~1865~1400012,00.html.
509. Bruce Schneier, "The Military are Spying on Americans," Schneier on Security, December 16, 2005. http://www.schneier.com/blog/archives/2005/12/the_military_is.html.
510. Agence France Presse, "Pentagon Admits Keeping Database on US Civilians Deemed Suspicious," December 15, 2005.
511. "Street Theatre Catches Eye of Pentagon," *Newsweek*, January 26, 2006. http://msnbc.msn.com/id/109655509/site/newsweek.
512. Schneier, "The Military are Spying on Americans," *supra* note 509.
513. Walter Pincus, "Pentagon Will Review Database on U.S. Citizens: Protests Among Acts Labeled 'Suspicious'," *Washington Post*, December 15, 2005.
514. Agence France Presse, "Pentagon Admits Keeping Database on US Civilians Deemed Suspicious," *supra* note 510.

515. Ibid.
516. See Schneier, "The Military are Spying on Americans," *supra* note 509 and Walter Pincus, *supra* note 513.
517. Ryan J. Foley, "Feds win Rights to War Protesters' Records," Associated Press, February 8, 2004.
518. ACLU, *Freedom Under Fire*, *supra* note 505, p. 2.
519. Ibid., pp. 5–6.
520. Jeanne Meserve and Phil Hirschkorn, "ACLU sues U.S. over 'no fly' list," CNN.com, April 6, 2004. http://www.cnn.com/2004/LAW/04/06/no.fly.lawsuit/.
521. Michelle Shephard, "How did this man land on a 'no-fly' list?; Air Canada 'flags' Toronto-born cartoonist; Airline has yet to address why it wouldn't sell ticket," *Toronto Star*, June 15, 2004.
522. Araminta Wordsworth, "If you're a David Nelson, you're a terrorism suspect," *National Post*, June 23, 2003.
523. CBS/AP, "Ted Kennedy's Airport Adventure," CBSNEWS.com, August 19, 2004. http://www.cbsnews.com/stories/2004/04/06/terror/main610466.html.
524. EPIC, "Passenger Profiling: EPIC Urges Suspension of Passenger Profiling System," December 15, 2005. http://www.epic.org/privacy/airtravel/profiling.html.
525. Associated Press, "Dozens of people from Canada turned back," January 24, 2005.
526. Statewatch, "U.K :E-Borders plan to tackle threats," *supra* note 283.
527. Independent Media Centers started during the 1999 anti-WTO protest in Seattle and spread into a global network of local, social-justice-oriented, Web-based alternative journalism centers. See www.indymedia.org.
528. Paul Weinberg, "Global agreements threaten media, privacy," *Rabble*, October 19, 2004. http://www.rabble.ca/news_full_story.shtml?x=34664. See also John Lettice, "Servers Seized By FBI Returned—but who wanted what?" *Register*, October 14, 2004. http://www.theregister.co.uk/2004/10/14/indymedia_servers_back/. See also, John Lettice, "Home Office in frame over FBI's London server seizures," *Register*, October 11, 2004. http://www.theregister.co.uk/2004/10/14/indymedia_servers_back/.
529. Ignacio Ramonet, "Terror Tactics," *Le Monde diplomatique*, March 2004, referring to a report by PEN International, *Antiterrorism, writers and freedom of expression, London*, November 2003.
530. Mark Bixler, "Carter Chides U.S. on Rights," *Atlanta Journal-Constitution*, November 12, 2003.
531. Amnesty International USA, "Colombia," *Amnesty Magazine*. http://www.amnestyusa.org/magazine/war_terrorism.html.
532. Reid Morden, "Spies, not Soothsayers: Canadian Intelligence after 9/11," *CSIS Commentary*, no. 85, November 26, 2003. http://www.csis-scrs.gc.ca/eng/comment/com85_e.html.
533. Available on the U.S. Department of Defense Web site, here: http://www.defenselink.mil/news/Aug2004/commissions_instructions.html.
534. Ben Hayes, *Statewatch Analysis: Terrorising the rule of law: the policy and practice of proscription*, June 2005.
535. Associated Press, "Anti-terror 'watchlists' merge to speed up access," *Toronto Star*, September 17, 2004. See also documents obtained by the Electronic Privacy Information Center through a Freedom of Information Act request. http://www.epic.org/privacy/air-

travel/foia/watchlist_foia_analysis.html. See also the testimony of FBI official Steve McCraw in "Can the Use of Factual Data Analysis Strengthen National Security? Part One," Hearing before the Subcommittee on Technology, Information Policy, Intergovernmental Relations and the Census of the House Committee on Government Reform, 108th Cong., May 6, 2003, Serial No. 108-72, p. 30. http://www.gpoaccess.gov/chearings/108hcat2.html.

536. Jay Stanley, *The Surveillance-Industrial Complex*, *supra* note 211, p. 19.
537. BBC News, "France 'confirms' fighter escorts," January 2, 2004. http://news.bbc.co.uk/1/hi/world/europe/3363291.stm.
538. Walter Pincus and Dan Eggen, "325,000 Names on Terrorism List," *Washington Post*, February 15, 2006.
539. Ibid.
540. James Gordon Meek, "13 Million on Terror Watch List," *New York Daily News*, April 8, 2003; Tom Godfrey, "5 million on [U.S.] terrorism list," *Toronto Sun*, January 20, 2004.
541. Jay Stanley, *The Surveillance-Industrial Complex*, *supra* note 211, p. 19.
542. Ibid., p. 19.
543. See Brian Braiker, "The 'Patriot' Search," *Newsweek Online*, June 3, 2004, and correction. http://msnbc.msn.com/id/5131685/site/newsweek.
544. The works of Czech writer Franz Kafka, published after his death in 1924, are notable for the recurrence of paradoxes or encounters with absurdity, and nightmarish predicaments. In *The Trial*, a man awakens one morning and, for reasons that are never clear, is arrested and subjected to the rigours of a mystifying judicial system for an unspecified crime. In *The Castle*, a land surveyor tries vainly to gain recognition from officials at a castle that dominates the life of a village. The word "Kafkaesque" has come to be used to describe situations characterized by surreal distortion, senselessness and often menacing complexity.

Chapter Eleven

545. Thomas Mathiesen, *supra* note 168, p. 29.
546. All of the information and quotations for this story come from Ellen Nakashima, "FBI Said Involved in Arrest of 8 Indonesians," *Washington Post*, January 14, 2006.
547. Omar Ahmed Khadr by his Next Friend Fatmah El-Samnah v. The Queen, 2005 FC 1976.
548. James Meek, "They beat me from all sides," *Guardian*, January 14, 2005. See also, James Gordon, "German's tale eerily similar to Arar's: Man said he was abducted, flown to Kabul where he claims U.S. officials tortured him," *Ottawa Citizen*, January 12, 2005.
549. Ibid.
550. Don Van Natta Jr., "Germany Weighs if It Played Role in Seizure by U.S.," *New York Times*, February 20, 2006.
551. Ibid.
552. Ibid.
553. Souad Mekhennet and Craig S. Smith, "German Spy Agency Admits Mishandling Abduction Case," *New York Times*, June 2, 2006.
554. See Swedish Young Left, *supra* note 504.
555. William M. Arkin, "U.S. Plans New Bases in the Middle East," *Washington Post*, March 22, 2006.

556. Anne Scot Tyson, "New U.S. strategy: 'lily pad' bases," *Christian Science Monitor*, August 10, 2004.
557. Walden Bello, International Civil Liberties Monitoring Group International Conference held in Ottawa, February 17, 2004. [Walden Bello]
558. Anne Scott Tyson, "New Plans Foresee Fighting Terrorism Beyond War Zones," *Washington Post*, April 23, 2006.
559. William M. Arkin, "Rumsfeld's New War Plan," *Washington Post*, January 25, 2006.
560. Tom Shanker and Scott Shane, "Elite Troops Get Expanded Role on Intelligence," *New York Times*, March 8, 2006.
561. Ibid.
562. Anne Scott Tyson, "New Plans Foresee Fighting Terrorism Beyond War Zones," *supra* note 558.
563. Tom Shanker and Scott Shane, *supra* note 560.
564. Anne Scott Tyson, "New Plans Foresee Fighting Terrorism Beyond War Zones," *supra* note 558.
565. Griff Witte and Kamran Khan, "Attacks Strain Efforts on Terror," *Washington Post*, January 26, 2006.
566. Associated Press, "U.S. kills al-Qaeda suspects in Yemen," *USA Today*, November 4, 2002.
567. When the European Commission finalized the deal amidst controversy, it ". . . argued that the alternative would have been chaos, with airlines facing fines and the loss of landing rights in the U.S., as well as trouble from E.U. data protection authorities." Ian Black, *supra* note 277.
568. Canada Department of Foreign Affairs and International Trade, *Fifth Annual Report on Canada's State of Trade, Trade Update: March 2004* (Minister of Public Works and Government Services Canada, 2004), pp. 3-4. http://www.dfait-maeci.gc.ca/eet/trade/state-of-trade-en.asp.
569. Maude Barlow, *The Canada We Want—A Citizens' Alternative to Deep Integration* (Ottawa: Council of Canadians, n.d.). http://www.canadians.org/documents/TCWW_eng.pdf.
570. Yap Swee Seng, Suaram and the Asian People's Security Network, "Impacts on the South: The Case of Malaysia," *Anti-Terrorism and the Security Agenda: Impacts on Rights, Freedoms and Democracy, Report and Recommendations for Policy Direction of a Public Forum organized by the International Civil Liberties Monitoring Group* (Ottawa: February 17, 2004), pp. 59–60. http://www.statewatch.org/observatory2ab.htm (Analysis No. 26)
571. Walden Bello, *supra* note 557.
572. See Seymour Hersh, "The Syrians' Bet," *supra* note 49.
573. In the various versions of the campfire story "The Monkey's Paw," a wizened, dismembered paw of a monkey grants its owner's wishes, but through some horrific interpretation of those wishes.

Chapter Twelve

574. Farewell Radio and Television Address to the American People by President Dwight D. Eisenhower, January 17, 1961. Available online at the site of the Dwight D. Eisenhower Library and Museum here: http://www.eisenhower.utexas.edu/farewell.htm.
575. Gwynne Dyer, *supra* note 9, p. 121.

576. Roch Tassé, Coordinator, International Civil Liberties Monitoring Group (Canada) and of the International Campaign Against Mass Surveillance (ICAMS).
577. American Association for the Advancement of Science, R&D Funding Update, March 4, 2005. www.aaas.org/spp/rd.
578. Ibid.
579. Statewatch, "E.U.: Security research programme to look at creating 'smart' biometric documents which will 'locate, identify and follow the movement of persons' through 'automatic chips with positioning,'" *Statewatch News online*, February 2004. http://www.statewatch.org/news/2004/feb/23Aeu-plan-security.htm.
580. For the full list of companies in the Group of Personalities, see "The Experts Looking Out for Europe's Security," *Intelligence Online*, no. 468. http://www.intelligenceonline.com/NETWORKS/FILES/468/468.asp?rub=networks.
581. Ben Hayes, *Arming Big Brother: the EU's Security Research Program*, Transnational Institute, TNI Briefing Series, no. 2006/1.
582. Commission of the European Communities, *Security Research: The Next Steps*, Communication from the Commission to the Council, the European Parliament, the European Economic and Social Committee and the Committee of the Regions, COM (2004) 590 (Brussels: COEC, September 7, 2004), p. 10. http://europa.eu.int/eur-lex/en/com/cnc/2004/com2004_0590en01.pdf.
583. Department of Finance Canada, *Enhancing Security for Canadians: Budget 2006*. http://www.fin.gc.ca/budget01/booklets/bksece.htm.
584. Department of Finance, Canada, Budget 2006, Chapter 3. http://www.fin.gc.ca/budget06/bp/bpc3de.htm.
585. Roch Tassé, citing Adam Mayle and Alex Knott, *Outsourcing Big Brother: Office of Total Information Awareness Relies on Private Sector to Track Americans*, Special report of the Center for Public Integrity, December 17, 2002. http://www.public-i.org/dtaweb/report.asp?ReportID=484.
586. ACLU, *MATRIX: Myths and Reality*, February 10, 2004: http://www.aclu/org/privacy/spying/14999res20040210.htm.
587. Madeleine Baran, *supra* note 397; Jim Defede, *supra* note 416.
588. Jim Defede, *supra* note 416. See also, Associated Press, "States build terror database resembling controversial federal project," SiliconValley.com, September 23, 2003. http://www.siliconvalley.com/mld/siliconvalley/news/editorial/6841676.htm.
589. Robert O'Harrow, "LexisNexis to Buy Seisint for $775 Million," *Washington Post*, July 15, 2004.
590. Lichtblau and Markoff, *supra* note 203.
591. Nick Wakeman, "Accenture secures U.S. Visit," *Washington Technology*, June 7, 2004.
592. Robert O'Harrow and Scott Higham, "U.S. Border Security at a Crossroads," *Washington Post*, May 23, 2005.
593. Ibid.
594. Schneier, "The Failure of US VISIT," Schneier on Security, January 31, 2006. *http://www.schneier.com/blog/archives/2006/01/the_failure_of_1.html.*
595. Ibid. Bruce Schneier makes a similar calculation.
596. Jay Stanley, *The Surveillance-Industrial Complex*, *supra* note 211, p. 28.
597. Goo and O'Harrow, *supra* note 428.

598. Richard Behar, "Never Heard of Acxiom? Chances Are It's Heard of You," *Fortune*, February 23, 2004.
599. Ibid.
600. Associated Press, "Takeoff Delay Slows Secure Flight," *Wired News*, February 9, 2006.
601. Patty Donmoyer, "DOJ Assails Secure Flight," *Business Travel News*, September 2005.
602. John Doyle, "EagleForce Gets TSA Contract for Secure Flight Data Tests," February 3, 2005. http://www.theeagleforce.com/TSA_Award.htm.
603. Steve Ranger, "Iris scans and passenger databases to protect UK borders: How are preparations for the £400 million e-Borders project shaping up so far?," silicon.com, February 16, 2006. http://www.silicon.com/publicsector.
604. "IBM wins Home Office e-Borders contract to strengthen UK border controls," PublicTechnology.net, November 4, 2004. http://www.publictechnoligy.net.
605. Robert Weisman, "Identity Crisis," *Boston Globe*, April 5, 2004.
606. See BioDentity Systems Corporation Web site homepage here: http://www.biodentity .com.
607. European Commission, "Sweden to start issuing biometric passports and e-ID cards in 2005," *eGovernment News*, September 2, 2004. http://europa.eu.int/ida/en/document/3247/355.
608. European Commission, "Danish Government to start issuing biometric passports by the end of 2004," *eGovernment News*, February 18, 2004. http://europa.eu.int/ida/en/document/2164/333.
609. Canada News-Wire, *Canadian Air Transport Security Authority Pilot Project Includes Bioscrypt Technology,* February 23, 2004. http://www.newswire.ca/en/releases/archive/February2004/23/c2728.html.
610. "Smart cards make inroads in Asia," *supra* note 225.
611. Oki Electric Industry Co., Ltd., "Iris Recognition System is Selected for Border Control at Frankfurt/Main Airport by the German Federal Ministry of the Interior," press release, February 13, 2004. http. //www.oki.com/en/press/2004/z03084e.html.
612. Brad Grimes, "Tech Success: Unysis, Daon help travelers fly through lines," *Washington Technology,* July 19, 2004. http://www.washingtontechnology.com/news/19_8/emerging-tech/24023-1.html.
613. Corporate Watch, "Company Profiles: Unisys." http://www.corporate watch.org.uk.
614. Citzenship and Immigration Canada Develop Biometrics Field Trial, CIC press release. http://www.cic.gc.ca/english/press/notice/notice-biometrics.html.
615. Canada News-Wire, "Bahrain Enhances Border Security and Takes the Lead With E-Visas Using SITA Technology," May 25, 2004. http://www.newswire.ca/en/releases/archive/May2004/25/c6965.html.
616. Siemens Business Services, *Integrated ID Solutions.* http://www.siemens.nl/sbs/getfile.asp?id=97.
617. Thales Secure Operations, *People's Republic of China Uses Secure Identification Technology for Smart Card Based ID Card.* http://security.thalesgroup.com/case_study/case15.htm.
618. Geoffrey York, "Rights Group Questions Trade Mission to China," *Globe and Mail*, September 21, 2004.
619. Electronic Privacy Information Center, "Air Travel Privacy." http://www.epic.org/privacy.airtravel.
620. George Monbiot, "The Perpetual Surveillance Society," *supra* note 253.

Chapter Thirteen

621. See the seminal article by Francis Fukuyama, *supra* note 136.
622. For an insightful treatment of imperialism, see Hannah Arendt, *Imperialism* (New York: Harcourt Brace Janovich, 1968 edition).
623. Tim Harper, "New name, same conflict," *Toronto Star*, February 11, 2006.
624. Steven Lee Myers, "Opponents Call Putin's Overhaul Plan a Step Back," *New York Times*, September 14, 2004.
625. Jeremy Bentham, *The Panopticon Writings*, ed. Miran Bozovic (London:Verso, 1995) pp. 29–95.
626. Michel Foucault, *Discipline and Punishment: The Birth of the Prison*, trans. Allan Sheridan. (New York: Random House, 1995) at p. 261.

Chapter Fourteen

627. Giorgio Agamben, Letter to the Editor [translation], *Le Monde*, January 11, 2004.
628. Stephen Grey, *supra* note 153.
629. See Anne Applebaum, *Gulag: A History* (New York: Anchor Books, 2003).
630. Stephen Grey, *supra* note 153; Estanislao Oziewicz, *supra* note 4.
631. Thomas Powers, "The Biggest Secret," *New York Review of Books* 53, 3, February 23, 2006.
632. Dana Priest, "CIA Holds Terror Suspects in Secret Prisons," *Washington Post*, November 2, 2005.
633. Stephen Grey, *supra* note 454; Estanislao Oziewicz, *supra* note 167. With respect to the CIA center in Jordan, see Associated Press, "Dozens of secret jails run by U.S., report says," *Toronto Star*, June 18, 2004. [Dozens of secret jails]. With respect to the CIA center in Qatar, see Jane Mayer, "Outsourcing Torture," *New Yorker*, February 14, 2005. [Outsourcing Torture]
634. Dana Priest, "CIA Holds Terror Suspects in Secret Prisons," *supra*, note 632. At the request of "senior U.S. officials," the *Washington Post* did not report the names of the European countries involved.
635. Ibid.
636. Ibid.
637. Stephen Grey, *supra* note 454. See also U.S. State Department country reports.
638. Stephen Grey, *supra* note 454.
639. Stephen Grey, *supra* note 454.
640. Estanislao Oziewicz, *supra* note 167. Another source put the number at 15,000 as of January 2004. Louise Christian, "Guantánamo: a global experiment in inhumanity," *Guardian*, January 9, 2004. J. Cofer Black, former head of the CIA's Counterterrorist Center, testified in late 2002 that there were at least 3,000 terrorist prisoners being held worldwide. The Sudanese intelligence service alone claimed to have turned over more than 200 captives in the two years following September 11, 2001. Stephen Grey, *supra* note 454.
641. Dana Priest, "Memo Okd Secret transfer of detainees: Experts say U.S. violated Geneva Conventions," *Washington Post*, October 24, 2004.
642. Association of the Bar of the City of New York and Center for Human Rights and Global Justice, *Torture by Proxy: International and Domestic Law Applicable to "Extraordinary*

Renditions" (New York: ABCNY & NYU School of Law, 2004), p. 15. www.nyuhr.org/docs/TortureByProxy.pdf.

643. Douglas Jehl, "Rule Change Lets C.I.A. Freely Send Suspects Abroad to Jails," *New York Times*, March 6, 2005. [Jehl, "Rule Change"]
644. Ibid.
645. Outsourcing Torture, *supra* note 633.
646. According to officials, the CIA is authorized to do this under the new directive. Jehl, "Rule Change," *supra* note 643.
647. Dana Priest, "Long-term Plan Sought for Terror Suspects," *Washington Post*, January 2, 2005.
648. Kareem Fahim, "The Invisible Men," *Village Voice*, March 30, 2004.
649. Stephen Grey, *supra* note 454. See also, Christopher Bollyn, "The Pentagon's Ghost Planes and Enforced Disappearances," *American Free Press*, January 17, 2005. [Christopher Bollyn], referring to articles written in the *Sunday Times*, *Washington Post*, *Boston Globe*, and *Chicago Tribune* trying to piece together facts about the fleet and its current operations.
650. Stephen Grey, *supra* note 454.
651. Third Geneva Convention, art. 122; Fourth Geneva Convention, art. 136.
652. Art. 2(i).
653. James Risen, David Johnston, and Neil A. Lewis, "Harsh CIA Methods Cited in Top Qaeda Interrogaton," *New York Times*, May 13, 2004.
654. Outsourcing Torture, *supra* note 633.
655. Human Rights Watch Briefing Paper, *The United States' "Disappeared": The CIA's Long-Term "Ghost Detainees,"* October 2004, p. 8. [*Ghost Detainees*] "Army General Paul Kern told Congress that the C.I.A. may have hidden up to a hundred detainees." Outsourcing Torture, *supra* note 633. For a complete copy of the report see: http://www.hrw.org/backgrounder/usa/us1004/
656. *Ghost Detainees*, *supra* note 655.
657. Jonathan Steele, "Bush is now thinking of building jails abroad to hold suspects for life: a global gulag to hide the world's secrets," *Guardian*, January 14, 2005. [Jonathan Steele]
658. Josh White, "Pentagon to Identify Detainees," *Washington Post*, February 25, 2006.
659. See, for example, David Rose, "How I entered the hellish world of Guantánamo Bay," *Observer*, February 6, 2005. [David Rose]
660. Testimony of Cofer Black, Hearing Before the Joint Investigation of the House and Senate Intelligence Committees, 107th Cong., September 26, 2002. http://intelligence.senate.gov/0209hrg/020926/witness.htm.
661. The United States has maintained that American constitutional guarantees for criminal process do not apply to the detainees there because they are aliens in foreign territory.
662. The Bush administration has alternately said that Geneva Conventions protections did not apply because the detainees were "unlawful combatants," that the Geneva Conventions did not apply to a war on terrorism, and that the Geneva Conventions did not apply because the Taliban was not the recognized government of Afghanistan and so not a party to the Conventions. See, Human Rights Watch, *Background Paper on Geneva Conventions and Persons Held by U.S. Forces, Human Rights Watch Press Backgrounder,* January 29, 2002. http://www.hrw.org/backgrounder/use/pow-bck.htm, referring to a statement made by Donald Rumsfeld on January 11, 2002. See also, Human Rights Watch, *Bush Errs in Geneva Convention Rules, Fails to Grant POW Status to Detainees,* February

7, 2002. http://hrw.org/press/2002/02/geneva0207.htm; and Amnesty International Report, *Human Dignity Denied: Torture and Accountability in the 'war on terror'*, October 27, 2004. http://web.amnesty.org/library/Index/ENGAMR511452004. [Amnesty *Human Dignity Denied*]. Finally, see *New York Times*, "A Guide to the Memos on Torture," *New York Times*. [A Guide to the Memos on Torture]. In particular, see descriptions of John C. Yoo's series of memorandums from January 2002 providing legal arguments to support the administration's assertions that the Geneva Conventions did not apply to detainees from the war in Afghanistan.

663. A Guide to the Memos on Torture, *supra* note 662. In particular, see descriptions of a March 2003 memorandum declaring that President Bush was not bound by either international treaty prohibitions regarding the treatment of prisoners or by a federal antitorture law because he had authority as commander in chief to approve any technique to protect the nation's security; and letter to the ICRC from Brig. Gen. Janis Karpinski, asserting that prisoners held as security risks could legally be treated differently from prisoners of war or ordinary criminals. Having taken prisoners to Guantánamo Bay from the theatre of war in Afghanistan and elsewhere, the United States has also maintained that although it is a signatory to the International Covenant on Civil and Political Rights, the Covenant does not apply there because Guantánamo Bay is not United States territory, but only leased by the U.S.

664. Military Order of November 13, 2001, "Detention, Treatment and Trial of Certain Non-Citizens in the War against Terrorism" 66 F.R. 57833 (November 16, 2001); Department of Defense Military Commission Order No. 1, released March 21, 2002 and No. 2 released April 30, 2002; Department of Defense Military Instructions Nos. 1-8, released April 30, 2002.

665. See United States v. Verdugo-Urquidez, 494 U.S. 259 (1990).

666. In the 1949 Geneva Conventions, there are no categories other than civilians and combatants in the law. The Third Geneva Convention covers combatants in international hostilities and divides them into various subclasses. While the Third Convention provides those who qualify as combatants with specific procedural and other rights as Prisoners of War, the Fourth Convention provides *comparable* rights to civilian prisoners. The only exception, which may apply to some of the detainees at Guantánamo Bay, are civilians (persons who do not qualify for combatant status under the Third Convention) who are "[n]ationals of a State which is not bound by the Convention . . . [or n]ationals of a neutral State who find themselves in the territory of a belligerent State, and nationals of a co-belligerent State . . . while the State of which they are nationals has normal diplomatic representation in the State in whose hands they are." In that case, they are entitled to such protections as their countries' diplomatic relations with the United States can provide them and to the protections contained in s. 75 of the First Additional Protocol to the Geneva Conventions. The United States is not a party to the First Protocol, but the rights it affords—against physical and mental torture, against degrading treatment, and to due process—are arguably part of customary international law.

667. The Human Rights Committee has for some time held the view that a state bears obligations under the Covenant wherever it has jurisdiction, reading disjunctively the second "and" in Article 2 of the Covenant which provides, "Each State Party . . . undertakes to respect and to ensure to all individuals within its territory *and subject to its jurisdiction* the rights recognized in the present Covenant. . . ."

668. Art. 2.

669. See in this regard Filartiga v. Pena-Irala, 630 F.2d 876 (2d Cir. 1980); Rodriguez Fernandez v. Wilkinson, 505 F. Supp. 787 (1980), aff'd on other grounds, 654 F. Supp. 1382 (10th Cir. 1981).
670. John Barry, Michael Hirsh, and Michael Isikoff, "The Roots of Torture," *Newsweek*, May 24, 2004. http://msnbc.msn.com/id/4989422/site/newsweek/ [December 20, 2004].
671. Ibid.
672. Outsourcing Torture, *supra* note 633.
673. Ibid. See also, A Guide to the Torture Memos, *supra* note 662.
674. Jonathan Steele, *supra* note 657.
675. Human Rights Watch, *Summary of International and U.S. Law Prohibiting Torture and Other Ill-Treatment of Persons in Custody*, May 24, 2004. http://hrw.org/english/docs/2004/05/24/usint8614_txt.htm. See also, Amnesty, *Human Dignity Denied, supra* note 662.
676. David Johnston and Neil A. Lewis, "Bush's Counsel Sought Ruling About Torture," *New York Times*, January 5, 2005. [Johnston and Lewis]
677. A Guide to the Memos on Torture, *supra* note 662.
678. Ibid.
679. Art. 2.
680. Outsourcing Torture, *supra* note 633.
681. A Guide to the Memos on Torture, *supra* note 662.
682. Human Rights Watch, "U.S.: Did President Bush Order Torture?: White House Must Explain 'Executive Order' Cited in FBI E-Mail," December 21, 2004. http://hrw.org/english/docs/2004/12/21/usint9925_txt.htm. [HRW, Did President Bush Order?]
683. Johnston and Lewis, *supra* note 676.
684. Outsourcing Torture, *supra* note 633.
685. Dana Priest and Charles Babington, "Plan Would Let U.S. Deport Suspects to Nations That Might Torture Them," *Washington Post*, September 30, 2004.
686. Ibid. See also, Nat Hentoff, "Torture as Foreign Policy," *Village Voice*, October 22, 2004 and ACLU, *"PATRIOT II" Provisions in H.R. 10 (As Passed by House)*, October 13, 2004. http://www.aclu.org/safefree/general/18692leg20041013.html. Article 3 of the Torture Convention prohibits states from sending persons to countries where there are grounds to believe they would be in danger of being subjected to torture. The bill shifted the burden of proof to the detainee and raised the standard of proof to "clear and compelling evidence": an impossible thing for most detainees to prove. The bill also required that the United States seek diplomatic assurances that the person would not be tortured; however, these are widely regarded as meaningless coming from countries with a long record of torture and human rights abuses. See Human Rights Watch, "Still at Risk: Diplomatic Assurances No Safeguard Against Torture," April 2005. http://hrw.org/reports/2005/ eca0405/.
687. Dana Priest and Charles Babington, *supra* note 685.
688. Human Rights First, "House and Senate Pass Intelligence Bill, Anti Refugee Provisions Struck from Final Version." http://www.humanrightsfirst.org/asylum/asylum_10.htm.
689. Nat Hentoff, *supra* note 686.
690. Ibid.
691. Rosa Brooks, "McCain to Bush: 'Don't try it pal'," *Boston Globe*, January 6, 2006.
692. Anthony Lewis, "The Torture Administration," *Nation*, December 16, 2005, p.14.
693. Rosa Brooks, *supra* note 691.

694. Ibid.
695. Presidential signing statement, Detainee Treatment Act of 2005, Title X of the Department of Defense Appropriations Act, 2006.
696. Rosa Brooks, *supra* note 691.
697. Editorial, "A Bad Bargain," *New York Times*, September 22, 2006; Adam Liptak, "Detainee Deal Comes with Contradictions," *New York Times*, September 23, 2006.
698. Editorial, "Rushing Off a Cliff," *New York Times*, September 28, 2006.
699. Michael A. Fletcher, "Bush Signs Terrorism Measure," *Washington Post*, October 18, 2006.
700. All the material and quotations for Diliwar's story come from the excellent article, Tim Golden, Ruhallah Khapalwak, Carlotta Gall and David Rohde, and Alain Delaqueriere, "In U.S. Report, Brutal Details of 2 Afghan Inmates' Deaths," *New York Times*, May 20, 2005.
701. Estanislao Oziewicz, *supra* note 167.
702. Estanislao Oziewicz, *supra* note 167. See also, Douglas Jehl, Steven Lee Meyers, and Eric Schmitt, "Abuse of Captives More Widespread, Says Army Survey," *New York Times*, May 26, 2004, citing U.S. Army summary of deaths and mistreatment of prisoners in American custody in Iraq and Afghanistan [Jehl, Meyers and Schmitt]; Dana Priest and Barton Gellman, "U.S. Decries Abuse but Defends Interrogations," *Washington Post*, December 26, 2002, p. A01. [Priest and Gellman]. See also, Dozens of Secret Jails, *supra* note 633 which describes the case of a CIA contractor who is accused of beating a detainee to death using his hands, feet and a flashlight.
703. In December 2002, the *Washington Post* interviewed American national security officials who suggested that pain killers had been given selectively to Abu Zubaida, one of the top Al Qaeda leaders, who was shot in the groin during capture. See Priest and Gellman, *supra* note 702.
704. Priest and Gellman, *supra* note 702. See also, Tim Golden and Eric Schmitt, "General took Guantánamo rules to Iraq for Handling of Prisoners," *New York Times*, May 13, 2004. [Golden and Schmitt]
705. Ibid.
706. Priest and Gellman, *supra* note 702.
707. Associated Press, "37 deaths of detainees in Iraq, Afghanistan probed," *Sunday Observer Online*, May 23, 2004.
708. Dan Eggen and R. Jeffrey Smith, "F.B.I. agents allege abuse of detainees at Guantánomo Bay," *Washington Post*, December 21, 2004.
709. As of May 2004, the Army had closed two homicide cases. One involved an Iraqi detainee who had been shot for throwing rocks at guards. Jehl, Meyers and Schmitt, *supra* note 702.
710. Neil A. Lewis, "Broad Use of Harsh Tactics," *New York Times*, October 17, 2004.
711. Jehl, Meyers, and Schmitt, *supra* note 702.
712. Associated Free Press, "C.I.A. renditions of suspects are 'out of control,'" *Nation online*, 2004.
713. David Rose, *supra* note 659.
714. HRW, Did President Bush Order?, *supra* at note 682.
715. Ibid. A Guide to the Memos on Torture, *supra* note 662.
716. A Guide to the Memos on Torture, *supra* note 662.
717. Scott Higham and Joe Stephens, "New Details on Scale of Iraq Prison Abuse," *Washington Post*, May 21, 2004.

718. Carl Huse and Sheryl Gay Stolberg, "Lawmakers View Images from Iraq," *New York Times*, May 13, 2005.
719. Ibid.
720. Ibid.
721. Eric Schmitt, "Rumsfeld and a General Clash on Abuse," *New York Times*, May 12, 2004.
722. Kate Zernike, "Accused Soldier Paints Scene of Eager Mayhem at Iraqi Prison," *New York Times*, May 14, 2004.
723. Agence France Presse, "Nearly 100 Dead in US Custody in Iraq, Afghanistan: Rights Group," February 22, 2006.
724. Outsourcing Torture, *supra* note 633.
725. Jonathan Steele, *supra* note 657.
726. Ibid.
727. Ibid.
728. Douglas Jehl, "Pentagon Seeks to Transfer More Detainees from Base in Cuba," *New York Times*, March 11, 2005. See also, *Dawn*, "Life Imprisonment without trial condemned," January 3, 2005. http://www.dawn.com/2005/01/03/int1.htm.
729. Dana Priest, "CIA Holds Terror Suspects in Secret Prisons," *supra* note 632.
730. Ibid.
731. Tony Johansson, "A Scandal in Sweden," ZNet (http://www.zmag.org), May 25, 2004.
732. Ibid.
733. Canadian Press, "Canada allegedly backed Bush on forced disappearances," January 19, 2006.
734. Wesley Wark, "America's Dirty Secrets," *Ottawa Citizen*, December 9, 2005.
735. Haider Rizvi, "Terror Policies Draw Outrage at Home and Abroad," Inter Press Service, June 2005. See also, Stephen Grey, "U.S. agents 'kidnapped militant' for torture in Egypt," *Times Online*, February 6, 2005.
736. Wesley Wark, "America's Dirty Secrets," *supra* note 734. See also STRATFOR, Daily Terrorism Brief, June 27, 2005. http://www.stratfor.org/products/premium/read_article.php?id=250690.
737. STRATFOR, *supra* note736.
738. STRATFOR, *supra* note 736.
739. Wesley Wark, *supra* note 736.
740. Tim Harper, "Ottawa okayed 'ghost flights'," *Toronto Star*, January 16, 2006.
741. Wesley Wark, *supra* note 736.
742. Tim Harper, "Ottawa okayed 'ghost flights'," *supra* note 740.
743. Anne Gearan, "Rice defends U.S. terrorism policy," Associated Press, December 5, 2005.
744. Human Rights Watch, *Empty Promises: Diplomatic Assurances No Safeguard against Torture*, April 2004. http://hrw.org/reports/2004/un0404/.
745. Human Rights Watch Briefing Paper for the 59th Session of the United Nations Commission on Human Rights, *In the Name of Counter-Terrorism: Human Rights Abuses Worldwide*, March 25, 2003. http://hrw.org/un/chr59. [HRW, *In the Name of Counter-Terrorism*]
746. Ibid.
747. Ibid.
748. Ibid.
749. Ibid.

750. Human Rights Watch, "Malaysia: Detainees Abused Under Security Law," press release, May 25, 2005.
751. Human Rights Watch, *In the Name of Security: Counter-terrorism and Human Rights Abuses Under Malaysia's Internal Security Act,* May 2004, vol. 16, no. 7 (C), p. 44. [HRW, *In the Name of Security*]
752. Ibid., p. 43.
753. Ibid., p. 45.
754. Ibid., p. 44.
755. Ibid.
756. Ibid.
757. Ibid., p. 43.
758. Christopher Bollyn, *supra* note 649.
759. Outsourcing Torture, *supra* note 633.
760. Christopher Bollyn, *supra* note 649.
761. Jim Lobe, "U.S. Militarizing Latin America," OneWorld.net, October 6, 2004.
762. Jack Epstein, "General Seeks Boost for Latin American Armies," *San Francisco Chronicle,* April 30, 2004.
763. HRW, *In the Name of Security, supra* note 751, p. 12.

Chapter Fifteen

764. Joint Inquiry Into Intelligence Community Activities Before and After the Terrorist Attacks of September 11, 2001, *Report of the U.S. Senate Select Committee on Intelligence and U.S. House Permanent Select Committee on Intelligence Together With Additional Views*, December 2002. http://www.gpoaccess.gov/serialset/creports/911.html. [Joint Inquiry Report].The Joint Inquiry referred to a long list of intelligence findings, which indicated that Al Qaeda was eager to attack the United States and that terrorists were interested in using airplanes as weapons. These included an intelligence briefing, prepared in July 2001 that said that bin Laden was looking to pull off a "spectacular" attack against the United States designed to inflict "mass casualties" and that "[a]ttack preparations had been made." A summer 1998 intelligence report suggested bin Laden was planning attacks in New York and Washington, and in September 1998, the head of the CIA briefed Congress and noted that the FBI was following three or four bin Laden operatives in the U.S. In December 1998 an intelligence source reported that an Al Qaeda member was planning operations against U.S. targets: "Plans to hijack US aircraft proceeding well. Two individuals . . . had successfully evaded checkpoints in a dry run at a NY airport." In December 1999, the CIA's Counterterrorism Center concluded that bin Laden wanted to inflict maximum casualties, cause massive panic and score a psychological victory. To do so, it said, he might attack between five and fifteen targets on the Millennium, including several in the United States. In 2000, the CIA had information that two of the 9/11 hijackers who had already been linked to terrorism were, or might be in the United States. In April 2001, an intelligence report said that Al Qaeda was in the throes of advanced preparation for a major attack, probably against an American or Israeli target. In August 2001, the FBI began to try to locate the two hijackers mentioned above.
765. Ibid., p. 7.
766. Ibid., pp. 7, 33.

767. Ibid. One intelligence source informed the Joint Inquiry that "a closely held intelligence report" for "senior government officials" in August 2001 stated that bin Laden was seeking to conduct attacks in the United States, that Al Qaeda maintained a support structure there, and that information obtained in May 2001 indicated that a group of bin Laden supporters were planning attacks in the United States with explosives. (p. 9). The Joint Inquiry's report also notes that in May 2001, "the U.S. Government became aware that an individual in Saudi Arabia was in contact with a senior al-Qa'ida operative and was most likely aware of an upcoming al-Qa'ida operation." (p. 111)
768. David Corn, "The 9/11 Investigation," *Nation*, August 4, 2006.
769. Bergman, Lichtblau, Shane, van Natta Jr., *supra* note 101.
770. Eric Lichtblau, "U.S. Seeks Access to Bank Records to Deter Terror," *New York Times*, April 10, 2005.
771. Ibid.
772. Associated Press, "LexisNexis theft much worse than thought," MSNBC.com, April 12, 2005.
773. Bob Sullivan, "Database giant gives access to fake firms," MSNBC.com, February 14, 2005.
774. Behar, *supra* note 598, pp. 140-144.
775. Bruce Schneier, "'I Am Not a Terrorist' Cards," *Crypto-Gram Newsletter*, March 15, 2004. http://www.schneier.com/crypto-gram-0403.html.
776. Eric Lichtblau, "F.B.I. Said to Lag on Translating Terror Tapes," *New York Times*, September 28, 2004.
777. Mark Trevelyan, "Head of Interpol highlights abuses in war on terror," *Statewatch News online*, October 2, 2003. http://www.statewatch.org/news/2003/oct/05interpol.htm.
778. Jim Lobe, "Development-U.S.: Guns Over Butter," Inter Press Service, February 8, 2006.
779. Summary and table from Wikipedia, Patterns of Global Terrorism. http://en.wikipedia.org/wiki/Patterns_of_Global_Terrorism.
780. Ibid.
781. Karen DeYoung, "Terrorist Attacks Rose Sharply in 2005, State Dept. Says," *Washington Post*, April 29, 2006. The figures were compiled by the NCTC and released with the annual State Department Country Reports.
782. Wikipedia, Car Accident. http://en.wikipedia.org/wiki/Car_accident.

Web Sites/Resources

SURVEILLANCE / CIVIL LIBERTIES / PRIVACY ISSUES

International Campaign Against Mass Surveillance
http://www.i-cams.org

Surveillance and Society
http://www.surveillance-and-society.org

War on Terrorism Watch
http://www.waronterrorismwatch.ca

Statewatch
http://www.statewatch.org

Statewatch Observatory on CIA "rendition"
http://www.statewatch.org/rendition/rendition.html

American Civil Liberties Union
http://www.aclu.org

Friends Committee on National Legislation
http://www.fcnl.org

Center for Democracy & Technology
http://www.cdt.org

PATRIOTWATCH
http://www.patriotwatch.org

Center for National Security Studies
http://www.cnss.org

Electronic Privacy Information Center
http://www.epic.org

Electronic Frontier Foundation
http://www.eff.org

European Civil Liberties Network
http://www.ecln.org

The Surveillance Project
http://www.queensu.ca/sociology/Surveillance

Homeland Security (Century Foundation)
http://www.homelandsec.org

Center for Constitutional Rights
http://www.ccr-ny.org

Office of the Privacy Commissioner of Canada
http://www.privcom.gc.ca

Privacy International
http://www.privacyinternational.org

NO2ID
http://www.no2id.net

European Digital Rights
http://www.edri.org

Campaign Against Criminalising Communities
http://www.cacc.org.uk

Schneier on Security
http://www.schneier.com/blog

Human Rights Watch
http://www.hrw.org

Human Rights First
http://www.humanrightsfirst.org

Index

⊙ ⊙

ABOUT THE AUTHOR

Maureen Webb is a human rights lawyer and activist. She was a litigator for some of the first constitutional cases heard under Canada's Charter of Rights and Freedoms, including the landmark freedom of association case, *Lavigne,* and a case challenging the powers of Canada's newly instituted spy agency, CSIS. She has also participated in cases before the House of Lords and Privy Council in the UK and before the U.S. District Court for the District of Columbia. In 2001 she was a Fellow at the Human Rights Institute at Columbia University, New York, where she also received her LL.M., graduating *summa cum laude.* She is Co-Chair of the International Civil Liberties Monitoring Group, a pan-Canadian coalition concerned with post–September 11 civil liberties and human rights issues, and Coordinator for Security and Human Rights issues for Lawyers' Rights Watch Canada. She has spoken extensively on post–September 11 security and human rights issues, most recently testifying before the U.S. House and Senate committees reviewing the Canadian Anti-Terrorism Act. She lives in Quebec.